NEW CENTURY BIBLE COMMENTARY

General Editors

RONALD E. CLEMENTS
(Old Testament)

MATTHEW BLACK
(New Testament)

ROMANS

THE NEW CENTURY BIBLE COMMENTARIES

*Not yet available in paperback
 Other titles are in preparation

NEW CENTURY BIBLE COMMENTARY

Based on the Revised Standard Version

ROMANS

MATTHEW BLACK

WM. B. EERDMANS PUBL. CO., GRAND RAPIDS

MARSHALL, MORGAN & SCOTT PUBL. LTD., LONDON

Copyright © Marshall, Morgan & Scott 1973
First published 1973 by Marshall, Morgan & Scott, England
Softback edition published 1981

Wm. B. Eerdmans Publishing Company
255 Jefferson Ave. S.E., Grand Rapids, Mich. 49503
and
Marshall, Morgan & Scott
1 Bath Street, London EC1V 9LB
ISBN 0 551 009 07 1

Library of Congress Cataloging in Publication Data

Black, Matthew.
Romans.

(New century Bible commentary)
Reprint. Originally published: London: Oliphants,
c1973. (New century Bible)
Bibliography: p. 13
Includes indexes.
1. Bible. N.T. Romans — Commentaries.   I.   Title.
II.   Series.   III.   Series: New century Bible.
BS2665.3.B5   1981   227′.107   81-5575
ISBN 0-8028-1905-2 (pbk.)   AACR2

CONTENTS

PREFACE

The author of 2 Peter was not exaggerating when he said that 'there are some things in them (the letters of St Paul) hard to understand' (ch. 3:16). In some respects the Epistle to the Romans contains probably the hardest of all Paul's thoughts about his gospel. Certainly it is this epistle which has presented generations of biblical scholars with their most challenging exegetical tasks. Moreover, the nature of some of the problems, where one may suspect, but can never be sure, that 'primitive error' or a textual corruption may be the source of the difficulties, does not make the exegetical task any easier.

The intention of the New Century Bible series is to provide, for the interested layman as well as for the clergy or theological students, an up-to-date account of the *status quaestionis* of the exegesis of the biblical writings, especially in those controversial areas of interpretation. In Romans this is a well-nigh impossible task; bibliographical items alone, over the past century, are more numerous than in any other New Testament book of comparable size. The attempt, nevertheless, has been made in the present commentary to give as wide and representative a selection of these as possible, from modern commentaries and articles which have appeared in the main European languages within the past seventy to 100 years. The reader has thus additional reference material for his own reflection and exegetical decisions.

I am grateful to my secretary, Miss M. C. Blackwood, for her outstanding services in preparing the manuscript, through several drafts, for the Press.

To my colleague, Dr. A. J. M. Wedderburn, who has himself a special interest in Romans, I am indebted for a careful reading of the commentary in proof. My gratitude is also due to the readers of the Press for their care and attention to detail, in particular in checking references and ironing out inconsistencies. For the many imperfections that remain I am alone responsible.

MATTHEW BLACK

St. Mary's College, St. Andrews
29th March 1973

ABBREVIATIONS

BIBLICAL

OLD TESTAMENT (*OT*)

Gen.	Jg.	1 Chr.	Ps.	Lam.	Ob.	Hag.
Exod.	Ru.	2 Chr.	Prov.	Ezek.	Jon.	Zech.
Lev.	1 Sam.	Ezr.	Ec.	Dan.	Mic.	Mal.
Num.	2 Sam.	Neh.	Ca.	Hos.	Nah.	
Dt.	1 Kg.	Est.	Isa.	Jl	Hab.	
Jos.	2 Kg.	Job	Jer.	Am.	Zeph.	

APOCRYPHA (*Apoc.*)

1 Esd.	Tob.	Ad. Est.	Sir.	S 3 Ch.	Bel	1 Mac.
2 Esd.	Jdt.	Wis.	Bar.	Sus.	Man.	2 Mac.
			Ep. Jer.			

NEW TESTAMENT (*NT*)

Mt.	Ac.	Gal.	1 Th.	Tit.	1 Pet.	3 Jn
Mk	Rom.	Eph.	2 Th.	Phm.	2 Pet.	Jude
Lk.	1 C.	Phil.	1 Tim.	Heb.	1 Jn	Rev.
Jn	2 C.	Col.	2 Tim.	Jas	2 Jn	

DEAD SEA SCROLLS (DSS)

1QIsª	First Isaiah Scroll
1QIsᵇ	Second Isaiah Scroll
1QLevi	Second Testament of Levi
1QpHab	Habakkuk Commentary
1QS	Rule of the Community (Manual of Discipline)
1QSa (= 1Q28a)	Rule of the Community (Appendix)
1QSb (= 1Q28b)	Collection of Benedictions
1QM	War of the Sons of Light against the Sons of Darkness
1QH	Hymns of Thanksgiving
4QFlor	Florilegium, Cave 4
4QpPs 37	Commentary on Psalm 37

4Qtest	Messianic Testimonia
CD	Fragments of a Zadokite Work (Damascus Document)
DSH	(now designated 1QpHab)

GENERAL

AV	*Authorized Version* (King James Version) (1611)
Bib.	*Biblica*
BZ	*Biblische Zeitschrift*
BZNW	*Beihefte zur Zeitschrift für die neutestamentliche Wissenschaft*
CBQ	*Catholic Biblical Quarterly*
CIL	*Corpus Inscriptionum Latinarum*
EGT	*The Expositor's Greek Testament* (ed. W. Robertson Nicoll), 5 vols. (London, 1897–1910)
Ev. Theol.	*Evangelische Theologie*
ET	*Expository Times*
FRLANT	*Forschungen zur Religion und Literatur des Alten und Neuen Testaments*
HThR	*Harvard Theological Review*
IEJ	*Israel Exploration Journal*
JBL	*Journal of Biblical Literature*
MM	J. H. Moulton and G. Milligan, *Vocabulary of the Greek Testament* (London, 1911)
Moffatt	J. Moffatt, *A New Translation of the Bible* (London, 1934)
NEB	*New English Bible* (1970; *NT* only, 1961)
Nov. Test.	*Novum Testamentum*
NTS	*New Testament Studies*
RB	*Revue Biblique*
RSV	*Revised Standard Version* (*NT*, 1946; *OT*, 1952)
RV	*Revised Version* (*NT*, 1880; *OT*, 1884)
SB	H. L. Strack u. P. Billerbeck, *Kommentar zum Neuen Testament aus Talmud u. Midrasch* (Berlin, 1922–61)
SH	(*see first item in Bibliography*)
SJT	*Scottish Journal of Theology*
Stud. Ev.	*Studia Evangelica*
Stud. Theol.	*Studia Theologica*

TU	*Texte u. Untersuchungen zur Geschichte der altchrist-lichen Literatur*, 3. Folge (1883—)
TWNT	*Theologisches Wörterbuch zum Neuen Testament*, hrsg. v. G. Kittel u. G. Friedrich (Stuttgart, 1933—)
TZ	*Theologische Zeitschrift*
Theol. Ltzg.	*Theologische Literaturzeitung*
Verb. Dei	*Verbum Dei*
ZNTW	*Zeitschrift für die neutestamentliche Wissenschaft*

SELECT BIBLIOGRAPHY

OLDER COMMENTARIES

The standard commentary in English is still: Sanday, W., and Headlam, A. C., *A Critical and Exegetical Commentary on the Epistle to the Romans* (*International Critical Commentary*), Edinburgh, 1895; 5th edn., 1902, with many subsequent reprints. A full list of older commentaries is given ibid., pp. xcviii ff. Special mention may be made of two:

Vaughan, C. J. (Dean of Llandaff, 1879–97), 4th edn (1874). Valuable for its philological learning, New Testament parallels, and Septuagint references.

Wordsworth, Christopher (Bishop of Lincoln, 1869–85) (1856–60). Especially valuable for its wide patristic learning.

To these should be added from the older commentaries:

Denney, James, *Commentary on Romans* (*Expositor's Greek Testament*, 2), London, 1900.

MODERN COMMENTARIES

Althaus, P., *Der Brief an die Römer* (*Neues Testament Deutsch*, 6) Göttingen, 1966.

Barrett, C. K., *The Epistle to the Romans* (*Black's New Testament Commentaries*), London, 1957.

Barth, K., *The Epistle to the Romans* (trans. by E. C. Hoskyns, Oxford, 1933). Also: *A Shorter Commentary on Romans*, trans. by D. H. van Daalen, London, 1959.

Best, Ernest, *The Letter of Paul to the Romans* (*Cambridge Bible Commentary on the New English Bible*), Cambridge, 1967.

Bruce, F. F., *The Epistle to the Romans* (*Tyndale New Testament Commentary*), London, 1963.

Brunner, E., *The Letter to the Romans: a Commentary* (translated by H. A. Kennedy), London, 1959.

Dodd, C. H., *The Epistle of Paul to the Romans* (*Moffatt NT Commentary*), London, 1932; Fontana edn, 1959.

Gaugler, E., *Der Brief an die Römer*, Zürich, 1952.

Häring, T., *Der Römerbrief des Apostels Paulus*, Stuttgart, 1926.

Huby, J., *S. Paul. Épître aux Romains: traduction et commentaire*, Paris, 1940; new edn with S. Lyonnet, Paris, 1957.

Kirk, K. E., *The Epistle to the Romans* (*The Clarendon Bible*), Oxford, 1937.

Knox, John, 'Romans', in *Interpreter's Bible*, IX, Nashville, 1954.

Kuss, O., *Der Römerbrief übersetzt und erklärt*, Regensburg, 1957.

Lagrange, M. J., *Épître aux Romains*, Paris, 1915, repr. 1950.

Leenhardt, F. J., *L'Épître de Saint Paul aux Romains*, Neuchâtel, 1957.

Lietzmann, Hans, *An die Römer* (*Handbuch zum Neuen Testament*) 4th edn, Tübingen, 1933.

Manson, T. W., 'Romans', in *Peake's Commentary on the Bible*, London, 1962.

Michel, Otto, *Der Brief an die Römer* (*Kritisch-exegetischer Kommentar über das Neue Testament*), 10th edn, Göttingen, 1955.

Murray, J., *The Epistle to the Romans* (*International Commentary on the New Testament*), Grand Rapids, 1959–65.

Nygren, A., *Commentary on Romans*, Eng. trans., London, 1952.

Pallis, A., *To the Romans: a Commentary*, Liverpool, 1920.

Rhys, H., *The Epistle to the Romans*, New York, 1961.

Ridderbos, H., *Aan de Romeinen*, Kampen, 1959.

Schlatter, A., *Gottes Gerechtigkeit*, Stuttgart, 1935; 2nd edn, 1952.

Schmidt, H. W., *Der Brief des Paulus an die Römer* (*Theol. Handkomm. zum Neuen Testament*), Berlin, 1962.

OTHER RECOMMENDED STUDIES

Allen, L. C., 'The Old Testament in Romans i–viii', *Vox Evangelica*, III, 1964, pp. 6–41.

Barrett, C. K., *Reading through Romans*, London, 1963.

Baur, F. C., *Ausgewählte Werke in Einzelaufgaben*, ed. K. Scholder, Stuttgart, 1963, I, pp. 147–266. Über Zweck und Veranlassung des Römerbriefes und die damit zusammenhängenden Verhältnisse der römischen Gemeinde, 1836.

Bultmann, R., *Theology of the New Testament*, London, 1955.

Cranfield, C. E. B., *A Commentary on Rom. 12–13* (*SJT Occasional Papers*, 12), Edinburgh, 1965.

Davies, W. D., *Paul and Rabbinic Judaism*, London, 1948.

Delling, G., 'Zum neueren Paulusverständnis', *Nov. Test.*, IV, 1960, pp. 95–121.

Deluz, G., *La justice de Dieu: explication de l'Épître aux Romains*, Neuchâtel, 1945.

Dinkler, E., *Predestination bei Paulus*, Neukirchen, 1957.

von Dobschütz, E., 'Zum Wortschatz und Stil des Römerbriefs', *ZNTW*, XXXIII, 1934, pp. 51–66.

Ellison, H. L., *The Mystery of Israel: an Exposition of Rom. 9–11*, Grand Rapids, 1966.

Friedrich, G. 'Römerbrief', in *Die Religion in Geschichte und Gegenwart*, V, col. 1137–44.

Goppelt, L., *Jesus, Paul and Judaism*, translated by E. Schroeder, New York, 1964.

Hunter, A. M., *Romans: the Law of Love* (*Torch Bible Paperbacks*), London, 1955.

Jeremias, J., 'Chiasmus in den Paulusbriefen', *ZNTW*, XLIX, 1958, pp. 145–56 (esp. p. 154).

Jewett, R., *Paul's Anthropological Terms: a Study of their Use in Conflict Settings*, Leiden, 1971.

Käsemann, E., *Perspectives on Paul*, London, 1971.

Knox, W. L., *St. Paul and the Church of Jerusalem*, Cambridge, 1925.

Knox, W. L., *St. Paul and the Church of the Gentiles*, Cambridge, 1939.

Leon, H. J. *The Jews of Ancient Rome*, Philadelphia, 1960.

Lütgert, W., *Der Römerbrief als historisches Problem. Beiträge zur Forderung christlicher Theologie*, 17 (ii), Gütersloh, 1913.

Rigaux, B., *Saint Paul et ses Lettres* (*Studia Neotestamentica Subsidia* 2), Paris-Bruges, 1962.

Schelkle, K. H., *Paulus: Lehrer der Väter*, Düsseldorf, 1956.

Schmithals, W., 'Zur Abfassung und ältesten Sammlung der paulinischen Hauptbriefe', *ZNTW*, LI, 1960, pp. 225–45.

Scroggs, R., *The Last Adam: a Study in Pauline Anthropology*, Oxford, 1966.

Schürer, E., *A History of the Jewish People in the Time of Jesus Christ*, 6 vols, Edinburgh, 1898–1903.

Schweitzer, A., *The Mysticism of the Apostle Paul*, Eng. trans., London, 1931.

Schweitzer, A., *Paul and his Interpreters*, Eng. trans., London, 1912.

Thackeray, H. St. John, *The Relationship of St. Paul to Contemporary Jewish Thought*, London, 1900.

Wiefel, W., 'Die jüdische Gemeinde im antiken Rom und die Anfänge des römischen Christentums: Bemerkung zu Anlass und Zweck des Römerbriefes', *Judaica*, XXVI, 1970, pp. 65–88.

THE STRUCTURE OF ROMANS

Bonnard, P., 'Où en est l'interprétation de l'Épître aux Romains?', *Rev. de Theol. et Phil.*, 3rd ser., I, 1951, pp. 225–43.

Dahl, N. A., 'Two notes on Romans 5', *Studia Theologica*, V, 1951–2, pp. 37–48.

Dupont, J., 'Le Problème de la structure littéraire de l'épître aux Romains', *RB*, LXII, 1955, pp. 365–97.

Feuillet, A., 'La Citation de Habacuc II.4 et les huits premiers chapîtres de l'Épître aux Romains', *NTS*, VI, 1959–60, pp. 52–80.

Feuillet, A., 'Le Plan salvifique de Dieu d'après L'Épître aux Romains: essai sur la structure littéraire de l'Épître et sa significance théologique', *RB*, LVII, 1950, pp. 336–87, 489–529.

Grayston, K., ' "Not ashamed of the Gospel": Rom. 1.16a and the Structure of the Epistle', in *Stud. Evang.*, II (*TU* 87), 1964, pp. 569ff.

Jeremias, J., 'Zur Gedankenführung in den Paulinischen Briefen', in *Studia Paulina* (de Zwaan Festschrift), Haarlem, 1953, pp. 146ff.

Klein, G., 'Der Abfassungswerk des Römerbriefes', in *Rekonstruction und Interpretation*, Munich, 1969.

Luz, U., 'Zum Aufbau von Röm. 1–8', *TZ*, xxv, 1969 pp. 161ff.

Lyonnet, S., 'Note sur le plan de l'Épître aux Romains' *Mélanges Jules Lebreton* (1951–2), pp. 301–16. (For other modern literature, see J. Dupont's article above.)

Manson, W., 'Notes on the Argument of Romans (Chapters i–viii)' in *New Testament Essays in Memory of T. W. Manson*, ed. A. J. B. Higgins, Manchester, 1959.

Ruijs, R. C. M., *De Structuur van de Brief aan de Romeinen: een stilistische, vormhistorische en thematische analyse van Rom. i:16–iii:23*, Utrecht–Nijmegen, 1964.

INTRODUCTION

to

Romans

INTRODUCTION

The Epistle to the Romans is one of the classic documents of the Christian faith, the theological epistle *par excellence* in the New Testament; the only other comparable New Testament writing, both in epistolary form and theological content, is the anonymous Epistle to the Hebrews. But Hebrews is an epistolary homily: its theology is subordinate to its homiletic purpose. Romans is a theological affirmation of the Christian faith, composed in the form of the literary epistle (*epistolē*) of the period.[1]

This does not mean that Romans is an exposition of Christian theology in the same sense as Barth's *Dogmatics* or Bultmann's *Theology of the New Testament*. A more accurate characterisation is that given by Michel:[2] Romans is 'epistolary catechesis', or instruction in Christian doctrine, a *Lehrbrief*, i.e. an Epistle written to instruct its readers. This is a valid definition in so far as the Epistle does embody *didachē*, or catechesis, in what St Paul regards as the essentials of Christian belief and its implications for Christian life and doctrine. Its central theme is Christian 'righteousness' (*dikaiosynē*) or 'salvation' (*sōtēria*). But this instruction is communicated within the framework of a sustained argumentation directed against the antithesis of Pharisaic Judaism, that 'righteousness' or 'salvation' had as its foundation obedience to a revealed *tôrāh*, or divine revelation. 'Salvation' was adherence, not to a divine Law, but to a divine Lord, apprehended by faith.[3]

1. DATE AND CIRCUMSTANCES OF WRITING

The date of the sending of Romans and the circumstances in which it came to be written can be determined with a fair degree of accuracy.[4] On the basis of a widely agreed interpretation of

[1] This is not to deny that Romans is also a 'real letter', with some of the formal characteristics of the letters of the period (see below, p. 29f., 39 n. 1 and 2). But its *Gattung* is that of the Jewish-style literary epistle.

[2] *Kommentar*, p. 5.

[3] Cf. W. D. Davies, *St. Paul and Rabbinic Judaism* (London, 1948), p. 148.

[4] But cf. J. R. Richards, 'Romans and I Corinthians: their Chronological Relationship and Comparative Dates', *NTS*, XIII (1966), pp. 14–30.

Rom. 16:23 and 1 C. 1:14, Paul is writing from *Corinth*, where he is the guest of his former convert Gaius, in whose house the Church in Corinth was accustomed to meet; moreover at 16:1 Phoebe, a deaconess of Cenchreae, the port of Corinth, is commended to the Roman Church. (She was probably the bearer of the letter.)

The actual circumstances of the writing of the Epistle are described at 15:22–32: Paul has now completed his work in Asia and Greece (v. 23), and is planning to mount a mission to Spain and, on the way, to visit Rome. But first he must 'back-track' to Jerusalem, with a relief fund subscribed by Macedonia and Achaia for the 'saints' there (the impoverished Jewish Christian community in the Holy City).

This statement of intentions and plans corresponds broadly with the account of St Paul's actual movements as reported by St Luke in Ac. 19:21–20:6. The Apostle's work in Asia, with his headquarters in Ephesus, is over or nearing its conclusion, and he is now planning to travel to Jerusalem via Macedonia and Greece; Luke even mentions Paul's intention to visit Rome after his journey to Jerusalem.

In this summarizing report (Ac. 20:2–6), Luke informs us that Paul carried out his projected plan, and went first to Macedonia and Greece; in Greece he spent three months, before resuming his journey to Jerusalem. There is little doubt that it was during these three months in Greece, almost certainly in Corinth, that Romans was written, probably in the year A.D. 58.

The reason for his circuitous journey to Jerusalem (via Greece) had no doubt to do with the 'collection' for the Jerusalem Church. When he left Greece again, however, it was to make the same wide detour—through Macedonia and across Asia—this time almost certainly to avoid the hostile reception awaiting him in Syria, probably at Antioch (he could have sailed direct from Corinth to Antioch or Caesarea; Ac. 20:3). He may also have been deliberately avoiding a confrontation with Jewish pilgrims to the Passover Festival, who would be travelling by the direct routes.

Paul set out after his three months in Greece for Macedonia, as we now know, from Corinth; and, since he left in order to reach Jerusalem for the Passover Festival, we may presume that it was the winter months he spent in Corinth. There he occupied himself by writing the Roman Epistle.

The Letter was written, therefore, at the close of Paul's so-called 'Ephesian ministry' (c. A.D. 57).[1] We are in the year A.D. 58 when the apostle sends his letter, perhaps in the early Spring.

The impression we receive from chapter 15 is that Romans was sent, among other reasons, to prepare the way for a future visit. Other, more powerful, motives, however, may have led to the conceiving and composing of this great Epistle. Paul was by no means certain he would ever see Rome: all reports underline the danger in which he stood, from the hatred of world Jewry and the tension and dissension in the Jerusalem Christian community (Rom. 15:31; Ac. 20:3). He could not be certain of the reception even a letter from him would get in Rome; and this may account for the absence of any greetings at Rom. 1:1, though mention is made of his amanuensis and other 'fellow-workers' at chapter 16 (Ac. 20:4, cf. Rom. 16:21-23). Paul bears sole responsibility for what he writes. He may also have thought that this, like his Master's last Passover, might well prove his own *via dolorosa et via crucis*. So, if he never preached in Rome, Rome (he determined) would, nevertheless, hear his 'Gospel' read to them, from his own living word. It really almost looks as if Paul set out, in these three months' breathing-space in Corinth during A.D. 57 to write his last will and testament[2]—his final literary and theological testimony to the world, the supreme *apologia pro vita et doctrina sua*, the classic exposition of the 'Gentile Gospel', the 'Gospel according to St Paul', his liberal faith for the Gentile world.

2. THE READERS

St Paul is writing to a Church which had been in existence a number of years, perhaps a whole decade, before he sent his Epistle from Corinth in A.D. 57-8. He is evidently himself a stranger to the Church in Rome, and had never been there

[1] The date, A.D. 57, for this stage in St Paul's career is fixed, first with reference to his encounter with Gallio at Corinth in A.D. 52—the one secure date supported by inscriptional evidence in the New Testament—and, there-after, by a rough computation of the period occupied by the events described in Ac. 18: 18-19: 20 (five years may be too long).

[2] Cf. G. Bornkamm, 'The Letter to the Romans as Paul's Last Will and Testament', *Austr. Bibl. Rev.*, XI (1963), pp. 2-14.

(1:10); he had certainly nothing to do with the founding of the
Church in Rome. Traditionally the Church in Rome is connected with St Peter, not St Paul; St Peter did probably at one
time visit Rome, and may have been martyred there, but the
actual founders of the Roman Church are unknown.[1] Their
names may have been preserved in the list of persons greeted by
the apostle at chapter 16, if that chapter is a genuine part of the
epistle; Paul refers to, among others, a certain Andronicus and
Junias who are 'of note among the apostles, and they were
in Christ before me' (16:7). It may have been one or more of
these notable pre-Pauline apostles who were the first to preach
the Gospel in the imperial city.

The actual date for the foundation of the Roman Church is a
matter for conjecture and inference. The main evidence is external,
not internal: it consists chiefly of the report of the Roman
historian Suetonius in his life of Claudius (25) of the famous
edict of Claudius of A.D. 49 banishing the Jews from Rome on
account of disturbances alleged to have been created by the
instigations of a certain 'Chrestus'; Suetonius is evidently report-
ing a garbled version of riots, probably within the large Jewish
community, produced no doubt by the preaching of the Gospel
by early missionaries; we are probably to think of a situation
similar to the riots which broke out about the same time in south
Galatia (Derbe, Lystra, Lycaonia) as a result of Paul's preaching
of the Gospel.[2]

Incidentally we read of two Jewish exiles from the persecutions
of Claudius at Ac. 18:1ff., the famous and well-to-do Jewish
couple, Priscilla and Aquila, who must already have been
Christians when they met Paul at Corinth.[3]

[1] Cf. H. W. Bartsch, 'Die historische Situation des Römerbriefs', *Communio
Viatorum*, VIII (1965), pp. 199–208. See also *Stud. Ev.* iv(1); *TU* cii, pp. 281–91.

[2] But cf. S. Benko, 'The Edict of Claudius of A.D. 49 and the Instigator
Chrestos', *TZ*, xxv (1969), pp. 406ff. Benko argues that the edict of Claudius
was occasioned by the Jewish-Gentile *Kulturkampf* in Rome (Chrestos was a
Jewish zealot agitator!). This was probably not the only occasion Claudius
had difficulties with the Jewish colony in Rome. Cf. F. F. Bruce, *New Testament
History* (London, 1969), pp. 279ff. on the report of Dio Cassius, *Hist.*, lx 6;
see also W. Wiefel, 'Die jüdische Gemeinschaft im antiken Rom und die
Anfänge des römischen Christentums: Bemerkungen zu Anlass und Zweck
des Römerbriefes', *Judaica*, xxvi (1970), pp. 65ff.

[3] Cf. A. Harnack, 'Probabilia über die Adresse und den Verfasser des
Hebräerbriefs', *ZNTW*, i (1900), pp. 16ff.

It is not surprising that there should have been a Christian Church in Rome at so early a period, for Roman Judaism presented a fertile soil for the Gospel. The Jewish community in Rome has been estimated in the first century B.C. at 40,000 to 60,000, with no fewer than thirteen synagogues.[1] The probability is that one of these was a Jewish-Christian synagogue; it is only in this way that we can satisfactorily account for the peculiarities of the early Roman Church.[2] A fourth-century Church Father, Ambrosiaster, has this to say about the ancient Roman Church:

> It is known that Jews lived at Rome in apostolic times, because they were subjects of the Roman Empire. Those of them who had become Christians passed on to the Romans the message that they should profess Christ and keep the Law . . . Without seeing displays of mighty works, or any of the apostles [a strange statement for a father of the Church to make], they accepted the faith of Christ though with Jewish rites.[3]

We have no reason to disbelieve this picture of the early Roman Church. When we add that, next to Jerusalem, it was probably the largest in the Empire (Tacitus, not many years later, speaks of Christians in Rome as an 'immense multitude'), we begin to understand the challenge it presented to St Paul. Sir William Ramsay was no doubt right in arguing that St Paul was anxious to plant the Christian flag in the capital of the Empire, though he tended to overlook the fact that a Christian flag had already

[1] Cf. H. J. Leon, *The Jews of Ancient Rome* (Philadelphia, 1960), p. 135ff. J. Juster, *Les Juifs dans l'empire Romain*, II (Paris, 1914), p. 170.

[2] Michel (p. 2, n. 3) thinks that there may have been several Christian centres, on the analogy of the numerous synagogues, and consequent on the Roman policy of 'decentralisation' of *'collegia'*, 'guilds', 'corporations'. See E. Schürer, *The Jewish People in the Time of Jesus Christ* (Edinburgh, 1901), II.ii, pp. 232ff.; J. B. Frey, 'Les Communautes juives à Rome aux premiers temps de l'Église', *Recherches de Science Religieuse*, XXI (1931); see also G. La Piana, 'Foreign Groups in Rome during the First Century of the Empire', *HThR*, xx (1927), pp. 183–403, and 'The Roman Church at the end of the Second Century', ibid., XVIII, (1925), pp. 201–77. For the strong links between Roman Jewry and Jerusalem, see G. F. Moore, *Judaism in the First Centuries of the Christian Era*, I (1927), p. 106. One of the Roman synagogues was known as the *synagōgē elaias*, the 'Synagogue of the Olive Tree', cf. Schürer, II, ii, pp. 74, 248. Was the first Roman Christian congregation an off-shoot? See Ch. 11, below, p. 145.

[3] Cf. Dodd, pp. xxvii f.

been planted there nearly a decade earlier—with a star of David, however, rather than a cross as its emblem. From St Paul's point of view the Roman Church was, like the Church in Jerusalem, a reactionary Church. He was ambitious to win Rome for his liberal Gospel, one prepared to admit Gentiles without first demanding that they become Jews. It is no coincidence that the main theme of Romans is 'Gospel and Law'.

Like all these early foundations, the Roman Church was of Jewish origin but of Gentile growth and, probably, of predominantly Gentile racial composition. It was, no doubt, a mixed community, socially as well as racially; some of the names at chapter 16 are those of emancipated slaves and freedmen, but others point to membership of the aristocracy ('the family of Aristobulus' at verse 10 is clearly a reference to members of the Herod family). The language of the Roman Church appears to have been mainly Greek, and Greek seems to have maintained its position till well into the second century, certainly as a literary and probably also as a liturgical language.[1]

In the light of the character of the Roman Church, the reasons for St Paul's letter are quite simply two: (i) the Roman Church was an important Church; and (ii) it was still (from Paul's liberal standpoint) an imperfect and immature Church, still probably little more than a sect within Judaism. Its main doctrine, no doubt, consisted of a belief in the Jewish Messiah, Jesus, crucified and risen, side by side with obedience to the Law. Paul preached the catholic Christ and emancipation from the Law; and he wrote to win over this influential centre to his Gospel.[2]

---

[1] Cf. further, K. H. Schelkle, 'Römische Kirche im Römerbrief: zur Geschichte und Auslegungsgeschichte', *Ztschr. für katholische Theologie*, LXXXI (1959), pp. 393–404.

[2] For modern discussion of the purpose of Romans (by Klein, Fuchs, Bornkamm, Marxsen, *et al.*), see K. P. Donfried, 'A Short Note on Rom. 16', *JBL*, LXXXIX (1970), pp. 441ff. No doubt Paul was anxious to have his authority as *the* Gentile apostle recognized by this powerful Gentile community (Klein). Romans may also have been aimed, indirectly, at Jerusalem readers; cf. J. Jervell, 'Der Brief nach Jerusalem: über Veranlassung und Adresse des Römerbriefes', *Stud. Theol.*, XXV (1971), pp. 61–73. One might add that in view of the close links with Jerusalem (see above, p. 22, n. 2), Paul's *apologia pro doctrina sua* in Romans, especially *vis-à-vis* the Law, would stand him in good stead in Jerusalem.

3. THE STRUCTURE OF THE EPISTLE[1]

While there is a general consensus among scholars, both ancient and modern, that Romans, in spite of its at times apparently digressive style, is not an entirely unplanned exercise—some more than others detect a carefully prepared 'outline' or 'plan'—agreement, even on the main structural lines of the epistle, has never been complete; and differences of opinion are not likely ever to be fully or finally resolved.

Chapter 16, with its long list of greetings, presents its own special problems; and it may be that 15:14–16:27 should be treated together as marking the conclusion of the letter (see further below, p. 25).

Traditionally, especially in Protestant exegesis, chapters 1–8 have been regarded as the doctrinal heart of Romans, presenting the essential doctrine of the epistle, 'justification by faith alone'. Within this section most exegetes have found a 'break', or 'caesura', in the developing argument at the end of chapter 5: chapters 1–5 deal with 'justification'; chapters 6–11, in the old Protestant terminology, with 'sanctification'—the Christian life ensuing on 'justification'.[2] Chapters 9–11 are regarded as a kind of appendix dealing with the problem of the final destiny of the ethnic Israel, so obdurately resistant to the appeal of the Gospel. Chapters 12–15 are Pauline *paraenesis*, i.e. attached Christian homiletic instruction.

Recent research has been challenging this traditional schema, especially in its analysis of the 'structure' of chapters 1–8, the 'great thesis' section; and, to judge from the amount of ink being spilled on the question, the debate is likely to continue. As will be evident from the commentary, the present author favours the division at chapter 5:11–12, following the arguments of Dodd, Dahl, Feuillet and Dupont among others (see the bibliography). The theme of 'justification', while it reappears at different points in the later chapters (e.g. 8:1), has been central and basic in this first section: 1:17 (statement of theme)–5:11. The Adam–Christ typology (5:12–21) lays the foundation for the doctrine of the Christian life (life 'in Christ', i.e. within the Body of Christ,

---

[1] For bibliography, see p. 13.
[2] Characterised as 'the classic plan' by Bonnard (p. 243); adopted by Godet, B. Weiss, SH, Goguel; and, among Catholic scholars, Lagrange, Huby. Cf. Dupont, p. 368. For Bonnard and Dupont, see bibliography.

the new Adam; or life 'in the spirit', 'eternal life', the present possession of the 'justified sinner') (6:1–8:39). Chapter 7 is hardly a digression, since it deals with the 'old Adam'.[1]

Probably the most convincing, and certainly the most influential, of the many studies on the structure of Romans are those of Professor A. Feuillet of Brussels. Few will disagree with Feuillet's statement ('Le Plan salvifique', p. 337) that the theme of the epistle is incontestably 'the salvation offered by God to all men through the faith of the Gospel'. This 'plan of salvation' the apostle envisages first with regard to individuals (chapters 1–8), then for its bearings on the agonizing problem of the unbelief of Israel (9–11). Feuillet further discerns a third section, viz. chapters 12–15, concerned with Christian life and community relationships. Chapter 15:14–16:27 is the conclusion of the epistle.

In recognizing these sections as each and all important parts of the 'grand design' of Romans, Professor Feuillet has made a significant contribution to the study of the epistle.[2] The view that chapters 1–8 contain 'the great thesis', while the rest is appendix, is not likely to have been the perspective of St Paul; the destiny of his own people, who were rejecting his Gospel, was an agonizing concern of the Apostle to the Gentiles. Similarly, chapters 13 and 14 dealing with attitudes within the typical hellenistic Christian community, including that at Rome, e.g. to the State and, especially, to fellow Christians ('the weak' Jewish-Christian, still concerned about *kosher* foods, and the 'strong' Gentile—probably proselyte—Christians, no doubt brought up under the restraints of the *tôrāh*, but now tending to throw off all restraint and taking up an antinomian or libertarian attitude).

Within chapters 1–8 M. Feuillet detects a structure, the key to which is supplied by Hab. 2:4, cited at Rom. 1:17 (the statement of the theme of the epistle).[3] Feuillet agrees with the exegesis

---

[1] For other views of chapters 6 and 7, see especially Dahl, Michel, Dupont: chapters 6 and 7 reply to questions about sin (6:1, 15) and the Law (7:7, 13), and together form a digression from the theme of chapter 5, which is resumed in chapter 8. (Cf. Nygren, *ad loc.*, for a further alternative.) On the 'question and answer' style, see below, p. 29f. These chapters can still contain replies to leading questions about sin and the law without being 'digressions'.

[2] Feuillet's arguments have clearly influenced the section divisions of the *Jerusalem Bible*; see Dupont, p. 365, n. 4.

[3] *NTS*, VI (1959–60), pp. 52ff.

which understands the text as: 'The "just-by-faith" shall live', and sees in the rest of the section a literary structure built on the two concepts of the text, viz. *justificatio sola fide* and (eternal) life in Christ. The words 'just', 'justice' and 'faith', coming from the first part of the quotation as given by Paul, are of very frequent occurrence from 1:17 to 5:11, and almost entirely absent thereafter. On the other hand, the terms signifying 'life' (and 'death') occur regularly in chapters 5:12 to 7:1.

Only at one point does M. Feuillet's division and exegesis seem to require some modification. No less than at chapters 9–11, St Paul in chapters 1–8, and, in particular, from 5:12ff, is concerned, not simply with the salvation of individuals, but with the societary aspect of 'salvation'; the emphasis of the doctrine of 5:12–6:23 is on the redeemed *mankind*; the 'justified sinner' is thereby incorporated into the Body of Christ.

There is always, of course, a danger in 'systematizing' St Paul, and in this connection the observations of Professor J. Jeremias are of great importance.[1] The Pauline method of arguing a case with an imaginary opponent or objector has suggested that we have in Romans a piece of living missionary experience of the apostle. Nevertheless, the arguments are conducted within the framework of the broad design of the epistle, and do not materially affect its underlying structure, with its four central (and equally important) themes: salvation by faith; Christian life; the destiny of Israel; and the obligations of the Christian, especially to his fellow Christians of 'weaker' faith.

4. THE INTEGRITY OF ROMANS

Scholars have argued for more than a century that chapter 16 is no original part of what St Paul wrote to Rome, but is a fragment of another letter which St Paul wrote to the Church in Ephesus.

(i) It seems surprising that St Paul should have known and sent greetings to so many Roman Christians (some twenty-six persons and groups of people are mentioned) considering that he had never himself been in Rome.

(ii) Several of the individuals named are associated with Asia and Ephesus, not Rome: at verse 5 a salutation is sent to Epaenetus described as 'the first convert in Asia for Christ', a

[1] See further below, p. 30.

description which seems more appropriate in a letter to Ephesus than to Rome.

(iii) Even more curious is the greeting at verses 3 to 5 to Prisca and Aquila and the Church in their house. According to 1 Cor. 16:19, Aquila and Prisca were domiciled in Ephesus, and it was in Ephesus that the Church met in their house; greetings are sent here from Aquila and Prisca to Corinth from Ephesus, where that epistle was written in A.D. 56.

To such internal considerations textual arguments have been added.

There is textual evidence that Romans circulated at one time without chapter 16. It consists of a reading of P^{46} (the Chester Beatty papyrus) which has the closing benediction of 16:25, not only at the end of this chapter, but also at the end of chapter 15. Since this benediction evidently formed the conclusion of the epistle, it is argued that Romans did at one time end at chapter 15. Several Vulgate texts do not have chapter 16, but end with the doxology at 14:23.

The internal arguments for a connection of chapter 16 with Ephesus as a separate fragment can be answered, though the counter-arguments have been felt by some to be at times somewhat forced.

St Paul may have met the persons greeted in chapter 16 as 'displaced persons' from the Claudian persecutions of A.D. 49. Priscilla and Aquila had been driven from their home in Rome in A.D. 49 (Ac. 18:2), and had moved from Rome via Corinth to Ephesus where they were domiciled in exile (giving hospitality to the Church there, as no doubt they had done in Rome). With the proclamation of the general amnesty on Jews and Christians by Nero (the dawn of the *aureum quinquennium* in A.D. 54) Priscilla and Aquila had returned to Rome, so that nothing was more natural than that Paul should send greetings to them in his letter to Rome written from Corinth in A.D. 57–8.

If we can believe this possible—and it does not seem an unreasonable hypothesis—and do not find insuperable the difficulty of St Paul's acquaintance with so many Christians in Rome, then there is no compelling internal reason to reject chapter 16.

The textual evidence is more easily explained. According to this theory of chapter 16, it is interpreted to mean that Romans originally circulated without it; that chapter 16 was not in fact an integral part of the text of Romans, and therefore that it must be part of another letter.

The textual evidence, however, is capable of the alternative explanation that Romans did originally contain chapter 16, which was later cut out simply because it consisted of a tedious list of names no longer of interest when the epistle was published and more widely circulated. This is, in fact, how the evidence is best interpreted. It was noted that Vulgate texts without chapter 16 ended at 14:23, which is just before a long Old Testament quotation. It is an unmistakable cut of the second century Encratite (ascetic) heretic Marcion, who 'criticized the New Testament with a sword' (*machaira*, Origen) (see SH, App.). It is probable that the other textual evidence is to be explained similarly, though the shortening of Romans in this way need not in every case be attributed to Marcion.

The possibility that chapter 16 was not an integral part of the original Roman epistle, or had been dropped at an early date, has given rise to various theories about Romans. Lightfoot thought that St Paul had shortened it himself, delocalizing it for general use; SH that Marcion shortened it for doctrinal reasons. These views are summarised in A. H. McNeile, *St Paul: His Life, Letters and Christian Doctrine*, pp. 185–8.[1] A different solution was proposed by Kirsopp Lake and accepted by F. C. Burkitt, that the short form of the letter was original. 'Written by St Paul at the same time as Galatians, in connection with the question of Jewish and Gentile Christians, for the general instruction of mixed Churches that he had visited.' 'Later on he sent a copy to Rome, with the addition of the other chapters, to serve, as we should say, as a covering letter.'

There remains the view (Moffatt) that the Church shortened Romans for general circulation; SH have shown conclusively that Marcion did so, though no doubt mainly for dogmatic reasons. Whether as the result of Marcion's influence or not, it is clear from P^{46} that Romans did circulate without chapter 16 and, in G, one manuscript at least lacks the personalia at 1:7, 15. Obviously the general character of the epistle, its suitability for all to read, and the obvious place to make a cut of unnecessary material led to the removal of chapter 16 (and the doctoring of

[1] Cf. J. Knox, 'A Note on the Text of Romans', *NTS*, II (1955–6), pp. 191–3.

the text earlier) in certain circles in the early Church. This is all
the explanation we require to account satisfactorily for the facts.[1]

5. THE STYLE OF THE EPISTLE

The epistles attributed to St Paul present a considerable diversity
of style. In some respects the Epistle to the Romans is unique:

> 'This epistle, like all the others of the group, is characterized by a
> remarkable energy and vivacity. It is calm in the sense that it is not
> aggressive and that the rush of words is always well under control.
> Still there is a rush of words, rising repeatedly to passages of splendid
> eloquence; but the eloquence is spontaneous, the outcome of
> strongly moved feeling; there is nothing about it of laboured oratory.
> The language is rapid, terse, incisive; the argument is conducted by
> a quick cut and thrust of dialectic; it reminds us of a fencer with his
> eye always on his antagonist.'[2]

A common explanation of this vivacious style of Romans is
that it has been influenced by the style of the spoken diatribe of
the period (see further below, p. 49). If it does show marks of
the diatribe, however, it is of a Jewish-style rhetorical discourse.

In his important contribution to the de Zwaan *Festschrift*,[3]
J. Jeremias drew attention to a formal characteristic of the style
of Romans which suggests that it owes much to the missionary
experiences of the apostle, in which he was frequently interrupted
in mid-course by a Jewish hearer, who raised an objection to
which Paul was obliged to give an immediate answer.

While it seems very likely that Paul did carry this debating
style into his correspondence—Galatians is an obvious example—
at the same time his 'controversial' style probably also owes not
a little to the current rhetorical practices of the Stoic diatribe of
the period, especially as adapted by Jewish controversialists.[4]

[1] See T. W. Manson, *Studies in the Gospels and Epistles* (Manchester, 1962),
pp. 227ff., and K. P. Donfried, 'A Short Note on Romans 16' (above, p. 23, n.
2) for recent discussion (and bibliography) on chapter 16. Cf. further, N. A.
Dahl, 'The Particularities of the Pauline Epistles', *Studia Neotestamentica et
Patristica* (Cullmann *Festschrift*) (Leiden, 1962), p. 270ff.

[2] Cf. SH, p. lv.

[3] See above, p. 16. Cf. also E. Trocme, 'L'Épître aux Romains et la méthode
missionaire de l'apôtre Paul', *NTS*, vii (1960–1), pp. 148–53.

[4] Cf. R. Bultmann, *Der Stil der paulinischen Predigt und die kynisch-stoische Diatribe*
(Göttingen, 1910).

The formal characteristics of this 'question-answer' style are:

(1) An objection is raised by the formula *ti (oun) eroumen* ('What shall we say?') (3:5; 4:1; 6:1; 7:7; 8:31; 9:14, 30), or *ti oun* ('What, then?') (3:1, 9; 6:15; 11:7). In the latter case, it would sometimes seem that *ti oun* is simply a contraction of *ti oun eroumen* (e.g. 3:9 (?); 11:7); on other occasions it is incorporated into the syntax of the sentence (e.g. 3:1).

(2) The objection is rejected with the formula *mē genoito*, which can be variously rendered: 'By no means', 'Heaven forbid!' (see note on 3:6) (3:4, 6, 31; 6:2, 15; 7:7, 13; 9:14; 11:1, 11).

At some places, Jeremias argues, Paul is replying to objections which are not expressly mentioned; e.g. chapter 4:1-2 is a reply to a 'hidden' objection that it was on the ground of his 'works' that Abraham was justified (the familiar rabbinical position—see note *ad loc.*).

The Jewish character of the Pauline diatribe or rhetoric is best seen in the extensive use the apostle makes, not only of the Old Testament to provide scriptural authority for his position, but of familiar Jewish methods of employing or interpreting the Old Testament,[1] or simply of rabbinical methods of argumentation.[2] Among these are the use of the composite quotation (see note at 3:10), the scriptural argument by 'analogy' (Jeremias, op. cit., p. 149), or the adaptation of Scripture and its interpretation (*pesher*) in the somewhat free method familiar at Qumran.[3] In general, as Barth (following Luther) maintained, the proper understanding of the Old Testament was one of Paul's main reasons for writing Romans.[4]

---

[1] E. Earle Ellis, *Paul's Use of the Old Testament* (Edinburgh, 1957); J. Schmid, 'Die alttestamentlichen Zitate bei Paulus und die Theorie von sensus plenior', *BZ*, III (1959), pp. 161–73; G. Schrenk, 'Der Römerbrief als Missionsdokument', in *Studien zu Paulus, Abh. zur Theol. des alten und neuen Testaments*, XXVI (1954), pp. 81–106.

[2] See Bonsirven, *Exégèse rabbinique et exégèse paulinienne* (Paris, 1939).

[3] See Ellis, op. cit. M. Black, 'The Christological Use of the Old Testament in the New Testament', *NTS*, XVIII (1970–1), especially pp. 8ff.

[4] *Epistle to the Romans*, pp. 10–11.

THE LETTER OF PAUL
TO THE
ROMANS

EPISTOLARY INTRODUCTION AND STATEMENT OF THEME, 1:1–18

(i) Apostolic Salutation 1–7
(ii) Thanksgiving and Personal Introduction 8–15
(iii) Adumbration of Theme 16–18

APOSTOLIC SALUTATION 1:1–7

The opening apostolic salutation is much more formal than in the other Pauline epistles (cf. the brief personal greeting at 1 Th. 1:1ff; Phil. 1:1), no doubt because St Paul was personally unknown to his readers. (Cf., however, chapter 16.) It also gives the writer the opportunity of stating his credentials as an apostle; these had been challenged elsewhere, and were possibly even more suspect in Rome than anywhere else, since Paul was also a stranger there. At the same time, he takes the earliest opportunity of giving, in summary form, the substance of his message, and in this way reassuring his readers about the soundness of his Gospel.

1. servant rather than 'slave' (*mg.*); the latter came to have degrading associations absent from the term as used by the writer. The expression 'servant of Christ' occurs not infrequently in salutations: this seems to be the first instance of it, but it is found also in the salutations of Phil., Jas, Jude and 2 Pet. Did St Paul set the fashion for other apostolic writers? The term does not here necessarily imply 'purchase by Christ', though St Paul does use this figure, and that of 'manumission' elsewhere (1 C. 6:19, 20; 7:22, 23). Cf. A. Deissmann, *Light from the Ancient East* (1910), p. 329.

The expression 'servant of God (the Lord)' is applied in the *OT* variously to Moses (Jos. 1:2), David (Ps. 89:3, 20), and the prophets from Amos onwards (Am. 3:7 to Jer. 7:25, Dan. 9:6 *et passim*). It is probably reading too much into the expression to suggest that St Paul is slipping the name 'Christ' without explanation into the place of 'God' or 'the Lord', or is thus placing himself in the succession of the prophets; that he regarded himself as 'bond-servant' of deity in his service of Christ goes without saying. For the expression applied to Christians by Paul, cf. Rom. 6:17, 22, 1 C. 7:22; Eph. 6:6; etc. The order 'Christ Jesus' is probably original, but it is doubtful if any great significance is to be attached to it (cf. SH *ad loc.*); both forms have become titular.

called to be an apostle: In his apostolic vocation St Paul emphasizes that it is a divine calling (as is also—verse 7—the call to all 'saints', i.e., Christians), cf. 1 C. 1:1; Gal. 1:1): in this he does stand in the line of the servants of God of the *OT* (Abraham (Gen. 12:1–3); Moses (Exod. 3:10ff.); Isaiah (Isa. 6:8, 9); Jeremiah (Jer. 1:4, etc.)). At Gal. 1:15 Paul applies to himself what Yahweh said to Jeremiah (Jer. 1:5).

The term 'apostle' can be used in a lower and in a higher sense; in the former, it can apply to all the first 'missionaries' of the Gospel (e.g. Rom. 16:7). St Paul applies it to himself in the higher sense: he sets himself alongside the Twelve 'pillar' Apostles, an apostolate which had been conferred on him, not by election of men, but by the sheer grace of the special calling and revelation of God (cf. again Gal. 1:1), its sphere the Gentile world (verse 5); see A. Fridrichsen, *The Apostle and his Message* (Universitets Årsskrift, Uppsala, 1947), III, p. 6: 'Obviously Paul pictures to himself the eschatological situation of the world [in his time] in this way: In this world, soon disappearing, the centre is Jerusalem, with the primitive community and the Twelve, surrounded by the mission field divided between two Apostles: one sent by the Lord to the circumcised, the other to the Gentiles. Peter and Paul themselves are the chosen bearers of the Gospel, flanking the portal of the world to come.'

set apart for the gospel of God: lit. 'separated' (or 'singled out') 'for [the proclamation of] the Gospel'. Like the prophet Jeremiah, St Paul thinks of himself as 'set apart' in the purpose of God 'from his mother's womb' (cf. Gal. 1:15, 16; cf. Jer. 1:5); but he is also represented as 'set apart' at his conversion and by the appointment of the Church for its Gentile mission (cf. Ac. 13:2). There may be a cryptic allusion in this particular word to Paul's Pharisaic background (Phil. 3): the name 'Pharisee' was popularly explained as meaning 'one separated off (from the world)' and so 'set apart' (*parush*). If St Paul is here alluding to his former Pharisaic status, he is now declaring that his dedicated

position is that of one separated from the world for the spread of
the Gospel.

gospel of God: the expression is a very common one in Paul
occurring some sixty times (with the variant 'gospel of Christ').
For an illuminating discussion of the term *euangelion* ('good news'),
see Deissmann, *Light from the Ancient East*, p. 370ff.

**2. which he (God) promised beforehand through his
prophets in the holy scriptures:** the words *epangellesthai* ('to
promise'), and *epangelia* ('promise') are key terms in the *NT* for
the 'promises' to Israel delivered by the Hebrew prophets, re-
corded in the sacred scriptures of the *OT*. These are now fulfilled
in the Gospel, which is the 'promise fulfilled', the 'good news'
of the advent of the Kingdom of God and His Messiah (cf. Mt.
4:23; Mk 1:14, 15; Ac. 13:32, 26:6; etc.). Note the characteristic paronomasia (*euangelion, proepēngeilato*). Cf. 2 Mac. 2:18;
Ps. Solomon, 7–9 (10) (the day of salvation *promised* to Israel),
12:7(6) ('the *promise* of the Lord' which the 'saints' will inherit).

3. concerning his Son: 'Son', 'Son of God', the highest
christological designation, Jewish-messianic in origin (cf. Dal-
man, *Words of Jesus*, p. 268ff., W. Kramer, *Christ, Lord, Son of God.
(SCM Studies in Biblical Theology* 50) (London, 1966), p. 183ff.,
F. Hahn, *Christologische Hoheitstitel: ihre Geschichte im frühen
Christentum* (Göttingen, 1963), p. 28off. and E. Evans, *Tertulliani
adversus Praxean liber* (London, 1948), p. 322. B. M. F. Van Iersel,
'Der Sohn' in den synoptischen Jesusworten, Nov. Test., Suppl. III,
(Leiden, 1961).

descended from David according to the flesh: St Paul is
contrasting Christ's messianic status, on the human side ('according to the flesh'), with his 'spiritual' status ('designated Son of
God', etc.). The Davidic descent of the Messiah was virtually
axiomatic in popular Jewish messianism. It was part of Paul's
gospel, according to 2 Tim. 2:8, and is appealed to as evidence
for Jesus' messianic claims at Ac. 2:30. According to Mk 12:35f.
and par., Jesus himself appears to have found difficulty with this
popular belief, and to have taken exception to it; he never used
the term 'son of David' of himself. See also E. Schweizer, 'Röm.
1:3f. und der Gegensatz von Fleisch und Geist vor und bei
Paulus', *Ev. Theol.*, xv (1955), pp. 563–71; and cf. E. Linnemann,
'Tradition und Interpretation in Röm. 1:3ff', *ibid.*, XXXI (1971),
pp. 264–75.

It is doubtful if the Gospel would ever have commended itself to Jews, Palestinian or hellenistic, without this accepted article of messianic belief. If it was not original and primitive, it must have been incorporated at a very early stage into the Apostolic *kerygma*.

4. designated Son of God in power according to the Spirit of holiness by his resurrection from the dead: these words can only be understood when interpreted as a whole.

designated: the usual meaning of this verb is 'to define', 'to determine' and so 'decree', 'ordain' (cf. Ac. 10:42; 17:31; and *The Greek Anthology*, trans. W. R. Paton (1916–18), IV, p. 363 (xii, 158, 7): 'destiny decreed (ordained) thee (Eros) a god'). This fundamental meaning would seem to rule out the otherwise contextually suitable 'revealed', 'proved to be' (Chrysostom) for which there are other, regular Greek equivalents. The English versions 'declared (to be)', 'designated' would seem to derive from this basic meaning; 'installed' (Moffatt) is a somewhat free rendering. What is left vague by these renderings is in what way —when or by whom—we are to conceive that Jesus Christ was 'declared to be Son of God'. A recent suggestion of L. C. Allen ('The Old Testament Background of *prohorizein* in the New Testament', *NTS*, XVII (1970–1), pp. 104ff.) is that the 'decree' proclaiming Christ's Sonship to which allusion is made here, is that of Yahweh at Ps. 2:6ff: 'I will declare the decree; the Lord hath said unto me, Thou art my Son: this day have I begotten thee.' We would then render: 'whom God decreed Son of God' ('with power . . . through resurrection'). For this use of the passive, where the subject is God, see below, p. 41. Ac. 13:32 similarly connects Ps. 2:6ff., the divinely decreed Sonship, with the Resurrection (verse 32 also stressing the preaching of the gospel of the promise made to the Fathers). See, further, below for this 'primitive' Christology; and on this verb, cf. M. E. Boismard, 'Constitué Fils de Dieu', *RB*, LX (1953), pp. 5–17.

in power: the 'Son of God', begotten from David's line on the human side, is also declared by divine decree 'Son of God' in power, on the side of the Spirit, the Holy Spirit—i.e. on the divine, supernatural side. The phrase 'in power' can be taken closely with 'Son of God', or as qualifying the whole expression 'decreed', 'miraculously decreed Son of God through Resurrection' (though the term is general, Christ's Resurrection is clearly meant).

according to the Spirit of holiness: St Paul is contrasting the
status of Christ's Sonship on the man-ward side (born of the seed
of David, according to the flesh) with his status on the 'spiritual'
(supernatural) side; Spirit (Holy Spirit) proceeds from God. The
expression could be interpreted to mean also: 'through the
operation of the Holy Spirit' and connected with 'through
resurrection'. According to common Jewish belief, the resurrection of the dead was to be the work of the Holy Spirit (cf.
I. Hermann, *Kyrios und Pneuma: Studien zur Geschichte der paulinischen Hauptbriefe* (1962), p. 117ff). Christ was divinely decreed
Son of God 'in power', i.e. miraculously, by a mighty act of God,
through the work of the Holy Spirit effecting his Resurrection;
cf. Lk. 1 :35.

'Spirit of holiness' is not the normal phrase for Holy Spirit
(*hagion pneuma*), and has been taken subjectively to refer to a spirit
of transcendent holiness possessed by Christ. This seems unlikely.
'Spirit of holiness' looks like a primitive 'hebraised' phrase
(*pneuma hagiōsynēs = ruaḥ haqqodesh*). For a similar expression, cf.
Test. of the Twelve Patriarchs, Levi xviii. 7. Cf. further B. Schneider,
'*Kata Pneuma Hagiōsynēs*', *Bib.*, XLVIII (1967), esp. pp. 377ff.

by his resurrection from the dead: 'by' can mean 'by reason
of', 'on the grounds of', 'through', or 'by' Resurrection; it may
also mean 'since'. The expression is a general one, 'Resurrection
from the dead', though the reference is to Christ's Resurrection.
But cf. S. H. Hooke, in *NTS*, IX (1962–3), pp. 370–1.

For the view that this verse implies a primitive Christology, see
Dodd, p. 4ff. Dodd holds that the christological position here
defined is 'scarcely a statement of Paul's own theology. He held
that Christ was Son of God from all eternity, that He was "in the
fullness of time" incarnate as a man, and that by His Resurrection
He was invested with the full power and glory of His divine status
as Lord of all. This is put most fully and clearly in Phil. 2:6–11;
but there is no reason to suppose that it belongs only to the later
period of Paul's theological thought. It is implied in this epistle
at 8:3, as well as in 2 C. 8:9 and Gal. 4:4. The present statement,
therefore, falls short of what Paul would regard as an adequate
doctrine of the Person of Christ. It recalls the primitive preaching
of the Church, as it is put into the mouth of Peter in Ac. 2:22–36.'
Cf. also Ac. 13:33. Was it a deliberate accommodation to an early
form of Christology current in the Roman Church? If so, it

was later corrected and developed; the *Apostolic Tradition* of
Hippolytus ('Canon of the Eucharist') reads: *quique in utero
habitus incarnatus est et filius tibi ostensus est* ex spiritu sancto *et
virgine natus* (emphasis mine); cf. R. H. Connolly in *JTS*, xxxix
(1938), p. 357ff.

Jesus Christ our Lord: for the history, background and
significance of this full title, see Vincent Taylor, *Names of Jesus*
(London, 1954), p. 22: 'in the majority of cases St Paul and St
Peter use "Christ" as a personal name'.

5. grace and apostleship: may be hendiadys, meaning
'grace of apostleship', thus referring to the peculiar character
of Paul's apostleship as due to the totally unmerited act of grace
in the divine revelation to him through Christ (cf. above, p. 34).
Cf. N. Turner, *Grammar of New Testament Greek*, Vol. iii, p. 335.
to bring about the obedience of faith: lit. 'an apostleship
for faith and obedience among all Gentiles'. The words define
the purpose and sphere of Paul's special apostleship: it was to
bring the Gentile world to an obedience which springs from
faith, in contradistinction to an obedience based on the external
observance of Law. The genitive is an adjectival one; Cf. G. H.
Parke-Taylor in *ET*, lv (1943–4), pp. 305–6.

As W. D. Davies has so well brought out (*Paul and Rabbinic
Judaism* (London, ²1955), p. 148), a great deal in Paul is only
fully intelligible if we replace the Jewish ideal of the *tôrāh*, or Law,
by the ideal (or Person) of Christ. The whole inspiration of
Jewish life was the Law and obedience to it; the inspiration of
Christian living is Christ, apprehended by faith, and obedience
to the Risen Lord.

among all the nations: perhaps implying the predominantly
Gentile character of the Roman Church.
for the sake of his name: Paul's apostolate to the Gentiles is
not only for their sake—never for less. It is also 'for Christ's sake',
unless, with Michel, we take 'name' as surrogate for God—it was
'for God's sake'.

6. called to belong to Jesus Christ: God calls; Christians
belong to Christ—a possessive genitive (cf. Barrett). Cf. verse 7:
who are called to be saints: the divine calling is not only to
the high office of the apostolate (cf. verse 1: 'called to be an
apostle'): it embraces all believers, described at verse 7 as 'saints'
(*hagioi*). The word 'holy' (*hagios*) originally denoted separation—

in particular, separation for the service of God. (Lev. 19:2 'You shall be holy: for I the Lord your God am holy . . .'). Then *hagioi* comes to be employed in the *NT* virtually as a proper name for Christians (8:27, 12:13, 15:25; 1 C. 6:1; Eph. 1:15; Col. 1:4; Phm. 5); it undoubtedly derives from the designation the '*saints* of the Most High' used to describe the Remnant or Son of Man at Dan. 7:13, 27 etc.

7. in Rome: one manuscript (G) omits the words here and at verse 15; at verse 7 G changes 'beloved of God' into 'in the love of God'. For the significance which has been attached to the omission, see note on the integrity of Romans, above, p. 28.

Grace to you and peace: this is a remarkable combination in what is a distinctive Pauline salutation. 'Grace' (*charis*) rings the changes on the common Greek salutation *chairein* ('greeting'), combining it with the Hebrew salutation *shalōm* ('peace'). 2 Mac. 1:2 is a precedent. Cf. Major on Jas 1:1 (p. 30ff.). Yet both terms also carry the full theological sense of the favour of God to man, and the cessation of hostility between God and man which was the work of Christ.

God our Father and the Lord Jesus Christ: Christ the Lord is joined with God the Father as equal in status: here is the germ of Trinitarian doctrine. It is also through Christ the Lord that God's Fatherhood has been revealed to man and assured for him.

THANKSGIVING AND PERSONAL INTRODUCTION 8–15

Paul's letters generally open with an epistolary prayer for the well-being of his readers, in which he singles out for thanksgiving some special characteristic for which they are noted.[1]

The simple form of the ordinary thanksgiving prayer in non-literary correspondence has been elaborated by St Paul into a formal literary pattern.[2]

The apostle occasionally may introduce the main theme (or

[1] For the Pauline epistolary thanksgiving prayer as a variation of a conventional epistolary form of prayer, see especially H. N. Bate, *A Guide to the Epistles of St. Paul* (London, 1949), p. 10ff.; W. Barclay, 'The New Testament and the Papyri', in *The New Testament in Historical and Contemporary Perspective; Essays in Memory of G. H. C. Macgregor* (Oxford, 1965), p. 70.

[2] See P. Schubert, *Form and Function of the Pauline Thanksgiving*, BZNW, xx (Berlin, 1939); J. T. Sanders, 'The Transition from Opening Epistolary Thanksgiving to Body in the Letters of the Pauline Corpus', *JBL*, LXXXI (1962), pp. 348–62.

themes) of his letter in this way (cf. 1 C. 1:7, 'spiritual gift').
At times there seems a deliberate irony in the characteristics of
the addressees singled out for thanksgiving: in Romans it is their
'faith' which is proclaimed 'in all the world'; in fact, they were
probably better known for their 'justification by works'. Thus,
as early in his epistle as this point St Paul introduces its central
theme.

In these verses Paul also intimates, prepares for, and justifies
his intended visit to Rome (cf. 15:24). He desires both to confer
and receive some 'spiritual gift', though hitherto prevented from
doing so, for he is filled with zeal to proclaim the Gospel in
Rome.

**8. First, I thank my God through Jesus Christ for all
of you.** First (of all): the adverb modifies the verb; Paul puts
thanksgiving to God first: yet the words also convey the thought
that he also puts his Roman readers first in his prayers. Or:
'my thanks to God for you all must come first'.

through Jesus Christ: Origen comments on these words: 'To
give thanks to God: this is to offer a sacrifice of praise: and therefore (Paul) adds: "through Jesus Christ", as it were through a
great High Priest.' (See SH, *in loc.*) This is probably to read a
great deal more into his words than Paul meant; the formula
'through Jesus Christ (our Lord)' means simply that the thanksgiving which Paul offers he makes, like his Roman readers, as
a disciple of Christ.

your faith is proclaimed in all the world: the Roman
Church was possibly better known throughout the Roman
Empire for its legalism than for its faith. See above, and Intro-
duction, p. 23.

**9. For God is my witness, whom I serve with my spirit
in the gospel of his Son:** the verb 'to serve' here (*latreuō*) is
especially associated with the 'liturgical service' of God, in Temple
or synagogue, by priest and people. The organ of Paul's service
is his 'spirit': its sphere the Gospel.

without ceasing: 'continually, without intermission'. The
adverb is stressed—so great is Paul's concern.

**10. asking that somehow by God's will I may now at last
succeed in coming to you:** 'at last' seems to imply that Paul's
Roman readers are aware of his plans to visit Rome; in fact they
are not apprised of these till chapter 15. Cf. J. Knox, in *NTS*,

II (1955–6), p. 191ff. Paul had often planned to visit Rome but
had been hindered hitherto (cf. verse 13). This is implied in this
verse, verse 11 emphasizing the intensity of Paul's desire to visit
Rome. Though he no doubt intended to do so (cf. 15:32), the
prospect is here left vague and uncertain: notice how indefinite
his words are—'if', 'perchance', 'at long last', 'sometime'. It was
no doubt his fears and anxieties about the results of his forthcoming visit to Jerusalem which accounted for this feeling of
uncertainty, as they would also for the words 'by God's will' (i.e.
if God so wills it); God's will for Paul in Jerusalem was still
unknown. There is certainly nothing here to suggest that St Paul
is coming to Rome; only that he has long wanted to. Cf. J. Knox,
loc. cit.

**11. For I long to see you, that I may impart to you some
spiritual gift to strengthen you:** the 'spiritual *charisma*' which
Paul's purpose is to share with the Roman Church is not necessarily to be defined as one or any of the 'spiritual gifts', e.g. those
listed by him at 1 C. 12:1ff. though Paul could claim possession
of miraculous gifts of the Spirit in a pre-eminent degree (1 C.
14:18). It is more probable that Paul is using the term in a more
general sense of the 'benefaction' of his Gospel for the Gentiles.

**12. to strengthen you, that is, that we may be mutually
encouraged by each other's faith:** *RSV* gives the correct
meaning, not *RV* ('to the end that ye may be established');
NEB: 'to make you strong'. The word is used of the inner
strengthening of mind and spirit imparted by God (cf. Rom.
16:25, 2 Th. 2:17, 3:3). The choice of the passive here may be
deliberate: 'Not that I (Paul) should strengthen you, but that
God should strengthen you.' For this use of the passive, cf.
Jeremias, *Eucharistic Words of Jesus*, Eng. trans. (Oxford, 1955),
p. 122ff.

The previous verse might sound patronizing, in spite of the use
of the word 'share' where Paul might have said 'impart' (which is,
no doubt, what he really meant); verse 12, with fine tact, qualifies
verse 11: it was a common or mutual encouraging, or heartening
or strengthening, he meant to be given and received 'among you',
and it was by their commonly held faith—theirs and Paul's—that
this strengthening and mutual encouragement was to be effected.

13. I want you to know: lit. 'I would not have you ignorant'.
This is a favourite phrase (cf. 11:25, 1 C. 10:1, 12:1, 2 C. 1:8,

1 Th. 4: 13) when St Paul wants to call attention to what follows; it is sometimes now referred to as a 'disclosure formula', or 'formula of transition'.[1]

in order that I may reap some harvest: there is an ambiguity in the meaning, which again is an instance of Pauline tact. Paul planned to get results at Rome as elsewhere in the Gentile world; but his words could mean that he planned to come to receive some benefit from the Roman Church, as he had also elsewhere in the Gentile world.

have been prevented: at 1 Th. 2:18 Satan was the hindrance; here it seems to be implied that it is God—or Providence—preventing Paul's firm intention being carried out.

14. under obligation: the noun is ambiguous: it can mean 'I owe a debt to', 'I am under obligation to'; and this fits well with the meaning of verse 13, that Paul planned his visit to Rome to *receive* some fruit from the Roman Church. The same noun, however, from meaning 'to owe something to' can come to mean 'to have a duty to' (cf. Gal. 5:3, Rom. 8:12), and this fits the other sense of verse 13. Paul planned his visit to Rome to impart the *charisma* of his Gentile Gospel; for he has a duty to Greeks and barbarians, wise and simple—to which latter category some Roman Christians may have belonged.

15. so I am eager to preach the gospel: the expression may be literally translated: 'as far as concerns me there is readiness', implying 'I am ready to do my part, whether or not you are'. Another version is: 'thus the readiness or inclination on my part (is) to preach the gospel', etc. This amounts, in effect, to the same as *RSV*, but the *impersonal* way of saying it may be deliberate: St Paul is keeping himself in the background.

It is not till chapter 15 that Paul discloses his plans, first to proceed to Jerusalem with his 'collection' for the saints (and all that this entails of trouble and delay), then to visit Spain via Rome. See J. Knox, in *NTS* II (1956-6), pp. 191-3.

---

[1] Cf. J. T. Sanders, 'The Transition from Opening Epistolary Thanksgiving to Body in the Letters of the Pauline Corpus', *JBL*, LXXXI (1962), pp. 348-62; J. L. White, 'Introductory Formulae in the Body of the Pauline Letter', ibid., XC (1971), pp. 91-7; also T. Y. Mullins, 'Disclosure: a Literary Form in the New Testament', *Nov. Test.*, VII (1964), pp. 44-50. White argues that the body of the Roman letter begins with verse 13, and that therefore the end of the Thanksgiving is at verse 12.

If we accept the argument of White that the body of Romans begins at verse 13 (see above, p. 42 n. 1), then Romans is, in fact, Paul's Gospel which he had failed to preach in person: verse 15 introduces it, verse 16 adumbrates it, and the remainder of chapters 1 to 8 defines it and enlarges on it.

PRELIMINARY STATEMENT OF THEME 16–18

The 'great thesis' of Romans, 'justification by faith alone' is adumbrated in these verses.

16. ashamed: to the Greek the gospel was 'foolishness' (1 C. 1:23); it took courage not to be ashamed of it in Imperial Rome. Cf. further, K. Grayston, ' "Not Ashamed of the Gospel" ', *Stud. Ev.* II (1964), pp. 569–73; O. Glombitza, 'Von der Scham des Gläubigen', *Nov. Test.*, IV (1960), pp. 74–80.

power of God: the word 'power' (*dynamis*) is especially associated in the *NT* with supernatural manifestations (e.g., miraculous occurrences like the Resurrection, cf. verse 4): in the plural, 'powers', it is a synonym of 'signs' (*sēmeia*) and 'wonders' (*terata*) (cf. Ac. 2:22). Thus the Gospel as the 'power of God' is a unique manifestation of supernatural reality. Older commentators compare it with natural forces such as heat and electricity, but, if we use this analogy or translate by 'force', 'energy', etc., it must be remembered (a) that such a force was conceived of in a category or concept of the supernatural—it emanated from beyond Nature as a divine force; and (b) that the divine 'force' or 'energy' of God which is the Gospel, by its very nature, is a *personal activity* of God on the human level—and this it is at the point of its manifestation, in Christ.

for salvation: the fundamental idea of 'salvation' (*sōtēria*) in Greek (profane or Biblical) is—like the word's derivatives—that of any kind of deliverance from physical danger or death (e.g. 1 Sam. 11:13). In Biblical Greek the word came especially to be appropriated to denote the great 'deliverances' of Israel by Yahweh, e.g. from the Egyptian bondage (Exod. 14:13, 15:2), the Babylonian Captivity and Exile (Isa. 45:17, 52:15). By a natural development, the word came to be used to describe the final deliverance of Israel when the Saviour or Deliverer came (e.g. Ps. Sol. x. 8, xii. 7); and this deliverance came more and more to be interpreted in terms of an ultimate deliverance from the powers of Satan, sin, and death. This is the connotation of the word in the *NT*: it is God's deliverance of man from sin, death, and judgement.

to every one who has faith, to the Jew first and also to the Greek: faith is the pre-condition of the effective working of the reality of God's saving power—and that reality goes out to every man, first to the Jew, since he was God's privileged man (cf. Ps. 80:17, where Israel is described as 'God's right-hand man', i.e. that branch of the human family specially chosen by God as the channel of his 'revelation'), then to Greeks; for this salvation by divine power given to faith is open to the believing Gentile no less than to the believing Jew.

17. the righteousness of God: 'righteousness' (and its cognates) has a wide range of meaning in the Bible. While it does have a connotation of 'integrity' ('uprightness', 'virtue'), in Hebrew thought, where ethics are 'relational', the emphasis tends to be on 'right relations' ('justice') within the societary unit (the tribe, nation, etc.) and, within the structure of a theocratic society, it includes the covenant relationship to God. It thus denotes the covenanted 'righteousness' under the *tôrāh*. It was thus also a 'soteriological' as well as an ethical concept: it denotes the true well-being (essentially, for the Hebrew mind, morally conditioned) of the God-fearing man who enjoys the divine favour and blessing (cf. Ps. 24:5; at Prov. 8:18 it means 'success', 'prosperity').

Since Paul can use the verb *dikaioun*, meaning 'to pronounce righteous' and so 'to acquit', at Gal. 3:11, in a context similar to the present one (also using Hab. 2:4 as proof-text), it is not surprising that the noun has come to be traditionally rendered by 'justification', in the forensic sense of *justificatio*, namely 'acquittal'.

'Righteousness' is also an attribute of God; the 'righteous God' performs acts of righteousness (Jg. 5:11). When attributed to God, 'righteousness' can mean 'right vindicated' (cf. *NEB*: 'God's way of righting wrong')—hence 'triumph, victory, the victory of the righteous cause'. The word thus comes to be nearly synonymous with 'salvation', stressing the more positive aspects, not 'deliverance from', but a vindication of, and so the *triumph* of, etc. (the righteous cause). The expression 'the righteousness of God' comes especially to be applied to the saving action or intervention of God in the deliverance of Israel from Egypt (e.g. Ps. 103:6), or the deliverance from the Babylonian captivity (Isa.

51:5: 'My righteousness (triumph) is near, my salvation is gone
forth.')

The 'righteousness of God' has been traditionally interpreted
in this context in two ways:[1]

(i) In view of the following 'proof-text' from Habakkuk which
stresses the righteousness of the individual, the 'righteousness of
God' is understood to be an individual righteousness, 'imputed'
or 'imparted' by God (*justitia imputata* or *infusa*), whereby, on the
sole condition of faith alone in Jesus Christ, the guilty party
is 'justified'. This is then said to be 'by faith and faith alone'.
Thus the theme of Romans is stated as: *justificatio sola fide*.

In support of this interpretation, Rom. 3:22 is cited: 'the
righteousness of God through faith in Jesus Christ'; where a
'righteousness proceeding from God' and 'imputed' or 'imparted'
on the grounds of faith in Jesus Christ seems the sense intended.
Moreover, since 3:24 employs the verb in the sense 'being
acquitted (freely by his grace)', the 'righteousness of God' in
verse 21 must at least bear the meaning of 'divine acquittal'. A
similar sense is claimed for Phil. 3:9, where Paul is again contrasting (as at Gal. 3:11) an 'acquittal' based on 'Law' (i.e. legal
works) with 'acquittal' which proceeds from God on the grounds
of Christian faith.

(ii) 'It is well to remember that St Paul had all these meanings
[of 'righteous' and its cognates] before him; and he glances from
one to another as the hand of a violin player runs over the strings
of his violin.'[2] The problem is to determine the meaning appropriate to each context. In spite of the arguments for a forensic
connotation at 1:17, the context (especially the parallel at verse 18
which stresses the revelation of the judgement (wrath) of God)
seems to favour the meaning: 'the triumph of God (over Satan,
sin and death)'.

is revealed: The verb *apokalyptetai* ('is being revealed') may be
taken as having a future reference to the Parousia. The tense of

---

[1] For a recent comprehensive discussion, see J. A. Ziesler, *The Meaning of
Righteousness in Paul* (SNTS Monograph Series, Cambridge, 1972). Ziesler
stresses the relational aspect of Christian 'righteousness' within the New
Covenant societary unit, the Body of Christ. Cf. also S. Lyonnet, 'De notione
justitiae dei apud S. Paulum [Rom. 1:17 et 3:21–26; Rom. 3:5]', *Verb. Dei*,
XLII (1964), pp. 121–52.

[2] SH, p. 34.

the synonymous verb, however, at 3:21 ('has been manifested')
clearly indicates that the triumph of God in the Gospel is already
a present reality. (Cf. Rom. 8:15, 23: 'adoption' as sons antici-
pates our final adoption as 'children of God'. See notes *ad loc.*)

through faith for faith: Barth interprets: '*unto faith* is revealed
that which God reveals from His faithfulness'.[1] Certainly the LXX
understood Hab. 2:4 in this way: 'The just shall live by *my* faith-
fulness'. Some may feel it unlikely, however, that Paul, however
skilful in his use of words, would have used the same word 'faith'
twice, in the same phrase, with a different meaning.

Similar phrases at 2 C. 2:16 ('from death to death' (i.e. 'from
total death'), 'from life to life' (i.e. 'from life that is life indeed');
cf. also Ps. 84:7) suggest some such meaning as 'through pure
faith' or 'through faith and nothing but faith' (so Nygren: *sola
fide*). Such an interpretation seems to rule out the sense: 'from the
faith (of a believer) to the faith of (others)—i.e. through the spread
of faith', or 'through the deepening of the faith of the individual'
(see SH *ad loc.*).

This is one of a number of phrases in Romans where J. Hugh
Michael suspects a corruption by 'vertical dittography': *ek pisteōs*
should be omitted as a dittograph from the following *ek pisteōs* in
Hab. 2:4.[2] This would certainly cut the Gordian knot, both of the
difficult phrase 'from faith to faith', but no less of the exegesis
of 1:17 as a whole. The verse would then be parallel to 16: 'a
righteousness of God is being revealed to faith'. The construction
would be analogous to 8:18: 'the glory that is to burst on us'
(Goodspeed).

He who through faith is righteous shall live: Hab. 2:4. The
original meaning of the Hebrew text of Hab. 2:4 is that 'the just,
or righteous man shall live (or survive) by his loyalty (to Yahweh),
i.e. the loyal Israelite shall escape or survive the impending politi-
cal catastrophe—in this case the Babylonian invasion or captivity
(586 B.C.). The text is quoted several times in the *NT*: by Paul
again at Gal. 3:11, where the context requires us to understand
'the righteous man' as the one who will be acquitted at the
Parousia on the sole grounds of his faith;[3] Hebrews 10:38 cites

---

[1] *The Epistle to the Romans*, trans. E. C. Hoskyns (Cambridge, 1953), p. 41.
[2] *JTS*, XXXIX (1938), pp. 150-4. See below, p. 48; also Michael's notes on
3:30, 4:12, 5:6, 6:16, 19, 10:9, 13:1, 4, 9, 14:12, 15:4, 5.
[3] Is there a possible suggestion here and in Romans that 'the righteous

the passage as: 'my just one shall live by faith (loyalty)'. The
thought is similar to Hab. 2:4: loyalty to God will save the
Christian (my just one), in this case, during the persecutions of
the Church in the Roman Empire. (Whether the loyalty is to God
or to Christ is not specified further.) 'Life' here has obviously
come to mean more than the survival of physical life from
disaster; it means: 'shall obtain or retain eternal life'.

How did St Paul understand Hab. 2:4 at Rom. 1:17? Notice
that he omits, in all places where the passage is cited, the *OT*
pronoun: '*his* faith', or '*my* faith'. Feuillet[1] considers this to be
deliberate: it has been done to enable Paul to take the words 'by
faith' (*ek pisteōs*) closely with the preceding 'the righteous man'
(*ho dikaios*), and to read, not 'the just shall live by faith', but 'the
just-by-faith shall live' (or as *RSV*). What St Paul is primarily
interested in is the kind of 'righteousness' by which a man is to
live, whether it is to be a 'righteousness' based on the Law, or a
new kind of righteousness in which the inner obedience of faith
replaces obedience to the external letter of the Law. The opposite
and contradictory proposition to 'the just-by-faith' (*ho dikaios ek
pisteōs*) would be contained in such words as 'the just-by-law'
(*ho dikaios ek nomou*). From the subsequent argument of Romans
it is clear that St Paul's main purpose is to substitute for the
obedience to the Law as the mainspring of life (cf. Dt. 30:15) a
living obedience by faith in the Risen Christian Lord (cf. 3:22,
Phil. 3:9); for Paul no less than for Hebrews, the 'life' to be so
gained is eternal life.

We must understand and render therefore: 'The just-by-faith
(in Christ) shall live (now and for ever)'—and the words, of
course, mean enjoy fullness of life, now and for ever.[2]

The key to an understanding of Paul's essential thesis is his
conviction of the total bankruptcy of contemporary Pharisaic
'scholasticism', which seemed to base the whole range of active
right relationships within the Covenant ('righteousness') on the

---

man' is a term for the Christian; cf. David Hill, in *NTS*, xi (1964–5), pp.
296ff.

[1] 'La Citation d'Habacuc ii. 4 et les huit premiers chapîtres de l'Epître
aux Romains', *NTS*, vi (1959–60), p. 52ff.

[2] Exegetes in favour of this view: H. Lietzmann, M. J. Lagrange, M. Goguel,
E. Kuhl, L. Cerfaux: for the older, traditional view, Th. Zahn, SH, C. H.
Dodd, O. Michel.

meticulous observation of the injunctions of the *tôrāh* as expounded
and expanded in the 'tradition of the elders'. This was 'legalistic
righteousness', a form of ethics based entirely on a code, external
and 'written', losing sight entirely of the gracious personal will
of a holy and good God, of which it was originally intended to be
the divine vehicle of expression. Paul would have had no quarrel
with the pious Jew who sought to do the will of God as revealed
in the *tôrāh*, without being hidebound at every turn by the
'prescriptions' of Pharisaic tradition. But he took a revolutionary
step forward by proclaiming a new personal intervention of God
in the history of salvation, Christ Risen and Returning, and faith
in this act of God as the sole grounds for salvation in the eschatological Now, in the impending, imminent Parousia.

Although the exegesis of this verse based on the assumption of
'vertical dittography' involves a conjecture—the omission of
ek pisteōs at verse 17—it seems to be the least unsatisfactory of the
many interpretations offered of this difficult passage. Verses 16
and 17 would then read:

> [16]For I am not ashamed of the Gospel. For it is the power of God
> for salvation to everyone who has faith, the Jew first, then the
> Greek. [17]For the triumph of God is revealed in it for faith, as it is
> written, 'The just-by-faith shall live'.

18. the wrath of God: verse 18 goes clearly with verse 17 and,
at the same time serves as a transition to verses 19ff. The same
verb is used of the 'revelation' of God's anger as in connection
with the 'revelation' of his 'righteousness'. God's wrath is the
manifestation of his righteousness. The God of the *OT* is on
occasion an angry deity, but his anger is never capricious or
arbitrary like the deities in Greek mythology: it is inflicted, for
instance, on rebellion against the Covenant (Lev. 10:1-2), or
on Israel for her transgression, on the Day of the Lord (Isa.
2:10ff.). In the *NT* the use of the term is 'eschatologized' (e.g.
Mt. 3:7; 1 Th. 1:10; Rom. 2:5; Rev. 6:16, 17). But this does
not mean that the wrath of God is manifested only on the great
Day of Judgement; God's way of 'setting things right', which is
also his judgement and the manifestation of his wrath, is also a
present eschatological reality in the visible consequences of here-
and-now evil-doing ('the observable situation in the latter part
of this chapter' (Barrett)). This is the element of truth in Dodd's

explanation of the wrath of God 'to describe an inevitable process
of cause and effect in a moral universe' (*ad loc.*). Cf. also G. Bornkamm, 'The Revelation of God's Wrath: Romans i–iii' in *Early
Christian Experience* (London, 1969), pp. 46ff.

is revealed: the verb here, as in verse 17, is best taken as a continuous present: 'is being revealed'. Paul is thinking of *the* great
eschatological drama as having begun already with the Resurrection: the *final* manifestation of God's wrath, viz. the Last
Judgement, will ensue when Christ returns at his Parousia.

from heaven: it is to be a Judgement 'out of this world'. This
is not God acting in history (as in the deliverances from Egypt and
Babylonia) but from 'beyond history'. The eschatology is a
'transcendentalising' eschatology.

ungodliness and wickedness of men: 'ungodliness' is the
human condition which brings down the divine wrath, since it
is a breach of the first commandment which is clearly Paul's
main thought in these verses: from 'godlessness' or 'idolatry' all
human wrong-doing springs.[1]

THE FAILURE OF LAW 1:19–3:20

THE CASE AGAINST THE GENTILES 1:19–32

The long section 1:19–3:20 is an indictment of the human race
for its tragic failure and folly. The first section (1:19–32) deals
with Gentile guilt. Though not possessing any revelation of God,
the Gentile world had a natural theology and a natural law: yet
it failed just as Israel failed.[2]

The literary structure of these verses is noteworthy. It is a
Jewish type of polemic by which St Paul carries forward his
argument, possibly influenced, in content and style, by Wis. 12:
27ff. (Cf. E. Norden, *Agnostos Theos* (Darmstadt, 1956), p. 128ff.)

[1] On the verse, see also C. E. B. Cranfield, in *SJT*, xxi (1968), pp. 330–5.
[2] Cf. S. Schulz, 'Die Anklage in Röm. 1:18–22', *TZ*, xiv (1958), pp. 161–
73. Cf. further H. Ott, 'Röm. 1:19ff als dogmatisches Problem', ibid., xv
(1959), pp. 40–50; F. Flückiger, 'Zur Untersuchung von Heiden und Juden
in Röm. i:18–ii:3', ibid., x (1954), pp. 154–8; A. Fridrichsen, 'Romans
i:19ff', in *ZNTW*, xvii (1916), pp. 159–68; M. Barth, 'Speaking of Sin:
Some Interpretative Notes on Rom. 1:18–iii:20', *SJT*, viii (1955), pp. 288–96.

Verses 28-32 read like part of a spoken diatribe, and might
well have come from a Pauline missionary 'sermon': they re-
semble, in some respects, the section in Attic comedy known to the
ancient rhetoricians as the *pnigos*, a long passage to be spoken in a
single breath. There is a word-play in the Greek at verses 28 and
31 ('see fit' (*edokimasan*); 'gave them up to' (*paredōken*); 'improper
(*adokimon*) conduct'; 'foolish' (*asynetous*), 'faithless' (*asynthetous*).
Note, too, the emphatic repetition of the word 'gave them up'
(*paredōken*) (verses 24, 26, 28) and 'exchanged' (*ēllaxan, met-
ēllaxan*) (verses 23, 25, 26). The central idea is that of God's
despair (*paredōken*, 'gave them up') at human perversion ((*met*)-
ēllaxan). Verses 18ff. develop the Stoic doctrine of knowledge
of God through His works.

19. what can be known: (See H. Rosin on Rom. 1:19, in *TZ*,
XVII (1961), pp. 161–5. Cf. also B. Gärtner, *The Areopagus Speech
and Natural Revelation* (Copenhagen, 1955); H. Bietenhard, 'Natürliche Gotteserkenntnis der Heiden', *TZ*, XII (1956), pp. 275–88;
B. Reicke, 'Natürliche Theologie nach Paulus', *Svensk Exegetisk
Årsbok*, XXII–XXIII (1957–8), p. 159; H. P. Owen, 'The Scope of
Natural Revelation in Rom. 1 and Acts 17', *NTS*, V (1958–9), pp.
133–43; J. L. McKenzie, 'Natural Law in the New Testament',
Biblical Research, IX (1964), p. 3ff.; D. M. Coffey, 'Natural Knowledge of God: Reflections on Rom. 1:18–32', *JTS*, XXI (1970),
pp. 674–91. For Stoic antecedents, see especially M. Pohlenz,
'Paulus und die Stoa', *ZNTW*, XLII (1949), p. 69ff.)
plain to them: lit., 'manifest in (or among) them'. What was
knowable about God was known to them. The sense 'plain in
their minds and consciences' may be preferred, since the argument
goes on to state that their minds 'had become darkened'.

20. Ever since the creation of the world: or: 'from the
created Universe', i.e. from things created. The first sense is
preferable, and the phrase is parallel to the expression 'from the
foundation of the world' (Mt. 25:34) and 'from the beginning
of creation' (Mk 10:6).

**his invisible nature, namely, his eternal power and deity,
has been clearly perceived in the things that have been
made:** note the oxymoron: 'invisible', 'clearly perceived' (lit.,
'seen'); and cf. Aristotle, *de Mundo*, 6: 'The invisible God is made
visible by his works themselves' (*atheōrētos ap' autōn tōn ergōn
theōreitai [ho Theos]*)', with Philo, *de Praem. et Poen.*, 7, for the

same paradox, no doubt a common place of Stoic natural theology; for the whole verse, cf. also Wis. 13:1ff., and for the connection with Wisdom, see Bornkamm, op. cit., p. 55. Bornkamm also rightly sees that 'natural revelation' for Paul is not the 'knowledge of God' by the use of rational faculties, but a God-given revelation to the mind of man (op. cit., p. 50ff.).

21. became futile in their thinking . . . were darkened: better 'became darkened' (note that both verbs are ingressive aorists). The *dialogismos* ('thinking') may refer to the 'arguments', 'debates', 'disputations' of the Stoic philosophers. We may paraphrase: 'they lose themselves (ingressive aorist) in their futile disputations, and are plunged (ingressive aorist) in mindless darkness.'

22. (On verses 22-32, see J. Jeremias, *Abba* (Göttingen, 1966), pp. 290-2. Cf. also E. Klostermann, 'Die adäquate Vergeltung in Röm. 1:22-31', *ZNTW*, xxxii (1933), pp. 1-6. (The usual paragraph division at verse 24 is to be rejected: the literary structure is: verses 22-4 (the sin of idolatry); 25-7 (divine punishment); 28ff. See also S. Lyonnet, 'Notes sur l'exégèse de l'épître aux Romains', in *Bib.*, xxxvii (1957), pp. 35ff.) **became fools:** again, ingressive aorist.

23. exchanged the glory . . .: men substituted idolatry for the worship of the true glory of God. In the background of the thought of this verse is Ps. 106:20, and also possibly Gen. 1:20; cf. Jer. 2:11; Dt. 4:15-18. Cf. N. Hyldahl, 'A Reminiscence of the Old Testament at Romans i. 23', *NTS*, ii (1955-6), pp. 285-8. Paul's thought is influenced here by Wis. 14:12, idolatry leads to moral depravity. He seems also to be familiar with pagan catalogues of the vices: they are grouped into (a) sensual vices (24-8), and (b) anti-social vices (29-31). See further, M. Hooker, 'Adam in Rom. 1', *NTS* vi (1959-60), pp. 297-306; xiii (1966-67), pp. 181-3.

24. lusts: in this context referring to sexual (or homosexual) passions.

among themselves: or 'between themselves'. This seems to mean 'with one another', and this yields a superior sense to the alternative interpretation which renders 'so that their bodies were dishonoured among them' (so SH).

images resembling mortal men: cf. J. M. Bover, ' "Imaginis" notio apud B. Paulum', *Bib.*, iv (1923), p. 174ff.

25. the truth about God for a lie: in the *OT*, 'lie', 'lies', can be used with the sense of 'false gods', 'idols' (e.g. Jer. 13:25) and this may be the sense here—'for idols' (collective singular). In that case, 'the truth of God' is not the 'truth about God' as virtually 'the true God' (abstract for concrete; cf. 1 Th. 1:9). This does not, of course, exclude other and wider meanings, such as 'the true revelation of God (which God gave)' and 'falsehood' (i.e. the false world of idolatry).

Bornkamm notes ('Revelation', p. 53) that Paul agrees with contemporary opinions that 'idolatry and immoral life are the results of irrational and deficient knowledge of God'.

who is blessed for ever: a brief Jewish form of doxology.

Verses 26–32 specify in detail the perversions which are consequent on idolatry. In 26–7 Paul describes the horrible homosexual practices of pagan society so obnoxious to Jews, though in specifying them first he may be giving them an even larger prominence than some of his compatriots did (cf. Letter of Aristeas, 152, in H. G. Meecham, *The Oldest Version of the Bible* (London, 1932), pp. 48, 297ff.).

26. dishonourable passions: lit. 'obscenity'.

27. in their own persons: lit. 'in (within) themselves'.

error: the Greek word is stronger: it means their foolish apostasy.

28. base mind: the word-play in this verse (see above, p. 50) is reproduced by Barrett (*in loc.*): 'And as they did not see fit to take cognizance of God, God handed them over to an unfit mind.' The original word means 'tried and rejected', a meaning which is reproduced exactly by the translation 'reprobate'. Kirk (Clarendon Bible) renders much more freely: 'as they recked nothing of God, he gave them over to recklessness'.

and to improper conduct: lit. 'to do the things that are not fitting' (*kathēkonta*). The expression is a regular Stoic term, e.g., Epictetus, II, xvii, 31; Polyb. VI. vi. 7. Cf. M. Pohlenz, *Die Stoa* (Göttingen, 1948–9), p. 487; and SH, *in loc.*

28–32. The list of vices may owe something to similar Hellenistic (or Jewish-Hellenistic) lists. There are similar 'catalogues' at Rom. 13:13; 1 C. 5:10f., 6:9ff.; 2 C. 12:20ff.; Gal. 5:19ff.; Eph. 4:31; 5:3ff.; Col. 3:5, 8; 1 Tim. 1:9f.; 2 Tim. 3:2–5. Cf. also 1 Clem. xxxv:5.

29. wickedness: (*adikia*); 'wrong-doing' or 'injustice' (*NEB*) is closer to the original. The word refers to all anti-social action or conduct, whereas evil (*ponēria*) is perhaps better rendered by 'wickedness': evil in general is meant. (*NEB* 'mischief' is too narrow a connotation for *ponēria*).

covetousness: *NEB* 'rapacity' is possibly too strong, though the Greek word can have this sense; in Plato it is the characteristic vice of the tyrant. The word means literally 'having more (than one's share)'—'selfishness', 'self-seeking', 'self-aggrandisement', 'greed', etc., according to context. A fairly common Pauline word; cf. Col. 3:5 where 'selfishness' is declared to be idolatry. This particular vice usually stands at the head of the hellenistic catalogue of vices, so that presumably it was one of the most common and most frowned-on of vices.

malignity: *NEB* 'malevolence'.

30. haters of God: the word could be understood in a passive sense meaning 'hated of God', as the Vulgate renders: *Deo odibilis*. Moreover, the word appears only to be attested in this passive sense (see Bauer, *in loc.*). On the other hand, the word is a comparatively rare one, and, as Barrett points out, the passage as a whole deals with human activities; the word, therefore, is better understood in an active sense: 'God-loathers'. (Cf. also I Clem. xxxv: 5, where the noun has an active connotation.) It has been further suggested that we should take the word as an adjective with the previous noun: 'God-hating (hated) slanderers', a suggestion of Pallis (*To the Romans* (1933); see Barrett, *in loc.*). The objection to this is that in the rest of the verse we have to do with single words (or compound expressions), all nouns (or nouns with a genitive), and this suggests that the word is to be understood as a noun by itself.

inventors of evil: an odd kind of expression. It is paralleled by Virgil's description of Ulysses as *scelerum inventor* ('crime-deviser'). Similar expressions at 2 Mac. 7:31 and in Philo (*In Flacc.* 20, 73).

31. foolish, faithless, heartless, ruthless: there is no logical link between the first two words: they are brought together for the sake of the word-play: *asynetous, asynthetous*.

32. There seems to be an anti-climax in Paul's 'not only . . . but': 'not only approve of those who do such things but do them themselves' would give the more appropriate sense: but the more difficult text is Paul's.

The Jews also are Attacked[1] 2:1-29

Verses 1–7 establish that only a good life counts in God's sight, and this applies equally to Jew and Greek (verses 9, 11). Obedience or disobedience to Law decide a man's destiny, and again nationality is of no account in God's sight, for the pagan world, though not possessing *the* Law, was not without some idea of law (their 'natural law', like their natural religion), obedience or disobedience to which would be rewarded or punished with the same impartiality as where there was a revealed Law (verses 11–16). The discussion about the equal responsibility of Gentile and Jew before God is continued in 2:17–3:20, with special reference to the alleged superiority of the Jew (3:1–9); 3:9–20 states the main conclusion, that both Jew and Gentile stand condemned in God's sight, and this is done with the help of a catena of *OT* quotations which clinch the argument with an effective rhetorical climax.

1. another: lit., 'the other man'; i.e., since Paul has the Jew in mind here, 'the Gentile'. The word here probably is to be understood in the sense of 'your fellow (man)', 'neighbour'.

2. We know: or, **'For we know . . .'** This is a familiar Pauline phrase (cf. 3:19; 7:14; 8:22, 28). Cf. the phrase *kathōs oidate* ('as you know'), especially in 1 Th. Paul can assume a body of Christian instruction. See N. A. Dahl, 'Anamnesis: mémoire et commémoration dans le christianisme primitif', *Stud. Theol.*, 1 (1947), pp. 69–95.

3. Do you suppose: lit. 'are you reckoning on this'.
you will escape: there seemed to be a widely held popular view among Jews that Jewish nationality by itself would confer exemption from judgement.

4. presume upon: lit. 'despise'. Cf. 1 Tim. 6:2 for a similar use.
riches of his kindness . . .: this expressive figure of speech occurs a number of times in different connections in the epistles: e.g. 9:23, 11:33; Phil. 4:19; Col. 1:27, 2:2; it is especially characteristic of Ephesians (1:7, 18, 2:7, 3:8, 16). The figure is

---

[1] That Paul has exclusively Jews in mind in this section has been challenged in recent discussion. Cf. H. W. Bartsch, 'Die historische Situation des Römerbriefs', *Stud. Evang.*, iv (TU 102, 1968), p. 286. See also Barrett, *ad loc.* (Jews and Stoic philosophers?)

not found elsewhere in the *NT*. 'The full force of this accusation
will be felt if we set beside it words from Wisdom (xiv, xv) (which
Paul evidently knew).' (Barrett)

is meant to lead you: this is an attempt to render what is called
a conative present: 'is seeking', ('striving', etc.) 'to lead'.

5. hard and impenitent heart: a hendiadys—'in your
obstinate, unrepentant state of mind'.

you are storing up wrath: lit. 'you are "treasuring" up wrath'.
The kind of 'treasure' here being amassed is contrasted with the
'riches' of verse 4. A 'treasury of wrath' was not what the Jew
here addressed believed he was accumulating. Cf. H. St. J.
Thackeray, *Relation of St Paul to Contemporary Jewish Thought*
(London, 1900), p. 81: 'Your obedience to the Law and disbelief
in the Gospel is not leading to a treasury of merits with God but a
treasury of wrath'. For this metaphorical use of the verb, cf.
Prov. 1:18 (LXX).

**on the day of wrath when God's righteous judgement will
be revealed:** lit. 'on the day of wrath and of the revelation of the
just judgement of God.' The word rendered 'just judgement' is a
rare one (*dikaiokrisia*), and it was this which probably led Moffatt
to render 'just doom'. It is a solemn and dignified expression: the
same meaning could have been conveyed by the two words 'just
judgement' (as at 2 Th. 1:5), but the style would have been the
poorer.

6. St Paul, here and at verse 13, assumes the current Jewish
doctrine of 'justification by works' (cf. 2 C. 5:10; Gal. 6:7;
Eph. 6:8). There is no necessary contradiction with his own
distinctive teaching about justification *sola fide*. The Pauline
doctrine deals with the conditions of entering on the Christian
life—that life rooted and grounded on faith alone. But in the life
that follows 'works', as the spontaneous expression of the life of
faith (the 'fruit of the spirit'), are no less an integral part of the
life which will one day be judged by God—only they are no longer
simply the result of an external conformity to a legal code.

7. to those who by patience in well-doing: the sense here
could be simply that of persistence or determination to do what
is right. The word rendered 'patience' has an active as well as a
passive sense in Greek; here it is not only the active pursuit of the
good life which is meant (*NEB*: 'steady persistence in well-doing'),
but possibly also the patient endurance under difficulties which

nevertheless continues to do right, like the 'goodness' which St Peter commends to the Christian slaves at 1 Pet. 2:20ff. (Cf. Heb. 12:1.)

seek for glory and honour and immortality: the last term is literally 'incorruption'. The motivation of Christian goodness is the same as its reward; the Christian seeks a glorious incorruption by his patient suffering and persistence in well-doing, and this is given to him in the eternal life which God bestows.

8. for those who are factious: the *NEB* rendering, 'for those who are governed by selfish ambition', is closer to the original meaning of the Greek. The same expression occurs at Phil. 1:17. The noun here used *eritheia* is rare and probably means 'selfishness', 'selfish ambition', rather than 'strife': but commentators are divided.

the truth: i.e. the way of truth.

wrath and fury: i.e. in the eschatological sense of these terms. Such evil-doers will be made to feel the full force of the terrible wrath of God in the coming Judgement.

9. tribulation and distress: these are both strong terms. The second means 'torturing confinement': *RV* 'anguish' is possibly better, because stronger, than 'distress': *NEB* takes the two words together as a hendiadys, and renders: 'grinding misery'.

for every human being who does evil: or who persists in evil-doing; the present tense may be pressed.

10. glory and honour and peace: a change in the earlier formula of verse 7. 'Peace' includes, if it is not confined to, the Pauline connotation of 'reconciliation with God' (cf. 5:1).

11. For God shows no partiality: lit. 'for there is no favouritism' (respect of persons, an *OT* expression) 'with God'–a principle enunciated also in *OT* Scripture, e.g., 2 Chr. 19:7; cf. also Sir. 35:13.

12. without the Law: i.e. outside the sphere of, or beyond the reach of, Law, but with the nuance 'lawlessly' and, in the second instance, 'as law-breakers (criminals) [perish]'. There is a deliberate parallelism in the clauses of this verse: the words might be a quotation from some well-known source. Moffatt brings this out well by rendering: 'All who sin outside the Law will perish outside the Law, and all who sin under the Law will be condemned by the Law.'

13. will be justified: i.e. will be acquitted at God's final assize.

14. Gentiles: i.e. *some* Gentile nations.[1] The absence of the article is significant: '*the* Gentiles' would mean all or most Gentile nations. But Paul would hardly concede that *the* Gentiles do naturally what the law enjoins—some Gentile nations certainly, and even this is subsequently qualified.

do by nature what the law requires: 'the law' here is clearly the Mosaic Law. As a rule in these verses when Paul speaks of 'law' (without the definite article), it is law in general he means, though it may also refer to the Mosaic Law as one form of 'law'.

It seems probable that the apostle is thinking of the Stoic 'natural law', i.e. reason, the immanent principle informing the *kosmos* (and converting it from *chaos* into *kosmos*), manifesting itself in the human mind as the power of discursive thought, able, among other things, to distinguish right from wrong. This is the meaning of 'conscience' in verse 15: it is the power of reason to make moral distinctions, and so decisions. See, further, note on verse 15.

The idea of 'natural law' goes back beyond Plato: in general it comes very close to the Hebrew ideal of the 'law written in the heart'. Cf. Plato, *Pol.*, iv. 425a, 427a, Isocrates, *Areopag.*, 41 ('law of the soul' contrasted with 'law of tables'—'let them fill their souls with justice and not the statute-books with new laws'); cf. also Plutarch (cited Wettstein); *quis custodiet custodes: lex rex mortalium et immortalium.* Cf. also Aristot., *Rhet.* i.xiii.14.

they are a law to themselves: lit. 'these men (or individuals)'. The masculine demonstrative pronoun shows that Paul is not really prepared to concede even that *some* Gentile nations could rise to these heights, but only that a few individuals might do so.

The words 'they are a law to themselves' mean the very opposite of the popular expression about 'being a law to oneself', namely, *have law within themselves.* Cf. Aristotle, *Nicom. Ethics*, iv. 1128a.31: 'the cultivated and free-minded man is, as it were, a law to himself', i.e. he does not require rules to be imposed from outside, but has his own self-imposed discipline. Cf. further, M.

[1] On this section, see J. Riedl, *Das Heil der Heiden nach Röm.* 2:14-16, 26, 27 (Vienna, 1965); cf. also *Scholastik*, XL (1965), pp. 189ff.; F. Kuhr, 'Römer ii:14f. und die Verheissung bei Jer. 31:31f.', in *ZNTW*, LV (1964), pp. 243-61.

Pohlenz, 'Paulus und die Stoa', *ZNTW*, XLII (1949), p. 69ff. See also W. Kranz, 'Das Gesetz des Herzens', *Rhein. Mus. für Philologie*, XCIV (1951), pp. 222–41.

15. They show: lit. 'inasmuch as they . . .'—giving the grounds for the statement of verse 14. There are several possible ways of construing these words: (a) inasmuch as they *manifest* (i.e., show as qualities of character) the conduct required by the law as (something) written in their hearts; (b) the word translated 'show' is used specially in a legal connection (the noun *endeixis* means 'proof', and gives us the English word 'indictment'): the verb here employed means 'prove', 'produce as proof'. We may then render: 'inasmuch as they produce as proof . . .'; in favour of this alternative are the legal metaphors in the rest of the verse ('bear witness', 'accuse', etc.).

what the law requires: lit. 'the works (coll. sing.) of the Law', i.e. the conduct required by the Law.

conscience: here personified and seen as an independent witness; see above on verse 14. The existence of a pagan 'conscience' (in the Stoic sense) is corroboratory testimony, supporting the proof or evidence already there of an inner law. Cf. for the same phrase, 9:1. See further B. Reicke, '*Syneidēsis* in Röm. 2:15', *TZ*, XII (1956), pp. 157–61.

and their conflicting thoughts: lit. 'and with one another, their debates'; or 'their mutual debates', i.e. 'their argumentations with one another', an alternative which may be preferable, especially in view of the prominence of the words 'with one another'. (Is the reference perhaps to the Stoic (or current philosophical) discourses in the form of the Platonic dialogues?)

16. on that day when: there is no justification for detaching the clause from its present place. (Moffatt places verse 16 after verse 13.) The thought is that the 'law on their hearts' will be their defence, and pagan 'reasonings'—from the dialogues of Plato to the latest Stoic diatribe—their witnesses, on the Day of Judgement.

God judges: or: 'God will judge'. The reference is to the future Last Judgement in this verse, as earlier in the chapter at verses 3, 5–6. See H. Saake, 'Echtheitskritische Überlegungen zur Interpolationshypothese von Römer 2:16', (1972–3) *NTS*, XIX, p. 486.

according to my gospel: this is sometimes connected with the following words 'by Jesus Christ', and to refer to the doctrine of the Parousia judgement as 'Paul's Gospel'. There is nothing, however, peculiarly Pauline about this idea.

St Paul's distinctive Gospel was his inclusion of the Gentiles within the purview of his Gospel. According to the immediately preceding verses, they stand equally responsible before God for their guilt, and will be judged or exonerated (on the grounds of their conscience) at the Parousia—according to *Paul's* Gospel. The words refer to verse 11 (there is no favouritism with God), expanded at verses 12–15: *all* men will be judged by God through Jesus Christ—Jews by Jewish standards, Gentiles by Gentile standards—according to Paul's Gospel.

by Jesus Christ: the judgement at the Parousia is meant.

17. The indictment is now brought *expressis verbis* to bear directly on the Jew. On 2:17-24 see especially O. Olivieri, in *Bib.*, XI (1930), pp. 188ff.

call yourself . . .: lit. 'bear the name of Jew'.

rely upon the law: lit. 'have the Law at your back', 'lean upon the Law' (cf. Mic. 3:11).

boast of your relation to God: *NEB:* 'are proud of your God'. Sanday suggests a connection with Jer. 9:24: 'Let him that glorieth glory in this, that he understandeth and knoweth Me, that I am the Lord' (SH, *in loc.*).

18. approve what is excellent: *NEB:* 'are aware of moral distinctions'; Moffatt: 'with a sense of what is vital in religion'; lit., 'prove the things that differ'. But proving leads to approving, and the latter to the making of distinctions. One might render: 'have acquired powers of moral discrimination'. Tyndale rendered: 'hast experience of good and bad'.

19. guide to the blind: cf. Mt. 15:14, 23:16, 24. Some think St Paul is alluding to these sayings; but they may have been proverbial.

20. the embodiment of knowledge and truth: *NEB:* 'the very shape of knowledge and truth'. It is rather the essence or substance of true knowledge, which the Jew found in the Law. There may be a hendiadys in the words 'knowledge and truth', and they should be rendered as a single expression, 'true knowledge'; at 2 Tim. 3:5, the noun *morphōsis*, here rendered by 'embodiment', means 'outward appearance', 'outward show'; but it seems unlikely that this is the meaning here.

22. rob temples: the Jews abhorred idolatry, but were not

above removing from pagan shrines their gold or silver idols for
their own private use and profit; cf. Josephus, *Antiq.*, iv. viii. 10
(207), and Ac. 19:37, where the Town Clerk declares that Paul
and his companion were not 'temple robbers'. This charge against
Jews must have been known all over the pagan world; anti-
Jewish propaganda made *Hierosolyma* (Jerusalem) into *hierosylia*
('temple-robbery').

24. For, as it is written: the words which follow are a free
adaptation of Isa. 52:5 'On your account continually is my name
blasphemed among the Gentiles.' Cf. J. A. Fitzmyer, 'The Use of
Explicit Old Testament Quotations in Qumran Literature and
the New Testament', *NTS*, VII (1960–1), p. 324; B. Lindars,
New Testament Apologetic (London, 1961), p. 22.

25. your circumcision becomes uncircumcision: the
meaning is not in doubt. It is worth noting, however, that the verb
gegonen ('becomes') here may reflect a rabbinical nuance
= 'is reckoned as', 'is in effect' (*logisthēsetai*, verse 26).

26. a man who is uncircumcised keeps: lit. 'if the uncircumcision keep': abstract for concrete.

27. those who are physically uncircumcised: lit. 'the
uncircumcision by nature'; again, abstract for concrete.
you who have the written code and circumcision: lit. 'you
with all your written code and circumcision'. The *dia* (here
translated 'with') is the *dia* of attendant circumstances.

28–9. These verses show the familiar characteristics of Hebrew
poetic style, and this seems intentional.

> It is not the outward Jew that is a Jew;
> Nor is external, physical circumcision true circumcision:
> He who is one inwardly is the (real) Jew:
> And circumcision is of the mind, spiritual not literal.

'Circumcision of the heart (mind)' is an *OT* expression; cf. Jer.
4:4; Dt. 10:16, 30:6. It means man's inward response to God,
e.g. in repentance, or 'man's humble response to God's gracious
love and election' (Dt. 10:15) (Barrett). Arguments for textual
dislocation in these verses are not convincing; see H. Sahlin,
'Einige Textemendationen zum Römerbrief', *TZ*, IX (1953),
pp. 92ff.

29. His praise is not from men but from God: Barrett

draws attention to a probable underlying word-play here: 'Jew' is
yehudi, 'praise' is *hodayah*. He tries to reproduce it by rendering:
'He is a Jew, whose due comes not from men but from God.'

THE ALLEGED ADVANTAGE OF BEING A JEW 3:1–9

'If what St Paul is contending is true,' an imaginary objector
states, 'then there does not seem to be any advantage at all in
belonging to the Jewish race.' St Paul replies to these objections,
taking the opportunity at the same time to reply to the standard
charges of antinomianism which were being brought against him.

The argument is conducted by a process of question and answer,
the question being asked by an imaginary opponent or objector,
and the answer coming from the apostle.

As Dr C. H. Dodd points out, the style is that of the contemporary popular preacher, the style of the *diatribē*, or philosophical
conversation. This seems largely to have been a technique
evolved by the Cynic and Stoic schools for popularizing philosophical and ethical ideas. 'The best familiar example of its use is
the *Diatribai*, or *Dissertations*, of Epictetus, which were actually
taken down from oral delivery by his pupil Arrian. (His better-
known *Enchiridion*, or *Hand-book*, is a compilation of selected
sayings.) They are distinguished by a familiar and lively inter-
change of question and answer, ironical apostrophe and personal
appeal.' (Dodd, pp. 148ff.; see R. Bultmann, *Der Stil der paulinischen
Predigt* on Rom. 9–11.) On the 'Question and Answer' style of
Romans, see especially J. Jeremias, 'Zur Gedankenführung in den
paulinischen Briefen'. This feature of Pauline style has been taken
as a guide to the literary structure of Romans, e.g., chapters 6 to 9
are the answer to three questions set out in 6:1, 7:7, 9:14; cf.
J. Dupont, 'Le Problème de la structure littéraire de l'épître aux
Romains'. Jeremias argues that the thought sequence of Rom.
1 to 9 is determined by these objections (p. 147). Cf. also H. E.
Stoessel, 'Notes on Rom. 12:1–2', *Interpretation*, XVII (1963),
pp. 161–75.

Verses 9–20 set out the general conclusion to this long indictment, viz. that the whole human race, Gentile and Jew, stand
condemned before God. This conclusion is most effectively stated
in a long *catena* of interwoven *OT* passages—a well-known rabbinical literary device (see below, note on verse 10ff.).

2. Much in every way. To begin with...: St Paul does

not get beyond his first point: his mind is typically diverted by the thought of the 'untrustworthiness' of the Jews, as suggested by their first great advantage or superiority—viz. that they had been entrusted with the Scriptures. A full list of the advantages of the Jew is to be found at 9:4ff.

are entrusted with the oracles of God: the word here rendered 'oracles' (*logia*) means (a) primarily, the promises, especially the *OT* promises, about the coming of Christ: but it can also mean (b) the Scriptures, or (c) oracles (divine), which include both ideas. (For a detailed study of the word, see T. W. Manson, *Studies in the Gospels and Epistles* (Manchester, 1962), p. 87ff.); J. W. Doeve, in *Studia Paulina* (de Zwaan *Festschrift*, Haarlem, 1953), pp. 111–23.

3. were unfaithful: the divine trust in Israel, in committing the Scriptures to her guardianship, recalls, by an association of opposites, Israel's faithlessness: the tense of the verb is the so-called 'ingressive aorist'—we may render, 'failed in their trust', 'proved untrustworthy'.

4. Let God be true: the connection is clearer if we render: 'God must be true' (i.e. faithful to his promise) 'though every man be false' (i.e. untrue, faithless, unreliable—see note on 'falsehood' at verse 7). The verse echoes the thought of Zeph. 3 (especially verse 5). The last words are taken from Ps. 116:11 (LXX).

The quotation from Ps. 51:4ff sits somewhat loosely to its context. '(Against thee, thee only have I sinned, and done that which is evil in thy sight), that thou mightest be vindicated in thy words (promises), and prevail when brought to judgement'. The purpose clause in Romans is attached loosely to the previous clause, simply confirming scripturally, in a general kind of way, the truth that God will always be found in the right over against men; cf. Barrett, p. 63: 'Paul, following the Psalmist, pictures a scene in court, where God and men plead against each other; when this happens, God is sure to leave the court in the right.'

5–8. The argument is a little tortuous, and very much in the disputatious style of rabbinical logomachy. But it enables Paul to reply to the charges of antinomianism to which he had been exposed. 'If', the argument runs, 'our unrighteousness proves God righteous, and, therefore, fulfils a divine purpose, how can God be a just God in punishing wrong-doing?' 'But how', Paul counters, 'can God act as the Judge of the world if he is unrighteous? For this function he must be righteous. If God's faith-fulness, nevertheless, redounds to his glory by my faithlessness, why am I still judged as a sinner? Can we not (as we are calum-niously reported and some say we declare) do evil that good may come? Of such persons the judgement which awaits them is well deserved.'

6. By no means: A familiar formula in the contemporary *diatribē*. It conveys a strong repudiation or denial of what has just been stated or agreed: 'Heaven forbid!' 'Never!' See Bauer, *Lex.*, s.v. *ginomai*, 3a, Michel, *ad loc.*, and Blass-Debrunner, §128 (v).

7. falsehood: the meaning of the Greek word is 'lie'; occa-sionally, but rarely, it is found in classical Greek meaning 'deceit', 'fraud'. In Biblical Greek (along with its cognates) it means 'unreliable conduct' and is used, e.g., of fraud and stealing (Hos. 7:1; Jer. 6:13, etc.). ('To do falsehood' is to practise deception, in word or deed.) The word then comes to have the semantic range of its Hebrew equivalents (especially *kazabh* = 'disappoint', 'fail', 'prove unreliable', e.g. Isa. 58:11 (of a spring)), and to mean 'unreliability', 'perfidiousness'. The masculine *pseustēs* means, not only a liar, but an unreliable, perfidious, faithless person.

9. What then? Are we Jews any better off? Both punctua-tion and translation of these words have caused great difficulty. The main problem centres on the meaning of the verb, whether middle or passive. If middle,.then its normal meaning is 'to put forward as a defence or excuse'. 'What then do we (i.e. the Jews) plead in defence?' makes excellent sense by itself, but the following answer: 'by no means', 'absolutely not' (*omnino non*), does not suit the question.

RV mg. has: 'What then? Do we excuse ourselves?' But it is doubtful if the verb can be so construed without the object it naturally takes.

Another solution is to give the middle an active force (cf. Vulgate: *praecellimus eos*), but we have then to ask why St Paul uses the middle in such a way without precedent? We may then, however, render: 'Have we then any advantage over them?' If we take the *ti oun* as short for 'What then shall we say?' (see *Intro-duction*, p. 30), we can render: 'What then shall we say? We have the advantage of them? Absolutely not; for our indictment was that Jews and Greeks all are under sin . . .' Grammatically the least unsatisfactory solution is to take the verb as a passive (see MM s.v., citing Plut. II, p. 1038c), as *RV:* 'are we in worse case than they?' (lit. 'are we excelled?').

It is possible to connect the interrogative with this passive sense if the *ti* ('what') is taken in the Biblical Greek and Semitic sense of *num* (asking a rhetorical question expecting an emphatic 'absolutely not' which the question gets). (For this construction and use of the interrogative, see the present author's *Aramaic Approach*[3], pp. 121ff.) Paul asks: 'Are we Jews then really outdone by the Gentiles?' To which the answer is: 'Absolutely not . . .' See further, O. Olivieri, 'Quid ergo amplius Iudaeo est?', *Bib.*, X (1929), pp. 44ff; and F. C. Synge, 'The Meaning of *Proechometha*' in Rom. 3:9', in *ET*, LXXXI (1969-70), p. 351.

I have already charged: *mg.* 'we', i.e., Paul, referring to the comprehensive 'charge' or indictment of human guilt which he has brought in 1:18-2:29 against *both* Jews and Gentiles.

10-18. This long *catena* of quotations which clinches the argument of this section is a familiar rabbinical practice. 'A favourite method was that which derived its name from the stringing together of beads *(charaz)*, when a preacher having quoted a passage or section from the Pentateuch, strung on to it another and like-sounding, or really similar, from the Prophets and the Hagiographa' (A. Edersheim, *Life and Times of Jesus the Messiah* (1959), I, p. 449). The first quotation, as we can gather from this instance, need not come from the Pentateuch: the present *catena* is made up as follows: Ps. 14:1-3 (verse 1 freely quoted, 2, abridged, 3, exactly, cf. also Ps. 53:1ff.), Ps. 5:9, exactly; Ps. 140:3, exactly, 10:7, freely; Isa. 59:7, 8, abridged; Ps. 36:1, exactly. The quotations are from the LXX. In the first quotation Paul himself introduces the words, 'There is no righteous man' (LXX: 'There is none who does good'), since they represent an essential part of the argument.

19. whatever the law says: The 'law' can refer to the whole *OT* revelation (cf. W. G. Kümmel, in *ZNTW*, xxxiii (1934), p. 112), and the reference here is to the composite quotation in the previous verses. It applies first to the Jews, but Paul has already argued that the Gentiles stand under the same condemnation, so that he can now conclude that the whole of mankind ('the whole world') stands condemned before the bar of God.

20. through the law comes knowledge of sin: 'clear knowledge' (SH). The idea seems to be a characteristically Pauline one: it is worked out more fully by St Paul at 7:7ff.

THE NEW GOSPEL 3:21–8:39

EXPOSITION OF JUSTIFICATION BY FAITH 3:21–6

These verses might almost be described as the *locus classicus* for St Paul's 'great thesis'. He returns more than once to the theme (5:1ff., 8:1ff., 10:1ff.) in the same, but also in other terms (at 5:1 he speaks of 'peace' with God, and of 'reconciliation' (5:10) rather than 'justification').

The thesis is developed against its antithesis, viz. the rabbinical doctrine of 'justification by works'. A basic assumption of contemporary rabbinical Judaism was that a man could be 'justified', i.e., acquitted before the Judgement Seat of God, on the grounds of his performance of works of the Law. This is categorically denied at verse 20: 'For no human being will be justified in his sight by works of the law . . .' (For a summary of the Jewish doctrine, see H. St. J. Thackeray, *The Relation of St Paul to Contemporary Jewish Thought* (London, 1900), p. 8off.) Now (St Paul argues, verse 21) a 'righteousness' has been manifested on the grounds, not of works, but of faith in Jesus Christ.

The basic principle of 'justification' or 'righteousness' by faith alone is set out in verses 21–3, where Paul is again at pains to underline the universal application of his Gospel (verse 22) and in terms which illustrate, in different ways, the nature of such 'righteousness'.

The supreme object of 'justifying faith' is defined at verse 25. It is the Person of Christ crucified as a means of propitiation or expiation, by whose blood God's wrath is averted, and his mercy dispensed in a total remission of past sin.

In these verses which follow verse 23 St Paul's thought moves forward, not in any logical sequence of argument, but in a series of images or pictures—from the *law courts*, the *slave-market* (redemption), and then the *altar*. They are all designed or selected to give expression to the Christian's experience of the 'liberation', the 'release' of 'absolution' through faith—it is like a guilty man **being pronounced 'innocent', a slave 'emancipated', a sinner** 'redeemed' by the sacrificial blood of the victim, slain on the altar. It is a fruitless task pressing the metaphors in an endeavour to elaborate, out of these, theories of the atonement. Paul thinks in 'film-strips', not in metaphysical propositions. On this whole section, see further J. Reumann, 'The Gospel of the Righteousness of God: Pauline Interpretation in Rom. 3:21-31', *Interpretation*, xx (1966), pp. 432-52; E. Käsemann, 'Zum Verständnis von Röm. 3:24-26' in *ZNTW*, XLIII (1950-1), pp. 150-4. A number of scholars have detected the presence of a pre-Pauline confession in these verses (possibly connected with the celebration of the Eucharist); see Bultmann, 'Neueste Paulusforschung', *Theol. Rundschau*, VIII (1936), pp. 1-22; also Reumann and Käsemann, op. cit.

21. the righteousness of God: see the note on 1:17. Here equivalent to (divine) acquittal; cf. verse 24, and Gal. 3:11.

apart from law: i.e. independently of the performance of any legal 'works'.

although the law and the prophets bear witness: again and again Paul is at pains to emphasize that the Gospel was a development, foreseen and provided for in the *OT*; cf. 1:2, 3:21, the whole of chapter 4, 9:25ff, 10:16ff., 11:1ff., 15:8ff., 16:26, etc.

22. through faith in Jesus Christ: (objective genitive). It is the believer's faith in Christ which is the ground of the newly manifested righteousness. For an alternative, but less acceptable, interpretation, see SH, *in loc.*

For there is no distinction: looking back to the argument of 2:1-16, and repeating the conclusion of the previous argument.

23. fall short: lit. 'be short of', 'be in want of' (cf. the use at Lk. 15:14), and therefore virtually 'have lost'. The middle form of the verb may have a special force here: man has not only lost the divine glory he once possessed, but he knows his loss.

the glory of God: The word for 'glory' (*doxa*) has undergone a remarkable change of meaning in Biblical Greek. In classical Greek it means 'opinion'; in Biblical Greek it means the divine brightness or 'glory' which radiated from the Presence of God (e.g., on Mt Sinai (Exod. 24:16), in the Pillar of Cloud (Exod. 16:10), in the Tabernacle (Exod. 40:34) or Temple (1 Kg. 8:11)). According to rabbinical tradition, it also shone on the face of Adam before the Fall, but, along with the divine image, was withdrawn at the Fall. The 'glory' in this sense was only to be

recovered when Adam's divine attributes were restored in
messianic times (see L. Ginzberg, *Legends of the Jews*, v (Philadelphia, 1925) (notes to vols I and II), p. 113 and 1QS IV. 24; V.
Taylor, *Names of Jesus* (1953), p. 126, n.8). It is sometimes mis-
takenly equated or confused with the divine image (cf. Dodd,
in loc.; Ginzberg, *loc. cit.*) Is it originally simply a poetic image
for the divine favour? SH interpret it to mean the divine perfection, 'the majesty or goodness of God as manifested to men', but
this seems a modern explanation.

At 2 C. 3:18ff, the 'glory' is restored to the believer by reflection
from the face of Jesus Christ; at 2 C. 4:4 the divine image is also
mentioned; the Christian's recovery of the 'glory' and the renewal
of the divine image come by faith in Christ, conceived as the
Second Adam. See the present writer's article, 'The Pauline
Doctrine of the Second Adam', *SJT*, VII (1954), pp. 170–9).

This highly poetic expression means virtually the same as the
preceding 'all men have sinned': all men are in the state of fallen
creatures separated from God, since they have lost the divine
favour (and know this loss).

24. they are justified by his grace as a gift: here is the key
verb to the Pauline doctrine. It means that men are freely
acquitted by the grace of God, and by nothing else or less.

through the redemption which is in Christ Jesus: The
word 'redemption' (*apolytrōsis*) means originally in Biblical Greek
the 'freeing', or 'liberation', of slaves or prisoners of war, generally
effected by a ransom (*lutron*). For the verb, cf. Exod. 21:8 (release
of a slave), Josephus, *Antiq.*, XIV. xiv. 1 (371). The noun, which
became established in Christian usage (see below), is found once
only in Biblical Greek at Dan. 4:34 (29, 32), of Nebuchadnezzar's
'liberation' or 'deliverance' from his madness. Though the
attestation is so slight, we may take it as fairly certain that the
word means, in general, 'deliverance' (from any form of oppres-
sion or evil). (Moffatt's rendering by 'ransom' is wrong: the
abstract noun does not necessarily imply any reference to
'ransom'.) While there does not seem to be any precedent in
Jewish Greek for the use of the noun in a religious sense, the verb
(and its cognates) is especially employed of God's mighty acts of
deliverance of his people, e.g. Dt. 7:8 (of the 'deliverance' from
Egypt), Isa. 51:11 (from the Exile). The use of the noun (and
verb) of the final 'deliverance' of mankind from the powers of sin

and death appears to be a Christian development and usage: it is almost a *terminus technicus* in this sense in the epistles (e.g., Rom. 8:23; Heb. 9:15; Eph. 1:7, 4:30; Col. 1:14). See further, K. Wennemer, '*Apolytrōsis* Röm. 3:24–25a', *Studiorum Paulinorum Congressus*, 1961, 1 (Rome, 1963), pp. 283–8; E. Käsemann, 'Zum Verständnis vom Röm. 3:24–26, *ZNTW*, XLIII (1950), pp. 150–4.

25. whom God put forward: the verb used here is susceptible of two alternative interpretations: (a) (*whom God*) '*proposed to Himself, purposed, designed*', and so 'ordained' (or 'foreordained')— as, e.g., Orig., Syr^vg. This is the most natural (and more usual) sense. The idea is also a Pauline one; e.g. 9:11 speaks of the divine 'purpose of election' (*prothesis*); cf. further Eph. 3:11, 2 Tim. 1:9. It is true that none of these passages refers to the *death* of Christ, but they nevertheless furnish close enough parallels for this meaning here. (b) '(*whom God*) *made a public show of*'. For this meaning, cf. 4 Mac. viii. 12 where the word is used to signify the display of the Syrian instruments of torture produced to intimidate the faithful Jews. In favour of this sense are the terms in the context denoting 'publicity', verses 21, 25, 26. Cf. also Gal. 3:1: Christ is 'placarded' on the cross, i.e. a public exhibition is made of Him. Is it possible that Paul meant to leave both possibilities open?

as an expiation by his blood: does expiation do justice to the word here used (*hilastērion*)? Older exegetes interpret by 'propitiation'; more recently it has been argued that ideas of propitiation are foreign to Biblical thought, and that we should understand these words solely in terms of expiation. The main exegetical issue, therefore, is whether we interpret as 'expiation', without implying 'propitiation' of the divine anger. The linguistic evidence seems to favour 'propitiation'; the closest parallel is 4 Mac. xvii. 22: '. . . through the blood of these righteous men and the propitiation of their death' (*dia . . . hilastēriou thanatou autōn*) lit. 'their propitiatory death') the divine Providence delivered Israel . . .' (See the discussions of Dodd and Manson; Moffatt, *in loc.*; *JTS*, XXXII (1930–1), p. 352ff., XLVI (1945), p. 1ff.; Leon Morris, *The Apostolic Preaching of the Cross* (1955), and in *ET*, LXII (1950–1), pp. 227ff.; T. C. G. Thornton, 'Propitiation', *ET*, LXXX (1968–9), pp. 53ff.; G. Fitzer, 'Der Ort der Versöhnung nach Paulus. Zu der Frage des "Sühnopfers Jesu" ', *TZ*, XXII (1966), pp. 161–83. Cf. also C. H. Talbert, 'A Non-Pauline Fragment at Rom. 3:24–26', *JBL*, LXXXV (1966), pp. 287–96, and further, S. Lyonnet and L. Sabourin, *Sin, Redemption and Sacrifice, A Biblical and Patristic Study, Analecta Biblica,* 48 (Rome, 1970).)

The word *hilastērion* may be taken in several ways: (a) As an adjective agreeing with some noun understood (e.g. *thuma,* 'as a propitiatory sacrifice'); cf. Josephus, *Antiq.,* XVI.vii.1 (182), of the propitiatory memorial (*hilastērion mnēma*) which Herod the Great set up outside the tomb of David after he had robbed it of 3,000 talents of silver; it was intended to be a kind of 'lightning conductor' for the divine anger. For a parallel to this expression, see B.P. Grenfell and A. S. Hunt, *The Fayûm Towns and their Papyri* (Oxford, 1900), p. 313, (no. 337). (b) As an adjective agreeing with the previous relative: 'Whom (Christ) God set forth as propitiatory, endued with propitiatory power': so Denney, in *EGT,* II, p. 611. (c) As a masculine noun in apposition to the previous relative, 'propitiator', and this is how the Reformers tended to interpret it, e.g. Melancthon ('propitiator'); Erasmus ('reconciler'); Cranmer ('the obtainer of mercy'); Purvey ('forgiver'); and, even earlier, Wyclif ('an helpere'). (d) As a neuter noun, the word is applied to any propitiatory offering or to the altar itself where such offerings were made. (e) Above all, in Biblical Greek it is employed to designate the 'mercy seat' in the Holy of Holies, the golden plate above the Ark, on which, annually, on the Day of Atonement, the High Priest sprinkled the sacrificial blood to 'atone for' the nation's sins. While for non-Jewish hellenistic readers the first meaning which would probably occur would be that of 'propitiatory offering', for Jews it would tend to be taken as 'the Mercy Seat'. We need not assume that these different possible interpretations are mutually exclusive.

A further point has been well brought out by T. W. Manson (*JTS,* XLVI (1945), p. 4ff). If we adopt the interpretation 'Mercy Seat' (or propitiatory offering), and combine it with the rendering 'displayed', a new and quite startling idea is being presented, especially if Day of Atonement associations are in the apostle's mind. The culminating moment of the Day of Atonement liturgy is the entry of the High Priest alone into the Holy of Holies. No one except the High Priest was ever permitted to see the Holy of Holies or the *hilastērion;* he went in on behalf of the people. The whole transaction was wrapped in mystery, and carried out in great secrecy. The startling thing in this verse is that Paul here speaks of the public display of the *hilastērion;* it is no longer simply

a piece of Temple furniture hidden behind the Veil to which
only the High Priest had access. This divinely appointed *hilastērion*,
Christ, in his Death (or through his blood) has been brought out
into the open, and all men can go, by faith, directly into this Holy
of Holies. 'Paul's application of Day of Atonement ideas to the
Gospel has, as its first fruits, the new and startling notion of the
display of the *hilastērion*. It is no longer hidden behind the veil:
it is brought out into the open for all to see. The Mercy Seat is
no longer kept in the sacred seclusion of the most holy place; it is
brought out into the midst of the rough and tumble of the world
and set up before the eyes of hostile, contemptuous, or indifferent
crowds.' (loc. cit., p. 5)

by his blood: it seems most natural to take this phrase along
with 'by faith'; it is our faith in the sacrifice of Christ which
atones. Most commentators, however, prefer to take these words
in close connection with *hilastērion*. They make precise the sense
in which St Paul speaks of Jesus *as a hilastērion:* it is above all the
dying Jesus, Christ crucified; cf. SH: 'the shedding and sprinkling
of the blood is a principal idea, not secondary'.

to be received by faith: The phrase here which now is simply
'by (through) faith' is to be taken closely with *hilastērion*, and this
is well brought out in the *RSV*. 'It (the phrase) stands here to
show that the benefits dispensed from the *hilastērion* are appropriated by believers.' (Manson, *loc. cit.*)

This was to show God's righteousness: the divine 'justice', or
'righteousness', required satisfaction, and this had to be demon-
strated to the whole world; cf. W. G. Kümmel, '*Paresis* and
Endeixis: a Contribution to the Pauline Doctrine of Justification',
Journ. for Theol. and the Church, III (1967), pp. 1–13. Cf. also S.
Lyonnet, 'Notes sur l'exégèse de l'Épître aux Romains', *Bib.*,
XXXVIII (1957), pp. 40ff.; H. Conzelmann, 'Current Problems in
Pauline Research', *Interpretation*, XXII (1968), pp. 171ff.

in his divine forbearance ...: God had passed over (the
original word means 'connived at', 'ignored') past sins, not forgiven them, but this he had done only in his long-suffering forbearance. In the long run, a righteous God could not 'connive at'
iniquity; and the full weight of his righteous anger bore down
upon Christ.

26. it was to prove: the death of Christ, as a divine 'act of
righteousness', proved that God is righteous yet merciful, for, in

the act of demonstrating that he is a just God, he also provides a means by which the believer can be acquitted.

27. boasting: i.e. the Jew's boasting in his exclusive privileges (cf. 2:17).

excluded: the verb implies that such boasting has been finally made impossible; Moffatt: 'It is ruled out absolutely'. Boasting about meritorious works is only possible in a system of legal works. When faith, not works, constitutes the ground of 'righteousness', there is no place for merit or pride.

on the principle of works: C. F. D. Moule ('Obligation in the Ethic of Paul', in *Church History and Interpretation: Studies presented to John Knox* (Cambridge, 1967), p. 393) distinguishes two different attitudes to, and uses of, *tôrāh*: the recognition that it is a revelation of the divine will, and the attempt to exploit it 'legalistically', to establish personal 'righteousness'. Cf. further SB, iii, pp. 186ff. (esp. p. 188): 'Der Nomismus des rabbinischen Judentums hat auch den Glauben völlig in seine Fesseln geschlagen.'

28. For we hold: 'accordingly we hold'. The verse recapitulates and summarises the Pauline position. It expresses in positive form the negative formulation at 3:20, again emphasizing the universal application of justification by faith: *any* human being is justified by faith.

30. since God is one: the central Hebrew tenet of the unity of God. There is only one God, and he is the God of the Gentiles as well as of the Jews. Hence he will acquit all impartially, Jew and Gentile, on the sole grounds of faith.

on the ground of their faith: cf. G. Friedrich, 'Das Gesetz des Glaubens, Röm. 3:27', *TZ*, x (1954), pp. 401-17.

31. Do we then overthrow the law by this faith? Paul is anxious to meet the possible objection that by such a doctrine he is doing away with the Law of Moses altogether. His reply is that, on the contrary, such a doctrine 'establishes' the Law. Either its deeper principles are being maintained, or we fulfil or make effective the provisions of the Law, i.e. produce obedience to it by our faith, and this he now proceeds to illustrate from the *OT* scriptures about Abraham.

On this section, see also G. Howard, 'Rom. 3: 21-31 and the Inclusion of the Gentiles', *HThR*, LXIII (1970), pp. 223-33. On the relation of 3:31 to chapter 4, see Barrett, *ad loc.*

ADDITIONAL NOTE ON ROM. 3:25

The main theological debate, in recent years, on this verse has focussed on the meaning of *hilastērion*: does it mean or imply 'propitiation' of the wrath of God, or can its meaning be confined to 'means of expiation', without any thought of the propitiation of an angry deity? The main protagonists of this latter view have been C. H. Dodd and T. W. Manson (see above), who conclude that *hilastērion* is the place or means of 'expiation', where or by which God shows his mercy to men.

This view has been challenged by Leon Morris, most notably in *The Apostolic Preaching of the Cross*. The verb *hilaskesthai* is used with propitiatory force in the *OT*; e.g. Moses' averting (propitiating) the wrath of God (Exod. 32:30ff) by offering his life for the people; the red heifer as a propitiatory offering (Dt. 21:1–9); Aaron's offering of the incense to avert the wrath of God, shown in the plague which had broken out among the people (Num. 16: 46–7). 'Such passages demonstrate that the word, even as used in the LXX, retained a certain association with the removal of anger', *ET* LXII (1950–51), p. 230f; 'the averting of anger seems to represent a stubborn substratum of meaning from which all the usages can be naturally explained . . .' (p. 231).

The context in Romans supports the sense of 'propitiation': both the immediate and remoter context (e.g. 1:18) are concerned with the wrath of God. 'The context demands the *hilastērion* should include an element of propitiation in its meaning, for St Paul has brought heavy artillery to bear in demonstrating that God's wrath and judgement are against the sinner, and while other expressions in verses 21–6 may be held to deal with the judgement aspect, there is nothing other than this word to express the averting of the wrath. Wrath has occupied such an important place in the argument leading up to this section that we are justified in looking for some expression indicative of its cancellation in the process which brings about salvation' (p. 232).

There is one further essential consideration in understanding the distinctive character of Christ's propitiatory offering of himself. Morris writes (*loc. cit.*): '. . . while the Old Testament is emphatic about the reality and seriousness of the wrath of God, the removal of that wrath is due in the last resort to God Himself'. It was God Who 'put forward' Christ as *hilastērion*, not only to dispense mercy, but as 'a means of propitiation'. The nature of this 'propitiation' is further characterized by the words 'in (by) his blood', which most exegetes agree goes with *hilastērion*—it was Christ's death which was the propitiatory deed. All this was a demonstration of God's 'righteousness'. But, above all, the unique feature of the Biblical idea of propitiation, without parallel in pagan religion, is that it is God Who Himself provides the means of propitiation and expiation. The saving deed which at once was a manifestation of the divine anger was, at the same time, an expression of the divine love and forgiveness: the very wrath of God visited on Christ for the sins of mankind was the expression of His saving love.

All this, in Paul, is expressed in the vivid language of figure and metaphor—the language of pictures, images, and poetry— 'redemption', or 'emancipation', recalling the slave-market, 'justification' the court-room, and *hilastērion* the altar. But it is the classic language of the religious consciousness; and it is the only language which can communicate the realities of divine justice and love. It is only in poetry and the language of poetry that an adequate medium exists for these unseen realities of the spirit; nowhere, for instance, is Paul's Gospel more adequately conveyed than in Augustus Toplady's 'Rock of Ages', much of its imagery borrowed from Romans.

THE CASE OF ABRAHAM 4:1–25

One of the main purposes of this chapter is to provide scriptural support for the doctrine of justification by faith (cf. Bultmann, *Theology*, 1, p. 280). For Paul's opponents, Abraham was the supreme exemplar of justification by works, the stronghold of the Jewish position; e.g. Gen. 26: 4ff. gave support to the doctrine that the blessing on Abraham and his seed ('I will multiply your descendants . . .') was a reward for Abraham's 'law-righteousness' (cf. also Sir. 44:20ff. and Dodd, *in loc.*; see further below, on verse 2). To counter this Paul quotes first Gen. 15:6: 'Now Abraham believed (*episteusen*) in God, and it was credited to him for righteousness.' Abraham's faith, not his works, constituted the grounds for his 'justification'. The argument is further reinforced by Ps. 32:1–2 (verses 7–8).[1]

[1] For a recent discussion, see U. Wilcken, 'Die Rechtfertigung Abrahams nach Röm. 4': *Stud. zur Theol. der alttest. Überlieferungen*. (Von Rad *Festschrift*).

Verses 9–12 seek to establish that, since this justification of
Abraham by faith was prior to his circumcision, it was intended
for the uncircumcised: 13–25 argues further that the blessing on
Abraham and his seed was for all who believe, circumcised or
uncircumcised, and was not dependent on Law, but on faith.
Righteousness likewise is by faith, as Scripture proves in Abraham's case (22–5).

1. **What then shall we say about Abraham, our forefather according to the flesh?** This verse is a notorious *crux*.
The *RSV* text follows the reading of only one MS. (B), which omits
altogether the word which creates all the difficulty, viz. *heurēkenai*
(lit. 'found' or 'gained'). The omission, however, may have been
purely accidental, and the more difficult reading (with 'found')
to be preferred. *RSV mg.* ('was gained by') is a somewhat free
rendering of the more difficult reading; the text reads literally:
'What then shall we say Abraham, our forefather after the flesh,
has found (has gained)?' We may complete the sense by understanding 'by his law-righteousness'. Alternatively, we may connect
the verb 'found' with the words 'according to the flesh', and
render: 'What then shall we say Abraham our forefather has
found (gained) *according to the flesh*, i.e. by his natural powers,
and so by the performance of works of the law, and not through
the grace of God?' None of these translations seems ideally suitable in the context.

It has been argued (cf. Michel, *ad loc.*) that the words 'What
then has Abraham . . . *found*' are an allusion to Gen. 18:3, where
Abraham asked God if he had found favour (grace) in God's
sight. The answer then to the question was: 'Favour (grace), *not*
justification by works.' If we could give a Hebrew sense to the
verb, we could render: 'What then shall we say befell Abraham
. . .?' Cf. Jos. 2:23, Ps. Sol. xvii. 18. The Hebraic word order—
verb first—might also be urged in support of this interpretation.

Neukirchen, 1961), pp. 111–27. For a splendidly lucid exposition, W. Neil,
'God's Promises are Sure: Rom. 4:21', *ET*, LXIX (1957–8), pp. 146ff. Further,
G. Klein, 'Heil und Geschichte nach Röm. 4', *NTS*, XIII (1966–7), pp. 43–7;
L. Goppelt, 'Paulus und die Heilsgeschichte: Schlussfolgerungen aus Röm. 4
und 1 Kor. 10:1–3', ibid., pp. 31–42; E. Käsemann, *Paulinische Perspektiven*
(Tübingen, 1969), p. 173 (Eng. trans. *Perspectives on Paul* (London, 1971), pp.
79ff.; N. A. Dahl, 'The Story of Abraham in Luke–Acts', in *Studies in Luke–
Acts: Essays presented in honour of Paul Schubert*, ed. L. E. Keck and J. L. Martyn
(London, 1968), pp. 139–58.

There could also conceivably be an allusion to Sir. 44:19. LXX
has: 'there was not *found* one like (to him) [i.e. Abraham] in his
glory.' In short, what Abraham found (acquired, gained) was an
unblemished 'glory'. This thought is continued in verse 2: Paul
at once concedes: 'Yes (*gar*), if it was by works Abraham was
'justified', then he has grounds for "boasting" (glorying) in his
achievement.' Cf. also 1 Mac. 2:52.

No solution hitherto proposed is without serious difficulties.
The text may, in fact, be beyond repair; and, since most solutions
are conjectural, textual emendation is defensible. One suggestion would be that the original read *euerestēkenai* (corrupted to
heurēkenai), i.e. 'In what then shall we say Abraham our forefather after the flesh proved well-pleasing (to God)?' (The conjecture is, in fact, the reading in the margin of two minuscules 4 and
23, reported by Tischendorf.) For other textual emendations,
see Michel, p. 115, n. 1, and R. R. Williams, *ET*, LXIII (1951–2),
p. 91f (for *heurēkenai eirgasthai*, i.e., 'What then shall he say? That
Abraham our forefather has worked (for his righteousness)?'

2. if Abraham was justified by works: the rabbinical
doctrine largely based on Gen. 26:5; cf. Sir. 44:20ff. Cf. also
Jub. xxiii. 10, B. T. Joma, 28b, etc.

he has something to boast about: according to Jewish
tradition, Abraham had cause to 'glory' both before men and God
(cf. Sir. 44:19ff. (Heb.), Jub. xxiv. 11).

3. Abraham believed God . . .: Gen. 15:6. The closest
parallel is 1 Mac. 2:52, where, however, Abraham's 'faith' is
his constancy under trial, and it is this which is 'imputed to him
for righteousness'. In the original Hebrew, it was Abraham's
willingness to believe the promise he had just received, of which
God approved. 'And he brought him outside, and said, "Look
toward heaven, and number the stars, if you are able to number
them." Then he said unto him, So shall your descendants be'
(Gen. 15:5). (St Paul takes up the thought of the promise at
verses 11ff.) Among the rabbis, Abraham's faith was included
among his good works and took a high place there; St Paul sets it
in antithesis to 'good works' as the ground of salvation, and
declares it was the ground of Abraham's 'righteousness' and is the
sole ground of all 'righteousness'.

it was reckoned to him as righteousness: a favourite
Pauline expression. The verb *logizomai* occurs 29 times in Paul

(apart from *OT* quotations)—11 times in Romans alone, and only 6 times elsewhere in the New Testament. For a study of the metaphorical use of the word in Paul, see W. H. Griffith Thomas, in *ET*, xvii (1905–6), pp. 211–14. The view that Abraham's 'faith' was 'reckoned to him' as *equivalent* to 'righteousness' is less convincing than to take 'for righteousness' as meaning that Abraham's faith was counted to his credit 'with a view to the receiving of righteousness'. (Cf. for this use of *eis* ('for'), Rom. 1:16, 3:22, 10:10.)

Paul is here making use of the rabbinical *gezera shawa* rule of exegesis, according to which the use of identical words in different quotations justifies interpreting one verse (e.g., here Gen. 15:6) in the light of another (Ps. 32:1–2, LXX). See J. Jeremias, *op. cit.*, p. 149ff. (see above, p. 30).

4. Now to one who works: a simple analogy from daily life: the worker is paid his wages as his due, not by grace and favour.

5. to one who does not work: the analogy has already broken down, like so many of Paul's figures; the 'one who does not work . . .' is the believer who does not rely on good works for salvation, but simply trusts in the God who acquits not the just but the impious, ungodly.

6. David pronounces a blessing . . . : neither this rendering nor that of the *NEB* ('David speaks of the happiness of the man, etc'.) is strictly correct. The Greek word 'blessing' does not mean 'blessedness' (or 'happiness') here, but 'the being pronounced blessed by God'. Therefore we should render 'David mentions the blessing (by God) of the man . . .'

7–8. It was good rabbinical practice to support a quotation from the Pentateuch by one from the Psalms (or Hagiographa): here the Psalm quotation both strengthens and further explicates the nature of the 'righteousness' which is imputed by God on the basis of faith.

ABRAHAM THE FATHER OF ALL WHO, LIKE ABRAHAM, ARE JUSTIFIED BY FAITH 9–12

9. St Paul is anxious to establish the point that the divine pronouncement of blessing which Abraham and his seed received was not just confined to the Jewish race (the 'circumcision'), but was upon all, Gentile and Jew alike, *whether circumcised or not*, who professed a faith like Abraham's.

10. To establish this, St Paul appeals to the historical fact that God's recognition of Abraham's faith preceded in point of time Abraham's circumcision (the rabbis reckoned on an interval of twenty-nine years, between Gen. 15:6 and Gen. 17:11 (Abraham's circumcision)). Faith-righteousness took priority over circumcision.

11. He received circumcision as a sign or seal of the righteousness . . . : lit. 'he received a sign consisting of circumcision' (gen. of apposition, definition or identity) 'as a seal of his faith-righteousness, which he received while still uncircumcised.' According to Gen. 17:11, circumcision was a 'sign of the covenant' (*sēmeion diathēkēs*); the Targums describe it as 'Abraham's seal'. In the latter, the idea of belonging to Abraham seems prominent: in Romans the idea is rather that of a seal which legitimizes.

without being circumcised: lit. 'all who believe "under" (*dia*, 'in a state of') 'uncircumcision' (*dia* of attendant circumstances); cf. 2:27.

12. who are not merely circumcised . . . : Paul is anxious above all to avoid giving the impression that Abraham was the father of the circumcised Jew who held that justification was by works. The category of Jew completely excluded here is that of those who are circumcised and rely on justification by works of the law alone. It was just this group which exclusively claimed Abraham for their father. Cf. further, L. Cerfaux, 'Abraham "père en circoncision" des Gentils', *Recueil Lucien Cerfaux*, II (Gembloux, 1954), pp. 333ff.

LAW AND PROMISE 13-17

In verse 13, St Paul turns to the divine promises made to Abraham (Gen. 15:5, 17:5, 22:17) summarized in verse 13b: 'The promise to Abraham and his descendants that they should inherit the world.' On the 'seed of Abraham', cf. M. Colacci, 'Il *Semen Abrahae* nel Nuovo Testamento', *Bib.*, XXI (1940), pp. 19ff. From the idea of the blessing on Abraham preceding his circumcision, Paul moves, by inference, to the wider idea that, therefore, the promise to Abraham (so closely related to the Blessing) was not given under a dispensation of Law, but under one where righteousness was a gift to Faith, not a reward of legal works. This promise was not given under any legal system, but under that of faith-righteousness. The Law is embraced in the Promise. Had the Law,

in current rabbinical Judaism, come to eclipse the thought of the
Promise and the Covenant? Cf. SB, III, pp. 188ff. Cf. J. Bonsirven,
Le Judaïsme Palestinien au temps de Jésus Christ, I (Paris, 1934),
p. 179.

The content of the promise is not exactly identical with anything in Scripture. It is not said in so many words to be the
possession of the promised Land (Gen. 12:7, 13:14ff, Exod. 6:8,
etc.), but it is clearly connected with the Promise in Gen. 15,
trust in which called down the divine blessing on Abraham—viz.
that he should have a son and descendants innumerable as the
stars. The words have also for Paul messianic overtones; the
promise was, that through one of these descendants the whole
earth would be blessed, and through him Abraham's true seed
would enjoy world-wide dominion.

14. adherents of the law: resembles a rabbinical phrase,
béné tôrāh, 'children of the Law', 'Torah-ites'; SH: 'dependants
of law', 'vassals of a legal system'. If it is the group of 'Torah-
ites' alone who are the heirs (ultimately of Israel's future messianic
kingdom), then clearly the faith of Abraham has been made null
and void, and the promise also cancelled. It has likewise been
made of no effect.

15. For the law brings wrath: this verse seems to be an
interpolation. All that the law (i.e. human legalism) produces,
or brings down on itself, is the wrath of God, His condemnation—
not salvation. Where law (i.e. human legalism) does not exist,
then transgression of law cannot exist; in such an ideal state there
there can only be the promise fulfilled in the Kingdom of God.

16. That is why it depends on faith: lit. 'for this reason it
is from faith'. Some supply 'all things are' before 'from faith'.

The style is 'telegraphic': cf. SH: 'In his rapid and vigorous
reasoning St Paul contents himself with a few bold strokes, which
he leaves it to the reader to fill out.' Some supply, instead of 'all
things', 'the inheritance is' (from verse 14) or 'the promise is'
(from verse 13). But St Paul leaves us with a kind of blank
cheque which we can fill out from the context, e.g. 'the divine
plan took its start from faith . . .'

may rest on grace: justification had to be by faith and pure
grace, since the only alternative system—justification by works—
has been shown by Paul to have broken down completely.

father of us all: cf. SB, III, pp. 185, 211.

THE FAITH OF ABRAHAM AND THE BIRTH OF ISAAC AS A TYPE OF THE RESURRECTION 17-25

These verses are a further exposition of Gen. 15:6ff., where God promises Abraham a son and that his descendants would be as numerous as the stars. At the time of this promise Abraham was childless and Sarah barren. Such a promise made a great demand on Abraham's faith: it was to believe in a God who can make the dead live and call into existence things that did not previously exist. This faith of Abraham was a type of Christian faith in the God who raised up Christ from the dead.

17. in the presence of the God in whom he believed: lit. 'in the presence of Whom he believed (namely) the God Who gives life to the dead . . .' The antecedent of the relative is attracted within the relative clause (cf. SH).

The commonest explanation takes these words as describing the posture in which Abraham is represented as holding colloquy with God (Gen. 17:1ff) (so SH). The words are usually, therefore, taken with the preceding verse; but, however they are construed, the connection is not very clear. *RSV* takes them after the word 'descendants' (verse 16), the words following, 'not only . . . nations', being a long parenthesis.

Alternatively we may understand them as closely following the quotation: 'Abraham is the father of many nations before the God in whom he believed . . .' 'Abraham is the father of Jewish and Gentile Christians, not in virtue of any human relationship with them, but *before God* . . .' So Barrett, *in loc.*

We may construe these words, however, not with the preceding verse or words, but with what follows. The thought of verse 17b (the miracle of the birth of Isaac from the dead womb of Sarah, etc.) is closely linked with that of verses 18ff., and especially with verse 23. Had the antecedent, 'the God who makes the dead live . . .', not been attracted within the relative clause, the words would have normally been taken with the following, not the preceding verse; and this is possibly how we ought to construe them, with the verb *episteusen* as the main verb (cf. verse 18), and with the participles alone belonging to the subordinate relative clause: 'In the presence of (before) the God who raises the dead and calls into existence the things that do not exist, he believed.' A parallel to the idea in these last words is claimed for 2 Mac. 7:28.

18. that he should become: his faith enabled him to become. **So shall your descendants be:** i.e. innumerable as the stars in heaven (Gen. 15:5).

19. He did not weaken in faith . . .: lit. 'Abraham did not fall ill with respect to his faith'. According to rabbinical tradition, Abraham did fall ill in connection with his circumcision. See L. Ginzberg, *Legends of the Jews*, v, p. 240 (n. 127). Is Paul deliberately contrasting the robustness of Abraham's condition when his faith was reckoned to him for righteousness with his weakness at the time of his circumcision?

21. what he had promised: The verb (*epangellesthai*) corresponding to the noun for 'promise' (*epangelia*) is always used in classical Greek for spontaneous promises; the other common verb 'to promise' (*hypichneisthai*) is used of pledges given under contract. The divine promise was a spontaneous act of God.

22. closes the argument with the Scriptural conclusion, Gen. 15:6.

23. were written not for his sake alone: the conclusion is now applied to the present-day faith of the Christian: Gen. 15:6 was not just written to preserve the glorious memory of Abraham and his story (Sir. 44:9ff.; Heb. 11:8ff.): these words were also written on our account who believe in the same active Creator God capable of performing such miracles as the awakening of life out of death; and this is evidenced by the Resurrection of Christ.

25. who was put to death for our trespasses: the closing words have been thought to derive from some early Christian hymn or confession: the Hebrew-type parallelism has been noted (cf. Dodd, p. 70): 'was put to death' is literally 'was surrendered up' (i.e., to crucifixion), a stereotyped Passion term (e.g. 1 C. 11:23; Rom. 8:32; Gal. 2:20; Eph. 5:2).

The term 'justification' (*dikaiōsis*) occurs once only again in the *NT* at Rom. 5:18. The neat parallelism appears to produce the doctrine of justification through the Resurrection, whereas elsewhere the Pauline doctrine is of justification, etc., on the grounds of Christ's propitiatory death. It seems unnecessary to suggest a pre-Pauline doctrine of justification in this embedded fragment; Death and Resurrection cannot be separated in Pauline theology.

LIFE IN CHRIST 5:1–21

Chapter five marks the transition from the thesis of Justification to that of the spiritual life of the Christian believer ('life in the spirit' or 'life in Christ'); 8–10 are the transition verses. Verses 12–21—Christ as the Second Adam—constitute a kind of 'bridge' between the first part of Romans ('justification by faith') and the second part ('sanctification' or the 'spiritual life' in Christ, i.e. in the Body of Christ, the Second Adam).

JUSTIFICATION AND SALVATION 1–11

Transition from doctrine of justification *sola fide* to Pauline teaching on the Christian life: life in the spirit (spiritual life) = *eternal* life, i.e. *en Christō*; life *in the Body of Christ*, the Second Adam.

Verses 1–11 recapitulate and develop further the Pauline doctrine of justification. This is a new state of 'reconciliation' with God which Christians now enjoy; the causes of hostility between them and God have been removed. Through Christ they have entered, by faith, into the state of grace in which they now stand. It is a state full of hope in which they should rejoice—the hope of again sharing in the divine glory. We can even exult in present sufferings, for they are productive of patience, and patience produces fortitude, fortitude character, and character hope— which is not an illusory hope, since even now we have the experience of the love of God being poured out into our hearts through our participation in the Holy Spirit. If, while we were enemies of God, we were reconciled to him by his Son, *a fortiori* we shall be saved by his life, and glory in God through Christ by whom we have obtained reconciliation with God. Cf. N. A. Dahl, *Stud. Theol.*, v (1951), pp. 37ff.

1. we have peace with God: *mg.* 'let us . . .' The textual evidence is overwhelmingly in favour of the subjunctive, 'let us'. On the other hand, 'let us have peace' seems to imply that a man who has been justified may thereafter choose whether or not he will be at peace with God, and this seems un-Pauline. The indicatives in the context also favour the present tense: in the next verse Paul says 'we have gained our access', 'we now stand', and in verses 10 and 11 'we were reconciled', 'we have been reconciled'. Exegesis, therefore, points to 'we have'. C. K. Barrett writes: 'He (St Paul) is not urging his readers to do and be what as Christians they ought to do and be, but reminding them of the facts on which all their doing and being rest.'

We could render: 'let us *enjoy* our state of peace with God', without introducing any un-Pauline thought; this is a meaning well attested for *echō* (= 'possess, enjoy'), and this may be the force of the subjunctive, On the whole, however, *echōmen*, the present tense, is preferable.

We may explain the subjunctive, *echōmen*, as an itacism, or as resulting from assimilation to the later subjunctive, 'let us rejoice' (*kauchōmetha*).

peace has the same meaning as 'reconciliation' at verse 11. It is a state of 'peace' through the removal of God's wrath towards man.

2. Through him we have obtained access: the word translated 'access' means 'introduction', and it has been claimed that the idea is that of introduction to the presence-chamber of a royal personage. (Cf. Xenophon, *Cyr.* VII. v. 45.) 'The rendering "access" is inadequate, as it leaves out of account the fact that we do not come in our own strength, but need an "introducer"—Christ' (SH). We need not limit the meaning to 'introduction' only, however: the word has also a special religious connotation describing the solemn 'approach' (e.g. as at festivals) to deity (cf. Herod. ii. 58). The word is found in a similar sense at Eph. 2:18, 3:12 (of 'approach' to God the Father). This seems preferable to the assuming of the (rare) meaning 'landing-stage', and the intention by the writer to suggest a nautical metaphor—'grace' being pictured as a 'haven' (cf. MM, s.v.). Some MSS. add 'by faith', but the best authorities omit.

this grace in which we stand: i.e. the condition of those who now enjoy the divine favour.

we rejoice in our hope: for this Pauline idea, cf. J. M. Bover, 'Gloriamur in Spe', *Bib.*, XXII (1941), pp. 41ff.).

glory of God: see note on 3:23.

3. endurance: not merely the passive quality, but the virtue of fortitude.

4. character: the word means literally the state of being proved and tested. Hence 'tried' or 'approved' character.

produces hope: cf. Jas. 1:12: 'Blessed is the man who endures trial, for when he has stood the test he will receive the crown of life which God has promised to those who love him.'

5. does not disappoint us: lit. 'does not put us to shame by proving illusory'. There is an allusion to Isa. 28:16 (LXX).

God's love has been poured into our hearts . . .: not our love to God, but, as is clear from verses 6ff., God's love for us. 'The idea of spiritual refreshment and encouragement is usually conveyed in the East through the metaphor of *watering*. St Paul seems to have had in his mind Isa. 44:3: 'I will pour water upon him that is thirsty, and streams upon the dry ground; I will pour *My Spirit* upon thy seed' (SH). Our hearts are refreshed by God's love to us, and this is the experience of His Spirit.

which has been given to us: the Christian believer becomes the recipient of the gift of the Holy Spirit from his baptism and the experience of the Spirit in this life is an 'earnest' of its full enjoyment. Cf. 2 C. 1:22. See further M. Dibelius, 'Vier Worte des Römerbriefs: 5:5, 12; 8:10; 1:30', *Symbolae Biblicae Upsalienses*, III (1944), pp. 3–17.

6. There appears to be textual corruption in this verse, and it is doubtful if the *RSV* (following the same traditional reading as the *AV*), has rendered the true text. There are two main difficulties: (a) *grammatical:* the subject of the main verb is in an unnatural position (within the subordinate clause); (b) *textual:* there is a redundant particle (*eti*, 'still') before the words rendered 'in due time'; and it is difficult to give a meaning to this second *eti*. Some inferior MSS. omit it, but this looks like an attempt at amelioration of the difficulty and the grammatical problem remains. Some 'Western' authorities, with Latin support (D[b] G it. vg. Iren.[lat.]) read 'For to what purpose (*eis ti gar* for *eti*) did Christ, while we were yet helpless, die at the right time for the ungodly?' Cf. J. Hugh Michael, *JTS.*, xxxix (1938), p. 152 (see above, p. 46). Vaticanus (B) alone has for *eti* the reading *ei ge*, and this makes good sense, and is the preferred reading of SH; the verse is then to be read closely with the preceding verse: '(. . . because God's love has been poured into our hearts . . .) since, in very truth, while we were yet helpless, at the right time Christ died for the ungodly.' The singularity of the reading suggests that it is a skilful amelioration of the scribe of Vaticanus. The 'Western' reading is preferred by Michael on the grounds that it explains the reading *eti gar* better than *ei ge* (*loc. cit.*); *eis ti* seems to be confined to Biblical Greek where it corresponds to Heb. *lammah* (Aram. *l[e]ma*); e.g., Jg. 13:18, 15:10 (LXX) (the more usual LXX

equivalent is *hina ti*); it occurs at Mk 14:4 (= Mt. 26:8) and
Mt. 14:31. Cf. A. T. Robertson, *Grammar of the Greek New Testament* (1914), p. 739 (Ac. 19:3 is doubtful). Another instance is
Mk 15:34. See further, N. Turner, *Grammar of NT Greek* (J. H.
Moulton *et al.*), III (Edinburgh, 1963), p. 267. The answer to
the question: 'To what purpose . . .' is given at verse 8: it is in
this way (by Christ's death, not for the good but for the bad) that
God 'commends his love to us'. On the whole, this does seem the
least unsatisfactory solution.

helpless: lit. 'weak'; but it is rather moral weakness which
is meant than weakness of faith: the parallel at verse 8 is 'sinners'.
The adjective may also convey the sense of human frailty (cf.
Ps. 6:3 (LXX), Wis. 9: 5), but it is here rather the 'weakness' of
the wicked: the adjective is rare in this sense, but the meaning is
attested for the noun, e.g. 1 Clem. xxxvi. 1, Hermas, *Mand.*,
IV. iii. 4.

9. much more shall we be saved: as Dodd points out, the
'much more' here (= *a fortiori*) has great significance. 'It shows
that, in spite of the emphasis which Paul felt he must lay upon
justification (partly because it was at this point he had to meet
opposition), he found the real centre of his religion in the new kind
of life which followed upon justification. It was life 'in Christ'
or 'in the spirit'; life in the love of God as mediated to us by 'the
Lord the Spirit' (*in loc.*).

10. reconciled: in keeping with the idea of 'peace' with God
(5:1), St Paul introduces the conception of reconciliation (the
noun at verse 11). Cf. 2 C. 5:18, 19—the only other passage
where the verb occurs in this connection.

ADAM AND CHRIST 12—21

Behind these verses lies the Pauline doctrine of Christ as the
Second Adam. They are to be supplemented by 1 C. 15:35-49,
where Christ is described as 'the last Adam', in contrast to 'the
first Adam' (verse 45) (the actual term '*second* Adam' is not
Pauline). (See the present writer's article on the subject in *SJT*,
VII (1954), pp. 170ff., for an exposition of the Corinthian passage.)
In our passage St Paul works out his doctrine of redemption
(or justification) in terms of this Adam-Christ typology: at 1 C.
15:45 he employs it in expounding his doctrine of the Resurrection. Christ as 'the Second Adam' is a key conception for St Paul;

it is closely related to his doctrine of the 'new creation' (Gal.
6:15; 2 C. 5:17), of Christ as the 'image (of God)' (2 C. 4:4, Col.
1:15), and of the reconciliation of Jew and Gentile in a new
humanity (the second Adam) (Eph. 2:15, cf. 4:24).[1]

As was pointed out above, Paul further prepares the way by
this doctrine for his exposition of the 'life' in Christ (i.e., in the
second Adam).

Sin entered the world by Adam and through sin death which
passed to all sinful men. (Even before the giving of the Law there
was sin, for death was on the throne from Adam to Moses.) God's
act of grace in Christ, however, was unlike Adam's act of disobedience: all men died through the one and all men have grace
richly bestowed on them through the other: judgement came by
one: but acquittal by the other. Death reigns under Adam; all
men reign in eternal life through Christ and unto a righteousness
leading to life. By one act of disobedience all were made sinners:
by one act of obedience all men become righteous. (The purpose
of the Law was to bring grace and life for death.)

12. Therefore as sin came into the world . . .: this verse
has proved a *crux interpretum*; for a useful bibliography of studies
on it, see E. Brandenburger, *Adam und Christus* (Neukirchen, 1962).
See also A. J. M. Wedderburn, 'The Theological Structure of
Romans 5:12', *NTS*, XIX (1972-3), pp. 339-54 (also contains
useful modern bibliographical material). For background, in
style and ideas, cf. Wis. 2:24. (Are both writers personifying Sin
and Death?) 'Now then', 'accordingly', 'it follows from all this'
(in referring back to the general sense of vv. 1-11); cf., however,
NEB. Michel (*ad loc.*) comments: 'So much has been claimed for

---

[1] See especially W. D. Davies, *Paul and Rabbinic Judaism*, pp. 53ff.; J. Bon-
sirven, *Exégèse Rabbinique et Exégèse Paulinienne* (Paris, 1939); pp. 269ff., R.
Bultmann, 'Adam und Christus nach Röm. 5', *ZNTW*, L (1959), pp. 145-65;
J. Murray, *The Imputation of Adam's Sin* (Grand Rapids, 1959); K. Barth,
Christ and Adam: Man and Humanity, in Rom. 5. (SJT Occas. Papers 5) (1956).
On the literary form of Rom. 5, see H. Müller, 'Der rabbinische al-wa-
homer-Schluss in paulin. Typologie. Zur Adam-Christustypologie in Röm. 5',
ZNTW, LVIII (1967), pp. 73-92; Felice Montagnini, *Rom. 5:12-14 alla
luce del dialogo rabbinico* (Brescia, 1971); A. Vitti, 'Rom. 5:12-21', *Bib.*, VII
(1926), pp. 132ff.; N. A. Dahl, op. cit. (p. 77); J. M. Bover, 'La justificación
en Rom. 5, 16-19', *Estudios Eclesiásticos*, XIX (1945), pp. 355ff.; F. W. Danker,
'Romans v. 12. Sin under Law', *NTS*, XIV (1967-8), pp. 424-39. For a summary of the history of interpretation, see C. E. B. Cranfield, 'On Some of the
Problems in the Interpretation of Romans 5:12', *SJT*, XXII (1969), pp. 324ff.

Jesus Christ that he may justifiably be seen as the beginner of a
new mankind. He cannot, therefore, be compared with any one
within the salvation-history of Israel, like Abraham or Moses, but
can only be set over against the one who began the old mankind.'
While Paul is undoubtedly thinking of Adam as an historical individual, he is also assuming that Adam (= *homo*) is also the head
and inclusive representative of the human race. Cf. H. W. Robinson, *The Cross of the Servant* (1926), and 'The Hebrew Conception
of Corporate Personality', in *Werden und Wesen des Alten Testaments
(Beitrag zur ZAW* 66, ed. J. Hempel (1936), pp. 49–62): '. . . the
whole group, including its past, present and future members
might function as a single individual through any one of those
members conceived as representative of it' (p. 49). Cf. also A. R.
Johnson, *The One and the Many in the Israelite Conception of God*
(Oxford, 1942), and also T. W. Manson, *Studies in the Gospels and
Epistles* (Manchester, 1962), p. 142, n. 1. For an example, cf.
Gen. 34:30.

world: in the sense of the entire human race.

through one man . . .: Paul assumes current rabbinical teaching.
Adam's Fall involved all his descendants; for this reason he can
say that in 'one man' all men die.

and so death spread to all men because all men sinned: so
all English versions (following the main exegetical tradition of
this verse); consult SH for the usual exposition. If so construed,
then the correlative to the 'as' clause ('as (*hōsper*) sin came into
the world . . .') is postponed till verse 19, where it is resumed and
completed: 'For as by one man's disobedience . . .' This exegesis
is supported by the main verb 'spread (to all men)', i.e. was
transmitted (from Adam) to all men.

The main difficulty with this understanding of the verse is then
the following clause, '*because* all men sinned', since we are then
involved in the contradictory proposition that, while death is
traced back to Adam's transgression, and thence was transmitted
to all men, at the same time it came to all men '*because* all men
sinned'. Cf. especially M. Dibelius, 'Vier Worte des Römerbriefs', *Symbolae Biblicae Upsalienses*, III (1946), pp. 7–8.

Alternative explanations of the 'because' (*eph hō*) clause are
given to avoid this contradiction; e.g. that we should understand
the words to mean 'in whom (i.e. in Adam) all men sinned', but
the antecedent is too remote for this to be grammatically de-

fensible. Origen and Augustine rendered 'in which', i.e. in death, but this is meaningless. Cf. the modern suggestion of E. Stauffer, *Neutestamentliche Theologie* (Stuttgart, 1941), pp. 248ff.; 'in the direction of which (i.e., death) all men sinned'; Stauffer compares 2 Tim. 2:14 for this use of the preposition.[1] Such an understanding of the words, is, however, strained and artificial. The *eph hō* means *propterea quod* (e.g., 2 C. 5:4, Phil. 3:12), or *quapropter* (see further below, pp. 88f).

More recently an alternative exegesis has been offered by Professor C. K. Barrett (*in loc.*), which takes the 'and so' clause in the sense of 'thus also', and makes it the correlative of the 'as sin came', and so on. With this exegesis the verb (*diēlthen*) would require to be rendered literally 'came', or possibly 'came severally', 'to all men, because all men sinned'. Barrett writes (p. 111): 'So far Paul has been describing the historical events (as he would deem them) of Adam's career, and established that he was responsible for the entry of sin and death into the world, at least as far as his own person was concerned. But once the connection between sin and death has been established, Paul moves onward: 'So also death came to all men, because they all sinned.' That is, all men sin (cf. 3:23), and all men die because they sin; but Paul does not add here that they sin, or that they die, because they are physically descended from Adam. Nowhere, even in verse 19, does Paul teach the direct seminal identity between Adam and his descendants which seems to be implied in the nearly contemporary 4 Ezra (especially 3:7, 21).' By 'seminal identity' Barrett appears to mean the natural involvement of all men in Adam's sin and its consequences by *physical* descent from Adam, i.e. their natural inheritance of sin and death, apart from their own personal responsibility. (Cf. St Augustine's belief that original sin was transmitted in the act of concupiscence.)

There appear to have been *two* doctrines about the origins of sin current in contemporary Judaism. The first is that of natural involvement in Adam's sin and its consequence, death; it is represented especially by the Jewish doctrine of the 'evil tendency (impulse)' (*yētzer hārā'*) inherent in human nature. Cf. 2 Esd.

[1] I have not been able to trace this note in the English edition. For other similar interpretations, see J. Cambier, 'Péchés des Hommes et Péché d'Adam en Rom. 5:12', *NTS*, XI (1964–5), pp. 242ff.

3:7: Adam sinned and God condemned him *and his offspring* to death; cf. also Sir. 25:24:

> From a woman sin had its beginning
> And because of her we all die.

On the other hand, the doctrine of individual responsibility, based on Ezek. 18:20, is found, e.g., in the Talmud (T. B. Shabb. 55a), side by side with this possibly more popular, more primitive view. Edersheim (*Life and Times of Jesus the Messiah*, I, p. 166, n. 3) argues that Jewish teaching, while admitting both —mutually exclusive—views, tended on the whole to favour the second (the doctrine of individual responsibility). See further Cambier, op. cit., pp. 219ff.

On Barrett's interpretation, Paul takes the Ezekiel position. If this is so, however, how are we to understand verse 19 or verse 15? 'Many' (i.e. 'all'; see below) 'died through one man's trespass', which assumes original or inherited sin.

There is no doubt that in verses 19 and 15 Paul takes the popular, primitive viewpoint—death came through Adam's sin (original sin). This is also the most natural interpretation of verse 12. Is it possible that at verse 12 Paul is making room for both doctrines? Cf. Wedderburn, op. cit.

The verb in 12c (*eiselthen*: 'came into', 'entered') should perhaps be given greater emphasis; through the first man, sin forced its way into mankind as through an opened door (cf. K. Heim, *Weltschöpfung und Weltende* (1952), p. 142). Adam's trespass was the *beginning* of sin and death among mankind: but this does not carry with it the *necessary* implication that, therefore, Adam's trespass was *the cause* of sin and death in the world. In this respect, every man is his own Adam (2 Bar. liv. 19), though bound by ties of heredity and descent from 'the first Adam (*homo*, 'man')'. Cf. Cambier, op. cit., p. 254.

A similar position is maintained by S. Lyonnet, 'Le sens de *eph hō* en Rom. 5:12 et l'exégèse des Pères grecs',[1] on the grounds that *eph hō* does not mean 'because' in this context: 'la locution désigne une *condition remplie*.' As is clear from Lyonnet's argumentation, the suggestion goes back to J. H. Moulton, *Prolegomena (Grammar of NT Greek*, I), p. 107, where *eph hō* is rendered: 'in view of the fact that'.[1]

---

[1] *Bib.* xxxvi (1955), pp. 452ff.: '. . . les hommes n'encourent la mort éternelle de l'enfer qu'à la condition, d'avoir eux-mêmes péché gravement:

Blass and Debrunner seem in doubt what precise meaning, other than 'because', to give to *eph hō*—even when the grounds given are a fulfilled condition (see *A Greek Grammar of the NT and other Early Christian Literature*, ed. R. W. Funk (Cambridge, 1961), § 235 (2)). Since Lyonnet showed, quite conclusively, that *eph hō* could also mean *quapropter*, *en suite de quoi* (depending on the context),[1] this alternative understanding could be original at Rom. 5:12, where it does make good sense in the context. 'Death passed from Adam to all men, *wherefore, from which it follows*, that all men, like Adam, sinned.' This exegesis is supported by verses 13 and 14; 13a asserts that sin was in the world before the Law (of Moses); 13b raises the objection to this proposition: 'But sin is not imputed where there is no Law', i.e. in the period where there was no Law, there could be no sin. Verse 14: '*But* death reigned supreme from Adam to Moses . . .'—incontrovertible proof of the presence of sin in this period.

13-14. The connecting links of the argument require to be supplied. Paul is arguing (with himself or with an imaginary opponent) in the style of the Stoic diatribe (cf. above, pp. 29f).

'(Death came to all men, wherefore all sinned.) Yes, (I tell you, *gar*) until the giving of the Law (of Moses) there *was* sin in the world, though you might argue that where there was no Law there could not have been any sin. But sin cannot be imputed (and therefore punished)—you will go on to object—where there is no law. Be that as it may (*alla*), death did hold sway from Adam to Moses (as it did from Moses onwards) even over those whose

_____

condition nécessaire, sans doute, mais dont Paul affirme, selon l'exégèse grecque, qu'elle a été de fait remplie. Et cependant, d'après la même exégèse, c'est le péché d'Adam qui cause cette universelle damnation du genre humain . . . Aucune antinomie, parce que la causalité des péchés personnels est secondaire par rapport à celle du péché d'Adam, subordonnée à elle: la puissance du péché introduite dans le monde par Adam produit son effet de mort éternelle à travers les péchés personnels, qui ratifient en quelque sorte la révilte d'Adam; elle ne produit même cet effet dans sa plénitude qu'à travers eux.'

[1] *Diodorus Sic.* xix. 98: '. . . from its centre (the Dead Sea) each year, it sends forth a mass of solid asphalt, sometimes more than three plethra [300 feet] in area, sometimes . . . less. That is why (*eph hō dē*) the barbarians who live near are accustomed to call the larger mass a bull, and the smaller one a calf . . .'

Cf. also J. Meyendorff, '*Eph hō* (Rom. 5:12) chez Cyrille d'Alexandrie et Thoédoret', *Stud. Patrist.*, IV (*TU* 79), Berlin, 1961, pp. 157-61.

sin was not exactly like the transgression of Adam—who is the type of the One to Come (the second Adam).'

13. is not counted: a book-keeping term: 'is not entered in the ledger against'. Cf. Phm. 18. (The inferior imperfect reading, 'was not counted', is clearly a mistaken correction to the tenses of the context.)

14. whose sins were not like the transgression of Adam: Hos. 6:7 uses the same word of Adam's 'transgressing', or breaking his 'covenant' with God. Presumably the other forms of 'sin' are of a lesser kind?

15. if many died . . . abounded for many: 'Many' is used here in the inclusive sense of its Hebrew equivalent, and should really be rendered by 'all' to avoid all possibility of misunderstanding. Cf. J. Jeremias, *The Eucharistic Words of Jesus* (London, 1966) on Mk 14:24, pp. 179ff.: 'While "many" in Greek (as in English) stands in opposition to "all", and therefore has the exclusive sense ("many but *not* all") Hebrew *rabbim* can have the inclusive sense of the whole, comprising many individuals.' E.g., Isa. 53:12; 2 Esd. 8:3, Mk 14:24 (see R. H. Lightfoot, *The Gospel Message of St Mark* (Oxford, 1950), p. 65). Cf. 5:12, 'all', 5:18, 'all men'. The point was noted by some of the early Fathers (see SH, *in loc.*). Richard Bentley pleaded for 'all' as a more accurate version: 'By this accurate version some hurtful mistakes about partial redemption and absolute reprobation had been happily prevented' (*Works*, ed. A. Dyce, III (1838), p. 244; cited in SH, p. 140). Cf. further, J. M. Bover, 'In Rom. 5:15: exegesis logica', *Bib.*, IV (1923), pp. 94ff.
grace . . . and the free gift may be explained as a hendiadys, i.e. 'the free gift of God in the grace . . .; or 'the gracious gift of God . . .' It seems more likely, however, that Paul is defining further that in which the divine 'grace' lay, viz. the free gift of righteousness; the 'free gift' is thus defined at verse 17. Some think that the expression 'the free gift in the grace' is to be taken as a unity, i.e. the free gift consisting of the grace of the one man Jesus Christ.
abounded . . .: Michel suggests that an old rabbinical commonplace about the mercy of God vastly exceeding the penalties for Adam's sin lies behind this verse.
for many: i.e. men in general (see note above).
16. Note the Hebrew-type parallelism and the compressed

style (*Lehrstil* (Michel)): trespass—condemnation—free gift—justification. Moffatt renders: 'Nor did the gift correspond in any way with the effects of one man's sin'; lit.: 'For the judgement (sentence) was pronounced upon one man, resulting in the condemnation (of all), but the gift of grace, following on many trespasses, had for its effect acquittal (for all)'.

17. death reigned: the same idea as above, at verse 14. By the transgression of the one man, death came to rule (*ebasileusen,* ingressive aorist), so *a fortiori* the recipients of the abundant grace etc. of the other will reign in life through the one man, Jesus Christ. We should expect the contrast to be 'death reigned': '(eternal) life reigned'; but Paul turns it round, so that it is the believers who reign in eternal life. For the idea of Christians as 'reigning', cf. 1 C. 4:8, Rev. 1:6, 20:4. Then, accordingly, it follows that Paul draws and states his conclusions:

18. acquittal and life: lit. 'acquittal of life', i.e. leading to (eternal) life.

19. as by one man's disobedience: the same fundamental ideas as verse 18 expressed in synonymous terms: 'trespass' = 'disobedience'; 'act of righteousness' = 'obedience'; 'led to condemnation' = 'were made sinners'; 'leads to acquittal and life' = 'will be made righteous'.

20. Law came in, to increase the trespass: cf. 3:20, where it is said that it was through Law mankind 'attained a deepening awareness of' or 'came to a recognition of' sin. The sense here is not that the multiplication of trespasses is a primary purpose of law, but that it is a secondary consequence (the *hina* clause is ecbatic, or consequential).

came in rather than 'was given'. The Greek verb means literally 'came in to take its place alongside things already existing'. 'St Paul regarded Law as a "parenthesis" in the divine plan: it did not begin until Moses, and it ended with Christ' (SH, *in loc.*).

21. repeats the idea of verses 14 and 17 in another variant form. Here it is not death which reigns, but 'sin-in-death', i.e. sin which has its inevitable outcome in death; and it is grace which reigns, but in a state of or under (*dia*) 'righteousness', which has as its consequence eternal life. And all this, as everything else in the Christian life, is 'through Jesus Christ our Lord' (again 'under' (*dia*), 'within the domain of').

CHRISTIAN FREEDOM FROM THE LAW 6:1-8:39

The second half of the 'great thesis' of Rom. 1 to 8 begins with chapter 6. St Paul develops in this second part his doctrine of 'sanctification', or of the 'post-justification life in Christ' or 'life in the Spirit' (Spiritual life)—life 'in Christ' being life in the Body of Christ, the Church. For a discussion of 6:1-11 see especially G. Wagner, *Pauline Baptism and the Pagan Mysteries* (Edinburgh, 1967); cf. also J. Knox, in *Chapters in a Life of Paul* (New York, 1950), pp. 141-59.

There are three main divisions in the section: (a) 6:1-7:6 deals with the death of the old mankind (the 'old man' in corporate terms) or the old selfhood (in terms of the individual) and the emergence of the new self—a 'death' and 'resurrection' which Paul conceives of as taking place through baptism. The new experience is further illustrated by analogies from slavery (15-23) and marriage and divorce (7:1-6); (b) 7:7-25 contains a psychological analysis of the experience of salvation, the death of the old Adam and the emergence of the new. (This chapter is often regarded as autobiographical; Paul is speaking, however, for every man, though his thought clearly comes out of his own Christian experience. See further, below, p. 101.) (c) 8:1-39, is a closing section on this new life 'in Christ', or a Spirit-filled (or Spirit-enabled) life.

DEATH OF THE OLD MAN 6:1-7:6

1. Are we to continue in sin . . .: or 'are we to persist in sinning, that there might be more and more grace?' This seems a natural enough consequence to draw from the principle laid down at verse 20 that, where sin increases, grace correspondingly increases, in 'geometric progression' ('abounded all the more').

2. By no means: a very strong denial. The idea is preposterous. See above, p. 63.

These verses serve as a transition to the main theme of this second part. The antinomian argument that one should become a persistent sinner in order to enjoy the grace of God more and more is rebutted by the statement that the baptised Christian is dead to sin.

The Pauline Doctrine of Baptism **3–11**

Rom. 6:3–11 is the *locus classicus* for St Paul's doctrine of baptism. The pattern of baptismal practice in the primitive Christian communities (e.g. in Acts) was the baptism of the catechumen by immersion (on his repentance and confession), accompanied by the laying on of hands and the gift of the Holy Spirit (cf. e.g. Ac. 2:38ff, 8:16ff.). Here Paul interprets the act of immersion in relation to the death of Christ (chapter 8 is concerned with the gift of the Spirit). Unlike the baptism of John the Baptist, Christian baptism for the remission of sins is integrally related to Christ's death for sins (cf., in addition to the present passage, 1 Jn 5:6 (cf. Jn 19:34), 1 Pet. 1:2, Heb. 10:22, 1 C. 6:11, Eph. 5:26, Tit. 3:5, etc.).[1]

3. all of us who have been baptized into Christ Jesus: in his baptism the Christian is plunged into the water—so, similarly, in our baptism, we are immersed 'into Jesus Christ'. The verb 'baptize' ('be baptized') is an intensive form of the verb *baptō* ('to dip'), and means, literally, 'to plunge'. Both Josephus and Polybius employ the verb of a 'sinking' ship (e.g., *Polyb.* 1. li. 6).

into Christ Jesus: what are we to understand by 'baptism into Jesus Christ'? Older commentaries (consult SH for a classic presentation) describe this incorporation by baptism into Jesus Christ as Paul's doctrine of 'mystical union', defined (SH, p. 163) as 'really faith, the living apprehension of Christ'. This is all (it is claimed) which lies at the bottom of the language of identification and union (cf. SH, p. 163). One cannot overestimate the value of such insights into the character (or one fundamental aspect of the character) of Pauline mysticism, but one may doubt if it does really get to the bottom of the language of 'identification and union'.

Nowadays it is generally recognized that the key to the Pauline meaning (and doctrine) lies in the understanding of 'Jesus Christ' here as *corporate* personality—the new redeemed, risen and glorified humanity of which he is the Head and inclusive Representative, i.e. the Body of Christ, or 'the second Adam'. To be baptized 'into' Jesus Christ is to be incorporated into the Body of Christ.

---

[1] Cf. L. Fazekas, 'Taufe als Tod in Röm. 6:3ff.', *TZ*, xxii (1966), pp. 305–18; R. Schnackenburg, *Das Heilsgeschehen bei der Taufe nach dem Apostel Paulus* (Münster, 1950); V. Iacono, 'La Palingenesia in S. Paolo e nell' ambiente pagano', *Bib.*, xv (1934), pp. 371ff.

The same expression occurs at 1 C. 10:1-2: 'I want you to know, brethren, that our fathers were all under the cloud, and all passed through the sea, and *all were baptized into Moses* in the cloud and in the sea . . .' Here 'to be baptized into Moses' cannot mean 'mystical union' of the Israelite with Moses. It means simply to become a member of the Israelite community redeemed from Egyptian bondage, of which Moses was the head and inclusive representative. The expression here, therefore, 'baptized into Jesus Christ', is synonymous with that at 1 C. 12:13, 'For by one Spirit *we were all baptized into one body*—Jews or Greeks, slaves or free—and all were made to drink of one Spirit.' The 'one body' is the Body of Christ.

The doctrine of baptism so expounded follows thus naturally and logically on the Adam-Christ typology at 5:12ff., which thus prepares the ground for Pauline baptismal teaching.

were baptized into his death: The Greek Orthodox church gives symbolical presentation to this doctrine in the shape of its baptisteries: they are fashioned in the form of a tomb. The 'sacramental dying' of the Christian in baptism is further explained at verse 6 as the 'crucifixion' of the 'old Adam'; see further below.

4. We were buried therefore with him by baptism into death: this total 'immersion' was also a kind of 'burial', more accurately 'into his death', and these words may go closely with 'by baptism', though they can be construed with the main verb (cf. Col. 2:12).

by the glory of the Father: commentators take 'glory' here as practically synonymous with 'power', and it is true that the two words frequently go together, especially in doxologies (cf. the Lord's Prayer). But it is doubtful if we can understand here 'through' (i.e. 'by means of') 'the power of God the Father'. The preposition describes, rather, attendant circumstances—i.e. the accompaniment of a manifestation of the glorious power of God. *NEB*: 'in the splendour of the Father'.

newness of life: The new 'life after death' (post-baptismal life) is characterized (a) negatively, by a freedom from sin; it is a sinless life (vv. 2, 6, 7); (b) positively, by 'newness of life' or 'new life'; Paul means a life which has the quality of 'everlastingness', i.e. eternal life (vv. 5, 8, 11); verse 8 (life like Christ's), verse 11 (alive to God in Christ).

For an analogous expression to 'newness of life', cf. Rom. 7:6: 'new life of the Spirit'. Though the character of this new life is not here further specifically defined, beyond the fact that it is a new eternal life of righteousness, without sin, the further ethical content of this new post-baptismal life is indicated at Gal. 3:27: 'For as many of you as were baptized into Christ have put on Christ...': baptized Christians have 'put on', or 'been clothed with', Christ, i.e. have become 'new men' (cf. Col. 3:12; Eph. 4:24; cf. Rom. 13:14), members of the Body of Christ, where racial, national, and all other distinctions have been abolished. (Is it possible that, even at this early period, the rite of baptism included, after immersion, the donning of a new (white?) robe?) Col. 3:10ff. describes the life of the 'new man', and its main features seem to come from the character of Christ as the early Church envisaged it. (The main lineaments of a 'portrait' of Christ can be traced in this passage in Colossians.)

5. united with him in a death like his: 'united by growth', lit. 'planted together'. The word exactly expresses the process by which a graft becomes united with the life of a tree. So the Christian becomes 'grafted into' Christ. The verse may be interpreted 'united with a death like his', i.e. Christians share in the death of Christ by growing up into a sacrificial life like his life.

we shall certainly be united with him in a resurrection like his: lit. 'in that case we shall indeed (become united with him in the likeness) of his Resurrection.'

6. our old self was crucified: lit. 'our old man': the expression occurs again at Col. 3:9; Eph. 4:22. Cf. Galatians 2:20: 'I have been crucified with Christ'. While *RSV* renders correctly, Paul also intends the phrase to refer to the 'old Adam' in all men.

sinful body: lit. 'body of sin': the genitive is more than adjectival; it means: '(the body) belonging to sin', 'under the dominion of sin'; 'belonging to' is the general sense, but the genitive has a special shade of meaning in different contexts; SH (cf. 7:24): 'this body which is given over to death'; Phil. 3:21: 'our body in its present degraded state'; Col. 2:11: 'the body which is the instrument of its carnal impulses'. So here: 'the body given over to sin'.

might be destroyed: 'should be "done away"', lit. 'annulled', 'cancelled out'. The verb is one specially appropriate in a legalistic context. Cf. verse 7.

7. freed from sin: lit. 'is acquitted from sin'; but the construction is a pregnant one: 'is acquitted, and so freed from sin and its consequences'; cf. E. Klaar, in *ZNTW*, LIX (1968), pp. 131–4. Are the aorists ingressive: 'he that takes death on himself' (cf. verse 6: 'has taken up his cross with (Christ)')?

Commentators are widely agreed that Paul is echoing, if not quoting, familiar rabbinical teaching: the sentence reads like a *halakah*. The idea that death ends all obligations under the Law is a familiar one among the rabbis. The idea that guilt is wiped out by death, and the sinner thereby freed from sin, is a widespread belief of the ancient world; cf. 1 Pet. 4:1.[1]

8 has been explained as coming from some early confession of faith. Cf. 2 Tim. 2:11. It seems more likely to have been a Pauline argument repeated by the author of 2 Timothy, who was no doubt familiar with the passage in Romans.

9. death no longer has dominion over him: the rabbis frequently represent man as under the absolute power of the Angel of Death.

10. once for all: Christ died to sin a death which is also 'final' so far as sinning is concerned (cf. verse 2); and this death of Christ was a unique event—single, singular, unrepeatable, possessing an unparalleled 'once-for-all' character. For this representation of Christ's death, cf. 1 Pet. 3:18; Heb. 9:12, 28.

11. dead to sin and alive to God: the Christian is 'dead and alive', but in a totally different sense from this familiar English phrase: 'dead', so far as sin is concerned; 'alive' with the new life of right living under God.

in Christ Jesus: cf. note above on verse 3. It is 'within' the Body of Christ we are truly alive, as members of the new human being. Cf., however, SH for the older interpretation of this verse as 'mystical union', 'in Christ', as living in an atmosphere we breathe (Christ in us).

The Analogy from Slavery: the Release from the Captivity of Sin and the New Captivity under Righteousness **12–23**

[1] See further S. Lyonnet, 'Qui enim mortuus est, iustificatus est a peccato', *Verb. Dei* (1964), pp. 17–21; R. Scroggs, in *NTS*, x (1963–4), pp. 104–8. Cf. also, K. G. Kuhn, 'Röm. 6: 7', *ZNTW*, xxx (1931), pp. 305–10.

12. passions: evil desires; cf. Rom. 7:7, Gal. 5:16. The old Adam 'lusts' to possess. The word is used here in a general sense; it includes both covetousness and lust.

13. Your members . . . as instruments of righteousness: lit. 'weapons of righteousness'. It may have been from his own rabbinical teachers or from Stoic philosophers that St Paul derived the image of the 'limbs' or 'bodily members' as weapons in the warfare against evil, and for righteousness. For a list of such 'bodily members' and the use to which they can be put as 'weapons of wickedness', cf. Rom. 3:13–18. We are probably to think of the 'members' here, not just as bodily organs, but as all our human faculties and powers. Cf. Col. 3:5, where 'earthly members' refers to everything in man's life and existence, outward and inward, which is 'of the earth' or lower nature.[1]

14. sin will have no dominion is a kind of promise, corresponding to the command at verse 12 (Michel).

15–23. *Analogy from slavery.* Cf. 1 C. 7:22.

15. Cf. verse 1—neither merely rhetorical questions, but here warding off misunderstanding. For the Jew, when the Law was was not paramount sin was rampant.

16. slaves of the one whom you obey states an axiomatic position. If you offer yourselves to anyone as his slave, you are bound to obedience to that master. So it is with sin: you become its slave, and die. Likewise with obedience: you become its slave, and come to right living.

The two masters here are Sin and Obedience; at verse 18 they are Sin and Righteousness. This apparent illogicality can be resolved by arguing that 'obedience' here ('you are slaves . . . of obedience, which leads to righteousness') is a 'slip of the pen', or an inadvertence in dictating, for 'righteousness': 'it is certainly not felicitous to suggest that the master who is obeyed is Obedience!' (Dodd). There is more, however, to it than this, and it seems likely that 'obedience' is here deliberately chosen in contrast to 'sin', this 'obedience' to which the Christian is enslaved being later defined as 'Righteousness'. For throughout this passage St Paul has a special kind of 'righteousness' in mind, the

[1] See also E. Schweizer, 'Die Sünde in den Gliedern', in *Abraham unser Vater: Juden und Christen im Gespräch über die Bibel* (*Festschrift* O. Michel), ed. O. Betz, M. Hengel, P. Schmidt (Leiden-Köln, 1963), pp. 437-9 (*Arbeiten zur Geschichte des Spätjudentums und Urchristentums*, No. 5).

'righteousness-by-faith', and this is or stems from obedience to Christ; so that the Christian convert yields his new loyalty to Christian obedience, which is Christian righteousness. Cf. C. K. Barrett (p. 131): 'Paul introduces this additional matter (slavery to 'obedience') because it is important to show that obedience has a place in the system of grace and faith.'

17. the standard of teaching to which you were committed: St Paul here further defines in different terms the object to which Christians yield themselves (or are committed) in obedience. It is to a form of doctrine handed down to them. In fact, of course, obedience is yielded to the Person who is proclaimed by Christian teaching, but Paul can vary his figure by further defining the obedience we obey as the Christian Gospel. The choice of verb, 'committed', is significant; it is the regular word for 'tradition' (handing on) but, instead of saying we are to obey the doctrine 'transmitted to us', he says 'we are handed over to' it, recalling the other common use of this verb of being 'surrendered up to', 'made captive to'—in line with the figure of slavery: the Christian has been delivered up captive to Christian doctrine.[1]

Notice that this verse is a thanksgiving for past deliverance (from sin) and present deliverance over to the Christian Gospel, which is slavery to the true righteousness (verse 18).

19. I am speaking in human terms, because of your natural limitations: usually, when Paul uses this phrase, he is apologizing for applying human terms to God. Was the state of the slave so degraded a condition that Paul had to apologize even for using it as an analogy? Or is he apologizing for specifying the typical Gentile 'sin' as 'impurity' and 'lawlessness'?

20. you were free in regard to righteousness: i.e. at that time you did not serve righteousness as your master. 'Righteousness' to which as Christians we are 'enslaved' is, in its aspect as the pure service of God, 'holiness' or 'sanctification'.

21. what return did you get: the question may end at 'get', and the answer be '(things) of which you are now ashamed'. The

---

[1] See further J. Kurzinger, 'Typos Didachēs und der Sinn von Röm. 6: 17ff.', Bib., xxxix (1958), pp. 156–76. Cf. also F. W. Beare, 'On the Interpretation of Rom. 6:17', NTS, v (1958–9), pp. 206–10; C. H. Dodd, in New Testament Essays in Memory of T. W. Manson, ed. A. J. B. Higgins (Manchester, 1959), p. 108.

return or wages of the service of unrighteousness is shame and shame's children. Their outcome is death, here for Paul, not only the consequence of evildoing, but the final judgement of God upon it.

22. Emancipation **from sin** and enslavement to righteousness means also that we have become God's slaves.

the return you get is sanctification . . .: *NEB* is closer to the Greek: 'your gains are such as make for holiness, and the end is eternal life'.

23. the wages of sin is death: though the word translated 'wages' can be used in the general sense of 'reward', the figure here is probably a military one, the reference being to the soldier's daily pay, lit. 'provision-money'. (Cf. the use of the term at Lk. 3:14, 1 C. 9:7.) The contrasting term here rendered 'free gift' is also used in the sense of a 'bounty' (*donativum*), cf. Michel, *ad loc.*, such as was distributed to the army on the accession to the throne of a new Emperor. Sin pays her mercenaries in the coin of death: the divine bounty is everlasting life in Jesus Christ our Lord.

Cf. further E. Käsemann, '*Römer 6:19–23*' in *Exegetische Versuche und Besinnungen*, I (Göttingen, 1960), pp. 263–6.

The Law of Marriage 7:1–6
Verses 1–6 of chapter 7 develop a further analogy from the institution of marriage illustrative of the Christian's emancipation from sin and the law of Moses. Cf. J. D. M. Derrett, 'Fresh Light on Rom. 7.1–4', *JTS*, xv (1964), pp. 97–108; C. L. Mitton, 'Rom. 7 reconsidered', *ET*, lxv (1953-4), pp. 78–81, 99–103, 132–5.

The general point of the analogy is clear; its details, like those of the allegory of the Wild Olive at chapter 11, are not to be pressed. A death has taken place which releases the Christian (= the wife whose husband has died) from the Law, so that he can then be legally united in marriage with another—namely his Risen Lord.

3. if she lives with another man: *NEB*; 'she consorts with another man'. The usage is Hebraic, and means 'becomes wife to another man' (lit. 'becomes the property of . . .', e.g., Dt. 24:2, Jg. 15:2, etc.).

4. Likewise, my brethren, you have died to the law through the body of Christ: the Christian believer has died

with Christ—his baptism is a kind of sacramental death—but will
also live with him (6:8, cf. 2 Tim. 2:11). This sacramental death
is 'through the body of Christ', i.e. through the death of Christ,
into which all Christians are baptised to become members of his
body. This means a final break with the Law, since such a death
releases the Christian from any further obligation to the Law.

that you may belong to another: the figure of marriage is
continued. Release from the Law (and the old partner, the old
Adam) means that the believer is free to contract a new union
with his Risen Lord, and obtain new progeny through this fresh
'marriage'.

5. to bear fruit for death develops the idea of bearing of
progeny (lit. 'fruit'). When life had no higher object than gratifi-
cation of the senses ('while we were living in the flesh'; cf. Gal.
2:20), then our sinful passions (which the Law calls forth and
aggravates) were active within us, to lead us into the kind of
actions that end in death ('our sinful passions . . . were at work
in our members to bear fruit for death').

6. But now we are discharged from the law: the Law
under which the old Adam was held down has become a dead
letter. It is God we now serve (not sin or the obedience of the Law)
in a new spiritual life, not in the old life of obedience to an external
code.

A similar attitude to the hopelessness of the natural life, even
with the Law, is found at 2 Esd. 3:20-22, cf. 9:36. But Paul
takes a step further than this author; for, whereas for the latter
the Law never loses its glorious character, for Paul it has become a
hindrance, even providing an impetus to sin. There seems little
doubt that such an apparent depreciation of the Law arose in the
course of controversy with Jewish opponents who could find
nothing higher than the Law.

the old written code: not, of course, the written *tôrāh*, but the
'letter of the Law', i.e. its strait-laced interpretation. Cf. E. Käsemann, *Perspectives on Paul*, pp. 138ff.

MAN'S SPIRITUAL PILGRIMAGE 7-25

The passage, verses 7-25, is generally regarded as autobiographical
(cf. Phil. 3:3ff.); Paul speaks in these verses about himself in the
first person. In general, this is true but, though it is indeed his
own spiritual experience St Paul is recounting in these verses, it is

equally clear that he intends us to understand them as a description of a typical human experience; it is for every man he is speaking in this famous passage; the 'I' in these verses is the unredeemed man. (See further W. Wrede, *Paul*, trans. E. Lummis, (London, 1907) p. 144ff. Wrede plays down the autobiographical emphasis, maintaining: 'The truth is, the soul-strivings of Luther have stood as model for the portrait of Paul' (p. 146).[1]

The question whether Paul is describing the pre- or post-conversion state has received a variety of answers. Nygren takes the latter position, Dodd the former. A. M. Hunter compromises: '14–25 therefore depicts not only the man under the law, but the Christian who slips back into a legalistic attitude towards God. The present tenses describe not only a past experience, but one which is potentially ever present' (*Romans*, p. 174).[2] Dodd's position is that 'it would stultify his (Paul's) whole argument if he now confessed that, at the moment of writing, he was a 'miserable wretch, a prisoner to sin's law' (p. 108). It is a convincing point (verses 23, 24). Advocates of the pre-conversion view include Origen, Wesley, J. Weiss. Cf. further, Bultmann, 'Romans 7 and the Anthropology of Paul', in *Existence and Faith* (Cleveland, 1960), pp. 147–57.

The passage stands in close connection with the doctrine of chapter 6:1ff. representing further reflection on the Christian experience of salvation as consisting of the death of the old self and the emergence of the new self (dying with Christ to live with Him); but this is now expressed in psychological terms, and as a typical human experience as well as the personal experience of the writer. Every man recapitulates in his own personal life the fall of Adam: he is beguiled (verse 11, cf. Gen. 3:13); the temptress is *hamartia*; and Sin in this passage, like the Law, is best

[1] Cf. further H. Jonas, 'Philosophische Meditation über Paulus Römerbrief, Kap. 7', *Zeit und Geschichte: Dankesgabe an R. Bultmann* (Tübingen, 1964), pp. 557–70; H. Braun, *Röm. 7:7–25 und das Selbstverständnis der Qumran Frommen* (Tübingen, 1963), E. Fuchs, 'Existentiale Interpretation von Röm. 7:7–12 und 21–23', *Glaube und Erfahrung* (Tübingen, 1965); J. M. Bover, 'Valor de los Términos Ley, Yo, Pecado en Rom. 7', *Bib.*, v (1924), pp. 192ff.; W. G. Kümmel, 'Röm. vii und die Bekehrung des Paulus', *Untersuchungen zum Neuen Testament*, xvii (Leipzig, 1929).

[2] Cf. also C. L. Mitton, 'Romans 7 Reconsidered', *ET*, lxv (1953–4), pp. 78ff., 99ff., 132ff. A survey of modern interpretations in O. Kuss, *Der Römerbrief* i (Regensburg, 1963), pp. 462–85, and K. Kertelge, in *ZNTW*, lxii (1971), pp. 105–14.

thought of as personified, corresponding to the Serpent in the Genesis allegory (Gen. 3:13: 'the serpent beguiled me, and I ate'). The penalty is death.

This central proposition is worked out in relation to the characteristically Pauline idea about the part played by the Law, or law, in man's spiritual odyssey. While good in itself, the Law proved less a help to man's salvation than in fact a stumbling-block, so that it became in the end the instrument of his downfall; the only result of the Law for man's life was to intensify his sense of sin or guilt (cf. 3:20). From this personal tragedy, repeated in the case of every man—the Fall of Everyman—we are saved, not by the Law, but *dia Iēsou Christou* ('through Jesus Christ'), verse 25, the conclusion of the passage and the main theme being developed in the following chapter.

7. What then shall we say: a transitional formula found, for example, at chapter 4:1, 5:1: in the present case it carries forward the argument by asking not only a rhetorical but a ridiculous question. Cf. also 8:31.

As we have seen earlier (above, p. 65), this idea that man came to know sin through the Law appears to be a distinctively Pauline thought; and here it is expounded and explained by an example. The meaning is that of personal knowledge or experience of evil desire rather than knowledge in any other sense; cf. G. B. Caird, *Principalities and Powers* (Oxford, 1956) p. 42, note 5. Cf. 2 C. 5:21, where the meaning appears to be, not 'him who knew not the meaning of sin', but 'him who had no personal acquaintance with sin'.

You shall not covet: 'If the Law had not said: "You shall not covet," Paul argues, 'we should not have known what the nature of "covetousness" was'.

The word *epithymia* here, frequently rendered 'covetousness', is much wider in meaning, and broad enough to include all evil inclinations among them, for instance, sexual desire, though *epithymia* is never purely sexual. Paul has probably in mind the 'evil inclination' of Jewish tradition or the 'evil heart' of 2 Esd. 3:20.

In Philo's exposition of the Ten Commandments (see especially *Decal.*, 142ff., 150, 173) there is a similar description of the power of *epithumia*; in Philo it is closely linked with *hēdonē* (lit. 'pleasure'), and both together are regarded as the root of all evil. There was probably an ancient Jewish tradition which linked evil desire, sin and death, as at Gen. 3 (cf. Jas. 1:15).

8. finding opportunity in the commandment: the word translated 'opportunity' here in the *RSV* means literally 'starting-point', (the corresponding verb means 'to make a start from' a place). The noun comes to be used in a military sense referring to a base of operations (Thucydides, 1. xc.2). St Paul's meaning is that the Law, or rather this particular commandment of the Law, was, as it were, a kind of bridgehead into human nature for the invading forces of Sin. Paul's argument is that Sin is 'dead'— that is to say, 'powerless'—apart from the Law.

9. apart from the law: there was a time when he once lived apart from the Law; but, whenever the commandment came into his consciousness, then Sin sprang to life (ingressive aorist), with the result that, instead of the Law being dead, he now died, and the commandment whose intention had been to bring life (cf. Dt. 6:24f., Ezek. 20:25) really proved to be a cause of the sinner's death.

10. the very commandment ... proved to be death to me: The commandment which should have led to life proved in my experience to lead to death: literally, 'the commandment which should have led to life was found for me (*heurethē*) (*leading*) to death'. We have here probably a LXX expression: 'was found' corresponds to Hebrew *nimsa* ('was found out to be', i.e. proved to be), cf. Mt. 1:18.

11. sin ... deceived me: verse 11 is a kind of allegorizing of the story of the Fall. Like Adam, Paul once lived in a time of innocence without benefit of Law; but the Law did come, as it did to Adam, in the form of a divine commandment. Sin then beguiled or tempted Paul, as the woman tempted Adam. (Note the verb 'deceived' (*exēpatēsen*), directly alluding to Gen. 3:13.) Cf. further 2 C. 11:3 and 1 Tim. 2:14. Dodd (pp. 105ff.) cites parallels from Philo and elsewhere, e.g. 2 Bar. 54:19. 'Each of us has been the Adam of his own soul'. Note that Eve or the serpent do not play any part in the Pauline analogy: in their place is the personified *Hamartia*, or 'Sin'.

Notice the close parallelism between verses 8 and 11. Both have the same main point—namely, the indictment of Sin which in this way makes use of the Law. Some commentaries give the impression that it was Paul's intention to attack the Law as calling forth 'evil desire'; in reality, as Gaugler emphasizes (*ad loc.*), it is above all *Hamartia* which is the object of Paul's attack in this chapter. As a spiritual reality, Sin may be said to have a Satanic or demonic character, because it uses a commandment of God's Law for its own ends (see further below).

12. the law is holy is finally the answer to the question of verse 7. Here Paul replies once and for all to his critics. So far as the Law is concerned, then it is holy, and its commandments are also holy, just, and good. It is not the Law or the commandment in itself that Paul indicts. For a similar statement about the Law, cf. verse 16 below, and 1 Tim. 1:8.

13. that which is good ... bring death: Did something good then become the death of me? Absurd. But Sin did become the death of me in order that Sin, which brings death as a consequence of its activity, might be exposed for what it really is, since it operates in this way through that which is good. Sin, I say, produced my death in order that Sin might be shown up and proved to be the wicked thing it was through the commandment.

Notice the two purpose clauses—both parallel and both conveying the same sense. By 'that which is good', Paul here clearly means the Law (cf. verse 16 below, and parallels in rabbinical sources (SB, 1, p. 809) in which the Law is the good *par excellence*.

14. the law is spiritual: the spiritual character of the Law is something of which we are fully aware (cf. 3:19). There is an alternative reading here, according to which the words were: 'for while I know that the Law is spiritual ... nevertheless I am "carnal", the purchased slave of sin.' (This is the preferred reading of Barth in his *Römerbrief*, following Zahn and others, and it is as early as St Jerome.) For a parallel to the latter phrase, cf. Jn 8:34.

By 'spiritual' here as a description of the Law, Paul evidently means that the Law comes from the Spirit of God—that is to say, that it has something divine in it. He means much the same as he has said earlier at verse 12, when he described the Law as holy—that is, the Law is God's Law. The statement 'I am carnal' implies, not only that the personal 'I' is enclosed in a physical body, but that this embodiment of personality is in fact in possession of tendencies which are the opposite of spiritual—that is, away from, not towards God. Behind this is probably the rabbinical doctrine of the 'evil inclination' which for St Paul appears to reside in the flesh (see below)—that is to say, the physical being of man is so tainted. Paul possibly took this idea of 'carnal' or 'of flesh', a concept more fully developed in the next chapter, from the hellenistic Judaism of his period. (See further below, p. 110.) Cf. also P. Althaus, 'Zur Auslegung von Röm. 7: 14ff.', *Theol. Ltzg.*, LXXVII (1952), pp. 475–80.

For a fuller discussion of the meaning of the word 'carnal', see the note on 'flesh' in the following chapter.

sold under sin: St Paul has evidently the slave market here in mind. Sin is the slave-owner, or master to whose possession the human person is delivered by the flesh with its impulses and appetites.

15. I do not understand my own actions: 'I do not even acknowledge my own actions as mine' (*NEB*). It may be suggested that the meaning of the verb *ginōskō* here is that of 'know' in the Biblical sense of 'choose'; see, for example, Philip Hyatt's note on Am. 3:2 in the revised *Peake's Commentary*. In that case, we ought perhaps to render it: 'I do not determine what I am about/am doing'; 'I do not determine my own actions'.

The verb here translated in the *AV* simply by 'do' refers to conduct and behaviour generally; it occurs at verses 15, 17, 18 and 20 in this chapter. It refers to the completed and overt action, acquired habit, and so can be used in general of 'conduct': 'I do not choose my conduct (behaviour)'.

For I do not do what I want, but I do the very thing I hate: similar analyses of this contradiction in human behaviour occur in hellenistic writers; the closest parallel is that of Ovid (*Metamorph.*, vii. 19f.: *video meliora proboque, deteriora sequor*). Here St Paul is not, however, simply indicating a curious psychological situation that occurs occasionally in human conduct: what he is thinking of is the whole existence of man as being involved in a conflict between what he, in agreement with the demands of the Law, wills to do, and what in fact his actual behaviour is under the compulsion of Sin. One may compare the further hellenistic parallels in Epictetus (*Dissertations*, IV.i.72), but this conflict goes much deeper in Paul than in these hellenistic writers, since it is a conflict between the ideal of obedience to the Law and the actual reality of human nature as under the pressure of an occupying power, Sin (see below). Between these two, for Paul, there is a wide gulf.

16. the law is good: the ideal, the Law, is good enough. It is not the Law that is inadequate; it is our own natural human weakness overcome by sin.

17. So then it is no longer I that do it, but sin which dwells within me: it is possible that 'dwell' (*oikein;* cf. Mt. 12:45 par., Rev. 2:13) has the sense of 'possess' ('demon possession'). (Cf. Bauer, *Lex.*, s.v., *katoikeō*.)

18. nothing good dwells within me: verse 18 repeats in other words this central Pauline idea where the term 'flesh' is applied to this aspect of human nature, left, as it were, to its own resources and devices. 'I can will what is right, but I cannot do it.'

19–20 repeat in parallel, but slightly different, ways these same leading thoughts. The will is present with me, but to accomplish the good is beyond me; and this is entirely due to that sin which dwells within me.

'It is difficult not to believe that the Apostle is there [Rom. 7] describing his experience as a Jew suffering under the *yêtzer ha-râ*' (W. D. Davies, *Paul and Rabbinic Judaism*, pp. 25ff.). While this familiar concept may well lie in the background of this chapter, it is nowhere explicitly mentioned. It is 'sin' which is the enemy, not the 'evil impulse'.

Paul's teaching in these verses (and in this chapter) can easily lead to misunderstanding. He appears to assume that Sin is a usurping force—personal, alive, and tyrannical—which exercises complete authority over human nature, indwells human nature (flesh); and Paul sees the human predicament in this light. Man is, as it were, caught up in this situation; he is an unwilling slave of this tyrannical force. James Denney has written (*Commentary on Romans*, pp. 641–2): 'That might be antinomian, or manichean, as well as evangelical. A true saint may say it in a moment of passion, but a sinner had better not make it a principle.' As Dr J. S. Stewart has reminded us in an article entitled: 'On a Neglected Emphasis in New Testament Theology' (*SJT*, IV (1951), p. 293), this warning of James Denney is entirely salutary; but he goes on to add that when 'a saint or for that matter a common sinner says this thing in a moment of passion, "It is not I who do the deed but sin that dwells in me"—as though some outside force getting hold of him were ultimately responsible—it is at once more Biblical and much nearer to the mark objectively than any psychological re-interpretation which suggests that Romans 7 and the perpetual predicament there mirrored can be dealt with under some such formula as "the divided self".' What is really at issue here is the 'whole mystery of iniquity', and for St Paul this is not simply a conflict within the human self only, between a higher self and a lower self, between personal integrity or dishonour. What is at issue here is the conflict between forces of evil in which man is caught up and the opposing powers of the Kingdom of God.

21. I find it to be a law: human nature has this kind of constitution. 'Law' here in the sense of 'principle'.

22. inmost self: the same expression again only at 2 C. 4:16 where, as the inner self which is daily 'renewed', it is contrasted with the 'outer man' that is perishing. The parallel with *nous* ('mind', verse 23) shows that it is of the 'higher (inner) self' Paul is thinking. Is this another expression for the 'new creation' (Gal. 6:15; 2 C. 5:17) or the 'new man' (Eph. 2:15; 4:24)?

23. members: *NEB* rightly paraphrases 'bodily members': it is 'the body' with its appetites Paul means.

Note the military metaphors, and cf. Jas 4:1; a law or principle in the body which is at war with (lit. 'campaigning against') the law of my mind and which brings me into captivity, etc.

law of my mind: Paul may again have the Stoic *lex naturalis* in mind. Cf. above on 2:14ff. This was also the 'Law of God' as much as the *tôrāh*. The ambiguous *nomos* is here used both for the higher law (the law of the mind = the *tôrāh*) and the lower 'law', or 'order', of sin which resides in the 'bodily members'.

24. Wretched man that I am: cf. J. I. Packer, 'The "Wretched Man" in Rom. 7', *Stud. Ev.*, II (1964) pp. 621-7.

this body of death: more than 'this mortal body'; *NEB*: 'this body doomed to death', i.e. by the operation of the 'law of sin' (scarcely as *NEB mg.*, 'doomed to this death').

25. This verse does not really supply an answer to the question asked in verse 24. That question is a rhetorical one, and the answer appears to be implied in verse 25. It is, in any case, supplied elsewhere in Romans. The answer is, of course: 'God through his intervention in Christ'. But all that we have in Paul is a thanksgiving which assumes the deliverance described elsewhere in Romans. In these circumstances, it is doubtful if *NEB's* rendering of verse 25 is legitimate, except as a free paraphrase. To the question asked in verse 24 *NEB* replies: 'God alone, through Jesus Christ our Lord. Thanks be to God.'

A problem may still be felt to remain here, so that the suggestion of Michel may be welcomed by many, namely, that we should take 8:2 immediately after the thanksgiving in verse 25. It is possible that there has been some dislocation in these verses. Verse 25*b*, for instance, would come much more logically within the argument of the previous verses if it followed immediately after verse 23. Chapter 8:1 would lead very naturally into verse 3.

THE SPIRIT-ENABLED LIFE 8:1-39

In the last two chapters, St Paul has been more concerned with the negative rather than with the positive aspects of salvation (freedom *from* Sin, freedom *from* the Law), though at more than one point the positive side has been mentioned (e.g. 5:18: 'absolution carrying with it life'; 6:8: 'we shall *live* with him'). In chapter 8, however, St Paul goes on to expand the theme of 7:25 (salvation through Jesus Christ), and to expound the more positive content of the Christian life, which is a life lived *in Christ*, i.e. as a member of the Body of Christ, by the power of the Spirit of God, the Holy Spirit, which enables us to fulfil the demands of the Law which under the old system of frail and unaided human nature man proved himself incapable of doing.

Cf. 6:1ff. Baptism is accompanied by the illapse of the Spirit. Having dealt in chapters 6-7 with the fundamental aspects of baptism as a 'death' and 'resurrection' of the believer within the Body of Christ—i.e. a new life in Christ—chapter 8 now goes on to develop the theme of the spiritual endowment of the Christian in his baptism.

Note on 'Flesh', 'Body', 'Spirit'

The basic meaning of 'flesh' (Greek *sarx;* Hebrew *basar*) is the same in all languages. It denotes primarily the muscular tissue, the fleshy substance common to men and all living creatures; cf. J. A. T. Robinson, *The Body: a Study in Pauline Theology. Studies in Biblical Theology*, 5, London, 1952); and also R. Bultmann, *Theology*, I, p. 232ff.; R. Jewett, *Paul's Anthropological Terms: A Study of their Use in Conflict Settings* (Leiden, 1971). In Hebrew thought, *basar* stands for 'the whole life-substance of men or beasts as organized in corporeal form', cf. Robinson, *op. cit.*, p. 13.

In Hebrew thought and in its applications to man, the word

basar or, in its Greek form, *sarx*, or *sōma* ('body'), came to denote, not just the physical body, but the whole human being, and in this it differed fundamentally from Greek ideas about the physical body (*sōma*), or its substance 'flesh' (*sarx*). As Robinson points out, '. . . the most far-reaching of all the Greek antitheses, that between *body* and *soul*, is also foreign to the Hebrew. The Hellenic conception of man has been described as that of an angel in a slot-machine, a soul (the invisible, spiritual, essential ego) incarcerated in a frame of matter from which it trusts eventually to be liberated. The body is non-essential to the personality: it is something which a man possesses or rather is possessed by.' 'The Hebrew idea of the personality, on the other hand,' wrote the late Dr. Wheeler Robinson in a sentence which has become famous, 'is an animated body and not an incarnated soul' (*The People and the Book*, ed. A. S. Peake (Oxford, 1925), p. 362). Man does not have a body; he is a body. He is flesh-animated-by-soul, the whole conceived as a psychophysical unity: 'the body is the soul in its outward form' (J. Pedersen, *Israel*, I-II (London, 1946), p. 171). There is no suggestion that the soul is the essential personality, or that the soul (*nephesh*) is immortal while the flesh (*basar*) is mortal. The 'soul' does not survive a man: it simply goes out, draining away with the blood.

A second important point of differentiation from Greek ideas, according to Robinson, is what he calls 'the principle of individuation' in Hebrew thought about the whole human personality. Greek thought, he contends, tended to set the *sōma* or body as that which sets off or isolates one man from another. The body is the most individual thing the soul possesses. In Hebrew thought the principle of individuation is not to be found in the outward appearance of the body; it is grounded solely on the individual responsibility of each man to God and the nature of the response each man makes to the demands of God; see Jer. 31:29f., and cf. Walter Eichrodt, *Man in the Old Testament*, Eng. trans. by K. and R. Gregor Smith (*Studies in Biblical Theology*, 4, London, 1951), pp. 9ff. and 23ff.; and J. A. T. Robinson, *The Body*, p. 15.

There is a further important aspect of this so-called principle of individuation. Hebrew thought, when it thinks of body or 'flesh', in this sense of the whole individual responsible to God, thinks, not only of the whole man as an isolated individual or unit, but the whole man as a social personality, just as in ancient tribal life, and especially the life of ancient Israel, there were no individuals—the unit was the tribe or group. So in later Hebrew thought, man's only life is the life of a social being. Thus J. A. T. Robinson writes (p. 15): 'The flesh-body was not what partitioned a man off from his neighbour; it was rather what bound him in the bundle of life with all men and nature, so that he could never make his unique answer to God as an isolated individual, apart from his relation to his neighbour. The *basar* continued even in the age of greater religious individualism, to represent the fact that personality is essentially social.'

Finally, 'flesh' comes especially to denote in the Old Testament weak mortal and perishable human nature; cf. especially Isa. 40:6–8: 'The voice said, Cry. And he said, What shall I cry? All flesh is grass, and all the goodliness thereof is as the flower of the field: The grass withereth, the flower fadeth: because the spirit of the Lord bloweth upon it. The grass withereth, the flower fadeth: but the word of our God shall stand for ever' (*AV*). 'All flesh' denotes weak and perishable mortality, in contrast to the life and power of God: it is man, as Robinson defines him, 'in his difference and distance from God'.

Paul builds on this Old Testament foundation. The further question has been raised whether, in addition to his Hebrew inheritance, Paul's concept of the flesh has also been influenced by trends in Greek philosophy—stemming ultimately from Plato—which, by setting matter over against mind, ended by regarding the 'flesh' or 'body', since it is composed of matter, as necessarily and inherently evil. Paul undoubtedly uses 'flesh' in what appears to be a 'theologically loaded' sense; he certainly can think of the 'flesh' (i.e. the natural life of man) as somehow the seat of evil desires (cf. verse 18). Jacob Licht (see below) contends that Paul is in the same tradition as Qumran, where 'flesh' seems to be inherently 'wicked' ('the wicked flesh'; cf. 1QS xi.9). It seems, however, that the Qumran concept represents an even more pessimistic point of view than Paul's (possibly a rationalisation of sexual disgust, not unnatural in an ascetic community). Paul's 'flesh' seems, by comparison, morally neutral, but, by virtue of its weakness, an unresisting 'host' to evil impulses. For recent discussion, W. D. Davies and K. G. Kuhn, *The Scrolls and the New Testament*, ed. K. Stendahl (London, 1958), pp. 157ff., 94ff.; Jacob Licht, 'The Doctrine of the Thanksgiving Scroll', *IEJ*

(1956), p. 90ff.; D. Flusser, *Scripta Hierosolomitana* (Jerusalem, 1965), pp. 246ff.

The subject is one which has, naturally, aroused a vast amount of learned debate; and some may feel that the straightforward position set out above may require amplification. Essentially the view presented is the Bultmann-Schweizer theory that life 'in the flesh' is neutral, whereas life 'according to the flesh' is evil. The theory has been challenged in recent studies.[1]

St Paul inherited ideas such as these from his tradition. 'Flesh' was fundamentally human nature in its weak creatureliness and mortality, in its distance and difference from God. But when St Paul thinks of the individual human being as 'flesh', just as when he thinks of him as *sōma* (or 'body'), requiring to be saved out of its weakness and mortality, he thinks in Hebraic terms, first of the whole personality responding morally to God, and so differentiated from others, and secondly of that whole personality as a social being. The individual cannot be rescued, so to speak, out of his fleshly and mortal weakness, so liable to the invasions of sin and amenable and doomed to mortality, as an isolated unit; that would be like raising oneself up by one's boot-strings. As a social personality he must be lifted out of the context of weak sinful mankind and placed into the new social context of the Body of Christ (the *sōma Christou*), the redeemed flesh, the 'second Adam'. In this sense, it is profoundly true that *extra ecclesiam nulla salus*.

In the psychology of the Old Testament, spirit (*pneuma, rûach*) is the supernatural divine element which breaks into human life over against the powerless and perishable flesh. All qualities in men which were deemed to be extraordinary are attributed to the workings of this divine power. Thus Samson's extraordinary physique and his physical prowess are due to the workings of the 'Spirit' of Jahweh; cf. Jg. 14:6f. ('and the Spirit of the Lord

---

[1] The literature on the subject is immense. Among more notable contributions are: H. W. Robinson, *The Christian Doctrine of Man* (Edinburgh, 1911); W. D. Davies, *Paul and Rabbinic Judaism* (London, 1962); O. Küss, *Römerbrief*; E. Schweizer, in *TWNT*, s.v. *sarx, pneuma*. For some additional recent discussion, consult E. Brandenburger, *Fleisch und Geist: Paulus und die dualistische Weisheit* (*Wissenschaftliche Monographien zum Alten und Neuen Testament*, Neukirchen, 1968); W. G. Kümmel, *Man in the New Testament* (London, 1963); E. Käsemann, *Leib und Leib Christi: eine Untersuchung zur paulinischen Begrifflichkeit* (Tübingen, 1933).

came mightily upon him'); and so also it is the Spirit of Jahweh which fills the artisans who fashion the furniture of the Tabernacle (cf. Exod. 28:3, 31:3). At Exod. 28:3 the translation: 'an able mind' is given in the *RSV*, where the other versions speak of 'the Spirit of wisdom', but this is precisely what the author means by the Spirit of Jahweh in such contexts. Similarly it is the Spirit of Jahweh which comes upon Joseph, and gives him his wisdom and gifts of administration in Egypt (Gen. 41:38). Above all, the prophetic spirit, the inspiration of the prophet, is conceived of as endowing men with the gift of understanding, wisdom and judgement; cf. Job 32:8: 'But there is a spirit in man: and the inspiration of the Almighty giveth them understanding' (*AV*). Here the 'spirit in man' is defined in terms of understanding, and it is as an endowment, as it were, of the 'breath of the Almighty'.

This typically Hebraic conception of man's divinely inspired nature and endowments is carried over into the Scriptures of the New Testament. The early Christian Church was uniquely conscious of the workings of this divine power in and through it; and the *fons et origo*, the source and inspiration, as well as the medium or channel, of this power was the Crucified, Risen and Exalted Lord. Christian spiritual life all down the centuries has been a life inspired by the Spirit of Jesus and drawing its spiritual resources from worship and obedience to the Risen and Ascended Christ. As a monk of the Greek Orthodox Church wrote in a little book called *Orthodox Spirituality* (London, 1945): 'The vitalising centre of the first Christian thought and devotion was neither a body of ethical teaching, simply relating the individual to his Father and Maker (Harnack, Tolstoi), nor a mere eschatological expectation (Schweitzer). Christianity was a stream of charismatic life flowing out with torrential might from Palestine upon the Greco-Roman world. It was a new spring-tide of the Spirit, out of faith in, nay, out of experience of, the Risen and Exalted Christ . . . grew the whole efflorescence of prayer and belief, of grace and self-giving, which we call the Holy Catholic Church' (p. 79).

St Paul speaks of the Spirit as the 'earnest' of the world to come (2 C. 1:22 and 5:5), and the author of the Epistle to the Hebrews (6:5) regards the Spirit as a foretaste of the powers of the age to come. Finally, the 'spirit' confers 'eternal life' (cf. 1 C. 15:45).

These powers found expression in such extraordinary super-

natural phenomena as 'speaking with tongues' (*en glōssē lalein*) and
in 'mighty works' (*dynameis*), but they also came to expression in
what St Paul regarded as the higher *charismata* or gifts of the
Spirit—that is to say, intellectual and moral endowments such as
(and here there is a close parallel with the Old Testament) the
words of wisdom (1 C. 12:8f.), of knowledge, and of faith, healings,
the gift of administration (*kybernēsis*), powers of discernment and
understanding (*diakrisis*), and so on; and, above all, what Paul
regarded as the chief and indeed the sum and perfection of the
gifts of the Spirit, the charisma of *agapē* ('charismatic love'). As
Rudolf Otto wrote in his book, *The Kingdom of God and the Son of
Man* (London, 1938), p. 342 (cf. pp. 351f. and especially p. 340):
'They are not magic powers, such as a *goētēs* (sorcerer) thought he
possessed. They are mysterious heightenings of talents and
capacities, which have at least their analogues in the general life
of the soul'; and Dodd writes: 'by Spirit Paul means the supernatural or divine element in human life and his test for it is the
presence of a love like the love of God in Christ' (*Commentary*,
p. 118). Perhaps it is Otto rather than Dodd who places the emphasis where it ought to be placed. While it is not denied that such
'endowments' are 'supernatural', it is equally important to recog-
nize that they are familiar human faculties, including the capacity
for *agapē* (which is more often toleration than passionate love). Perhaps too great emphasis has been placed on the Spirit as the (Holy)
Ghost, and too little on the Spirit as *Geist*, the higher life of the
spiritual being (intellectual gifts as well as qualities of character).

Sin, the Incarnation and Life in the Spirit 1-4[1]

1 There is consequently *now* no condemnation for those in Christ
Jesus.
2 For the order of the living (and life-giving) Spirit in Christ Jesus
has delivered us (set us free) from the order of sin and death.
3 For what the Law was incapable of effecting—in so far as it was
weak by reason of the flesh—God sent His own Son resembling
sinful flesh and as a sin-offering (or, for sin), and condemned
(abolished) sin in the flesh.

[1] On these verses, see S. Lyonnet, 'Le Nouveau Testament à la lumière
de l'Ancien, à propos de Rom. 8:2-4', *Nouvelle Revue Théologique* (Louvain),
xcvii (1965), pp. 561-87. Cf. also N. A. Dahl, *op. cit.* (p. 77); J. Tibbe, *Geist
und Leben. Eine Auslegung von Röm. 8* (*Bib. Studien*, 44) (Neukirchen, 1965).

4 that the just requirements of the Law might be fully realised in us who no longer conduct ourselves according to the flesh (by the order of unredeemed human nature) but according to the Spirit.

1. no condemnation for those who are in Christ Jesus: i.e. within the Body of Christ, the Church. Cf. note on 6:3 above

2. the law of the Spirit: Paul can use 'law' in a wide variety of senses (cf. 7:23 above). But does it mean here 'authority'? (SH) Is it not rather the 'order', 'principle' (of the living/life-giving Spirit)? It is this new order of things, the 'spiritual order' which frees from the old 'natural order'. T. W. Manson writes (*Peake's Commentary, in loc.*): 'Moses' law has right but not might; Sin's law has might but not right; the law of the Spirit has both might and right.' See also S. Lyonnet, 'Rom. 8:2-4 à la lumière de Jér. 31 et d'Ez. 35-39', *Mélanges E. Tisserant*, I (Vatican, 1964), pp. 311-23.

3. what the law . . . could not do: a pendant nominative. The logical continuation would be: '. . . what the Law could not do (or, what was impossible under the Law), the Holy Spirit enables us to accomplish; because, with the help of the Spirit, we were empowered to fulfil the demands of the Law.' What Paul, in effect, does is to introduce the thought of *the means* by which all this was made possible, viz. through the incarnation of the Son of God, Who imparts the enabling Spirit.
sending his own Son: cf. E. Schweizer, *ZNTW*, LVII (1966), pp. 199-210, for the 'sending' formula. Cf. further *ibid.*, 'Dying and Rising with Christ', *NTS*, XIV (1967-8), pp. 1-14.
in the likeness of sinful flesh: Origen: *ostendit nos quidam habere carnem peccati: filium vero dei similitudinem habuisse carnis peccati non carnem peccati.* For the phrase 'sinful flesh', cf. 1 QS xi.9.
and for sin: mg. 'or *and as a sin offering*'; cf. Lev. 4. Origen understands 'an offering': *hostia pro peccato factus est Christus.* Cf., however, SH: '. . . we need not suppose the phrase *peri hamartias* here specially limited to the sense of 'sin-offering'. It includes every sense in which the Incarnation and Death of Christ had relation to, and had it for their object to remove, human sin' (p. 193).
4. the just requirement of the law: cf. Tyndale: 'the righte-

wesnes requyred of' (i.e. 'by') 'the lawe'. *NEB:* 'the commandment of the law'.

Life in the Spirit (The Spiritual Life) 5–11
The literary structure of these verses is similar to that at 5:12–21,
and the balance of lines and clauses here is particularly noteworthy:

5 Those whose being is on the level of the natural life
Concern themselves with affairs of the natural life.
Those who live by the Spirit mind the things of the Spirit.
6 The natural frame of mind leads to death,
The spiritual mind is (eternal) life and peace;
7 Because the natural mind is at enmity with God,
It is not subject to the divine law, nor is it capable of becoming
so (v. 3).
8 Those who are in the natural state of life are incapable of pleasing
God.
9 But you are not in that state but in the Spirit (spiritual);
Since, I tell you, the Spirit of God dwells in you; and if anyone does
not possess the Spirit of Christ, he does not belong to him.
10 But if Christ be in you then, as your body is dead for sin
11 Yet your spirit is alive for righteousness, and if the Spirit of Him
who raised up Jesus from the dead dwells in you,
He that raised up Jesus Christ from the dead will endow with life
your mortal bodies through the Spirit that dwells in you.

**5–7. live according to the flesh . . . live according to the
Spirit . . . hostile to God:** these and the following verses are of
fundamental importance for Pauline Christology, no less than for
his doctrine of the Spirit, with its important ideas about the inner
character and inspiration of Christian life. The latter is a 'pneu-
matic', or spiritual, life, a consciousness in which the frame of
mind is one of divinely-aided obedience to the law of God, the
divine agent in obedience being the Holy Spirit. Conformity to
the mind or will of God (pleasing God), so achieved or attained
by the *charisma* of the Spirit, comes from the 'being in the Spirit'
(cf. verse 9ff.) or having the Spirit in one.
8–11. Verse 9a defines the Spirit as the 'indwelling Spirit of
God' (*pneuma theou*). Verse 9b speaks of the Spirit as 'the Spirit of
Christ' (*pneuma Christou*), and 10a refers to the experience as
'Christ in you' (*Christos en hymin*). See also M. Dibelius, *op. cit.*
(see p. 86.) All these expressions are related and, one might

almost say, synonymous, terms for the same spiritual reality of the Christian character or 'spiritual' frame of mind (*phronēma;* cf. verse 6). C. H. Dodd writes (*Commentary,* p. 123f.): 'This apparent equation, "Spirit of God" = "Spirit of Christ" = "Christ within you", is characteristic of Paul among New Testament writers. We may perhaps trace the lines of his thought thus. First, for Paul as for all Christian thinkers, Christ was in the fullest way the manifestation of God, and His whole life and person the expression of the divine Spirit. Further, it was the common postulate of primitive Christianity, as we have seen, that the Church was a fellowship of the Spirit, a community of those who had received the Spirit of God through faith in Christ. The one Spirit constituted the one Body. But, for Paul, with his mystical outlook, that Body was the Body of Christ, manifesting the new humanity of which He was the inclusive Representative. Hence in every member of it, possessing the Spirit of God, Christ was in some measure present and active, since the man was a member of His Body (as the whole of any organism is in some sort active in every part of it). Thus the community might be indifferently regarded as constituted by the Spirit of God, or by Christ as a 'corporate personality'; and the individual as possessed by the Spirit of God, or by Christ dwelling in His member. Christ Himself, as the 'second Adam' was a 'life-giving Spirit' (1 C. 15:45), and Paul could speak, not only of the *Spirit of the Lord,* but, in the next breath, of the *Lord the Spirit* (2 C. 3:17-18).'

The doctrinal presuppositions of St Paul's use of this 'spiritual equation', i.e. these virtually synonymous terms, 'Spirit of God', 'Spirit of Christ', 'Christ in you', may be more simply formulated in terms of the apostolic doctrine of baptism. In baptism the believer was not only forgiven—that is, in Pauline terms, released from the order of sin and death—he also received the Spirit through his faith in Christ. It was the gift of the Pentecostal Christ; and it was Christ's Spirit yet also coming from God, the Spirit of God (cf. Ac. 2:33; 'Being therefore exalted at the right hand of God, and having received from the Father the promise of the Holy Spirit [the promised Holy Spirit], He [Jesus] has poured out this which you see and hear'; and Eph. 4:4ff.) The 'Spirit of God' was mediated by Christ to His disciples.

From the point of view of Pauline 'mysticism', it may also be described as a kind of faith union—Christ *in* you—but this was

not for St Paul an individual and purely mystical experience in
the sense of Evelyn Underhill ('The flight of the Alone to the
Alone'. *Mysticism* (London, 1911), p. 68); it was always an
experience in Christ—that is, within the Body of Christ, the new
man, the Church. It was to share in the upsurge of charismatic
life which flowed within and from the Christian community; it
was essentially a *social*, not an *individualistic*, phenomenon (cf.
supra, p. 109ff).

Dodd adds: 'Behind this rather subtle train of thought there
must have been direct experience. Paul was immediately aware
that when he was in close touch with Christ, that divine energy or
power which he recognized as the Spirit was released within him;
and conversely, the full moral effect of that power was realized
only through reference to Christ as revealing the eternal Love.
In Christ, in the Spirit, the Spirit within, Christ within were in effect
only different ways of describing the one experience, from
slightly different points of view. This is not to say that Paul, in a
strict theological sense, identified Christ with the Spirit.

'But his virtual identification of the experience of the Spirit
with the experience of the indwelling Christ is of the utmost
value. It saved Christian thought from falling into a non-moral,
half-magical conception of the supernatural in human experience,
and it brought all "spiritual" experience to the test of the historical
revelation of God in Jesus Christ' (p. 124).

In other terms, the 'spiritual mind' (verse 6) is the 'mind of
Christ' (cf. Phil. 2); and to possess this 'frame of mind', 'attitude',
or 'outlook' is to be concerned or involved socially—to belong,
not to the old order of humanity (the 'old Adam'), but to the new
humanity.

Christians as Sons of God 12-30

Verses 12 and 13 mark a transition from the section on the Spirit
to a section the main purpose of which is to present Paul's doctrine
of the status of Christians as no longer servants or slaves but as in
the category of free sons of God, and this he attributes to the
workings of the Spirit in us. Verses 12 to 17 are a Pauline paraenesis meant to encourage Christians in their faith and hope; this
exhortation follows from the previous doctrine and bridges the
two parts of the chapter—namely, first the doctrine of the Spirit,
followed by the doctrine of Christians as sons of God.

12. we are debtors: we do not owe anything to the natural life; if we live on this level, then we are bound to die. In his choice of verb ('we have no duty, obligation to (the flesh)'), it is as if Paul was countering the argument that what is natural is right, and, therefore, we owe it its 'due'.

13. you will die: if you put to death the works of the body, then you will achieve eternal life (the latter being the force of the verb here); by 'the works of the body' Paul is referring to the category of the vices of the 'flesh', listed, for example, at Gal. 5:18ff.

14. All, on the other hand, who are 'led', that is to say, whose lives are ruled by the Spirit of God—these Paul declares to be sons of God, and in the following verse he contrasts the two spirits: one the spirit of slavery, which is the state of the man under the Law, and which leads to fear—fear of the consequences of the failure to fulfil the Law—with a spirit which he describes as that of adoption, that is to say, a status of full sonship. The thought is already expressed at Gal. 4:5ff, and more fully developed here.

15. For you did not receive (at your baptism) **the spirit of slavery,** here obviously referring to that state of mind, contrasted with the new freedom of Christian sonship. It is no slavish spirit Christians received at their baptism, a spirit which, as in the old system under Law, relapses into fear, a fear-ridden state of mind like that of any slave.

spirit of sonship: 'adoption' here implies the conferring of the right to inherit, as in Babylonian and in Greek law (in Roman law it meant the acquisition of the *patria potestas*). It is this same feature of inheritance which is stressed in certain Egyptian documents. Cf. L. Mitteis and U. Wilcken, *Grundzüge und Chrestomathie der Papyruskunde*, Leipzig-Berlin, 1912, II.i, p. 274ff.; O. Eger, *ZNTW*, XVIII (1917–18), pp. 94ff.; and also F. Lyall, 'Roman Law in the Writings of Paul—Adoption', *JBL*, LXXXVIII (1969), pp. 458–66.

It seems probable that the Aramaic *abba* was in widespread liturgical use, possibly as a survival from its use in the Aramaic form of the Lord's Prayer. When Christians say: '*abba*'— that is to say, 'my Father'—Paul declares that this is the work of the Spirit in them, and the testimony that they have achieved the status of sonship. Some have suggested that the strange Aramaic word *abba* itself may have been regarded as an ejaculation of the Spirit,

like Amen, or Hosanna, or Hallelujah; cf. Dodd, p. 129, and
further below.

spirit of slavery . . . sonship: cf. Gal. 4:7; Heb. 1:2. It was
only the son, and not the slave, who had the right to inheritance.
Abba! Father!: if, as is suggested above, there is a reference here
to the Christian experience of baptism, then there may be a
reference to the use of the Lord's Prayer, possibly even in its
Aramaic form, as one of the mysteries of admission into the
Christian Church; it is well known that in the early centuries the
catechumen had to profess the Lord's Prayer. It may be that, if this
was said in the original baptismal ceremonies in Aramaic, it was
taken to be a sign of the possession by the Spirit; cf., further,
F. H. Chase, 'The Lord's Prayer in the Early Church', *Texts and
Studies*, 1, iii (Cambridge, 1891), p. 14; and also J. Jeremias on
'*Abba*' in *The Central Message of the New Testament* (London, 1965),
pp. 9-30, and in *Abba: Studien zur neutestamentlichen Theologie und
Zeitgeschichte* (Göttingen, 1966), pp. 15-67.

16. bearing witness with our spirit: Two witnesses, according to the *OT* injunction, establish the truth of any statement,
and here the witnesses are, first, the Holy Spirit, which the
Christian experiences in baptism, and then the Christian himself.
They testify to the status of Christians as children of God.

17. fellow heirs with Christ: Paul here goes on in an argument *a minori ad maius* to argue that, since Christians enjoy the
status of full membership of the family, then they must also be
heirs and joint heirs of God and fellow-heirs with Christ—that we
are indeed children of God. (Note the force of the emphatic
position of the 'we are'; cf. 1 Jn 3:1.) There is no difference in
Paul's use of the words 'sons' and 'children' in this passage (verses
14 and 16); cf. Jn 1:12. The usage corresponds to the Semitic
usage of the word, and 'children' of course, refers generally to the
sons of the family. It does, however, include all members of the
family, and perhaps this is the reason for Paul's use of 'children'
(*tekna*) as well as 'sons' here, i.e. he is using the word with the
wider Greek sense to include the daughters as well as the sons of
God within the family of God.

Being a full son implies the right to inherit, even if that right is
acquired by adoption (verse 15).

provided we suffer with him: or lit. 'if, in very truth, we
suffer with him'. Verses 18 and 36f. appear to imply that the

sufferings are not by any means hypothetical but present realities;
cf. Phil. 3:10, 1 Pet. 1:6, 4:13, 2 Mac. 6:30, and see E.G. Selwyn,
1 Peter (London, 1955), p. 127f.

The words 'if in very truth' are not a conditional sentence, and
ought perhaps to be rendered 'since, as is the case'; they give the
grounds for the Christian's common inheritance with Christ—
namely, their common fellowship in his sufferings. A similar use
of the conjunction occurs at 2 Th. 1:6; Rom. 3:20, 8:9.

in order that we may also be glorified with him: just as
Christ is now glorified after his passion and death, so too Christians
will share in that inheritance of glory, as they actually do now
share in the fellowship of his sufferings.

The next section, verses 18 to 25, takes up the theme of the
Christian's 'glorification' as 'son of God' through participation
in sufferings like Christ's. The status of sonship is attained, through
the Holy Spirit's agency, in our baptism. The reality of sonship,
which is the final goal in eternal life—that is, virtually becoming
like the angels in heaven (cf. Lk. 20:36)—is a process of emancipation through suffering from corruption and death which the
children of God share with the whole animate creation. According
to verse 15, we 'received' adoption as sons through the Spirit in
baptism; according to verse 23, we are still waiting in hope for
this adoption—that is to say, its realization as sons of God, a goal
which will only be reached through our final deliverance from
our bodily life in the new reality of eternal life.

Verses 26 to 27 resume the theme of the Spirit as co-operating
with us in all things for good, and verses 28 to 30 outline the 'plan
of salvation': first the call of Christians; then their acquittal;
and finally their 'glorification'.

18. the sufferings of this present time: the simplest
understanding of this verse is the rendering: 'for I do not count
our present sufferings worth considering in comparison with the
glory which is destined to be revealed'. SH is right in understanding the words 'to us' as of the glory which is to reach and
include all Christians in its 'radiance'; but are the authors correct
in understanding 'the glory' here of the heavenly brightness of
Christ's appearing? Is it not rather the glory or glorification of the
individual Christian in which he is to participate? Cf. verse 1
above. This is the recovery of the divine image or glory originally
lost at the Fall, but restored in Christ; cf. note on 3:23 above.

19. The word translated here in the *AV* as 'the earnest expectation (of the creation)' is highly expressive. The verb means 'to
strain forward', 'to await with outstretched head'; it appears
again at Phil. 1:20, combined with the word for 'hope'. Cf. G.
Bertram, in *ZNTW*, XLIX (1958), pp. 264–70. See also, L. C.
Allen, 'The Old Testament in Rom. i–viii', *Vox Evangelica*, III
(1964), p. 18.

The usual understanding of 'creation' here is that it refers to the
whole of the created universe and that, when Paul goes on in
verse 20f. to speak of the emancipation of the creation from its
enslavement to corruption, he is thinking of the redemption or the
renovation of nature, and in the background of his thought are
such passages as Isa. 65:17ff. (see the *excursus* in SH on this
understanding of the term).

An alternative interpretation is to understand the word here
as the equivalent of the Hebrew word *beriyyah*, which means 'the
creature' as well as '(the) creation' (see G. H. Dalman, *Words of
Jesus* (Edinburgh, 1902), p. 176f., and cf. G. H. Box, *The Ezra
Apocalypse* (London, 1912), p. 142).

This understanding of the word is preferred by E. Brunner in
Revelation and Reason (London, 1947), p. 72, n. 16, where he argues
that the term here does not refer to the cosmos, but to man as the
creature of God: 'It is not the creation which is 'fallen' but man;
the revelation in the creation has not been destroyed but by sin
man perverts into idolatry that which God has given him.' This
meaning certainly fits in well with verse 21, where the creature
himself, in this sense, will be emancipated from the slavery of
corruption into the glorious freedom of the sons of God. On the
other hand, the whole context seems to imply, especially at
verse 22f., that it is the entire created universe which St Paul has
in mind.

A further possibility would be to take verse 22 as referring to
'the entire creation', but verses 19 and 20 as meaning 'the creature',
man, who is part of creation.

For further discussion, see G. W. H. Lampe, 'The New Testament Doctrine of "Ktisis"', *SJT*, XVII (1964), pp. 449–62.
Bultmann admits that this is one place where redemption goes
beyond the salvation of men (*NTS*, I (1954–5), p. 13 (cf. E.
Schweizer, *NTS*, VIII (1961–2), p. 3.)

20. for the creation was subjected to futility: what is

'futile' in the Biblical sense is what is 'without result', 'ineffective', 'something that does not reach the end for which it was created'. The word is here used of the disappointing and frustrating character of present existence, and it is assumed that the whole created world had been subjected to this state of frustration, not because it wanted to, but because of its Creator Who so subjected it, in the hope that creation itself would one day be freed from its mortality and decay like man himself, who would achieve an immortal destiny within the redeemed creation.

22. We know: i.e. as part of the well-known tradition of Jewish apocalyptic prophecy. Cf. W. D. Stacey, 'God's Purpose in Creation: Rom. 8:22-33', *ET*, LXIX (1957-8), pp. 178-81.

groaning in travail together until now: Dodd: 'sighs and throbs with pain': there could be a reference to the birth-pangs of the Messiah (messianic age). The figure of speech is a familiar one in 1QH iii. 7-10, possibly with a similar reference to the birth-pangs of the Messiah or the messianic people. (Cf. M. Black, *The Scrolls and Christian Origins* (London, 1961), p. 149.)

23. first fruits of the Spirit: cf. 2 C. 5:4-5, where also 'we groan' in the 'covering' ('tent') of our physical bodies, though we have been given (verse 5) a 'first instalment' (*arrabōn*) of the life 'in the spirit'. *Aparchē* ('first-fruits') is possibly not to be pressed in its literal meaning in this context (Moulton, *Voc.*, s.v.); it means simply 'foretaste' or, even more generally, 'gift'. It is probably best taken as synonymous with *arrabōn* at 2 C. 5:5—i.e. first instalment, issue, of the Spirit. It is a favourite word of St Paul; cf. Rom. 16:5; 1 C. 15:20-23, 16:15. Cf. C. C. Oke, 'A Suggestion with regard to Rom. 8:23', *Interpretation*, II (1957), pp. 455-60.

as we wait . . . bodies: 'wait': the same word as at verse 19, indicating a 'longing expectation'. We received 'adoption' as sons at our baptism (cf. verse 15,) but this apparently does not prevent us 'longing for' our 'adoption'. This can only mean our 'complete adoption', i.e. transformation into 'sons of God'; and this is further defined as the 'deliverance' of our body (for the word, cf. above, on 3:24). Cf. further, P. Benoit, 'Nous gémissons, attendant la délivrance de notre corps', *Rech. de Science Religieuse*, XXXIX (1951), pp. 267-80.

24. For in this hope we were saved: lit. 'by hope'. The meaning may be simply: 'in hope we attained our salvation', i.e. one of the integral elements of Christian 'salvation' is the Christian

hope, the deliverance of verse 25. This seems preferable to taking
the dative as instrumental or as referring to the content of
Christian hope as, in some sense, the means or instrument of
'salvation'. 24b stresses the essential character of Christian hope
as a grasping, by faith, of the unseen.

25. with patience: again the stress is on an earnest longing
for the fulfilment of the Christian hope, but one that is accompanied by patience or endurance, by holding out.

26. Likewise the Spirit helps: similarly, i.e. as we 'groan' in
our longing expectation, the Spirit comes to the assistance of our
weakness, with the same deep longing, also expressed 'with
unutterable groanings'. Whether we are to interpret 'weakness'
here of human frailty in general (elsewhere the word has an
ethical connotation) or, in the light of 26b of the imperfection of
the devotional life, is difficult to determine (cf. Dodd, p. 135).
Certainly, as an intercessor, the assistance of the Spirit is in
prayer, but wider aspects of that divine help cannot thereby be
excluded, since prayer itself is the inner strivings of the human
spirit to transcend its weakness, strivings manifested in conduct.
Probably too, as Dodd comments, prayer is here conceived as the
working of the Spirit within us; our inarticulate groans and
sighings mingle with the sighs and groans that cannot be uttered
in the Spirit's joint intercession with us (cf. Dodd, p. 135). Implied
is the value of inarticulate prayer; cf. T. W. Manson (in an un-
published meditation): 'The prayer that comes tripping from the
tongue does not always come from the depths of the heart; and
prayer that does not come from the depths is not likely to climb
very high . . . those very longings and aspirations which reach
upwards towards something that mere formal prayers can never
reach are inspired; they are themselves the work of the Spirit of
God.' See, further, E. Käsemann, 'Der gottesdienstliche Schrei
nach der Freiheit', *BZNW*, xxx (1964), pp. 142–55; and
Perspectives on Paul, pp. 129ff. Käsemann argues that a com-
munal groaning is meant—that is, the inarticulate 'sighs and
groans' of the whole congregation, similar and related to the
glossolalia phenomena in 1 Corinthians; this was a form of the
Roman Christians' 'enthusiasm'. Cf. also K. Niederwimmer, 'Das
Gebet des Geistes', *TZ*, xx (1964), pp. 252–65.

27. the mind of the Spirit: St Paul seems to regard the
action of the Holy Spirit as personal and distinct from the action

of God. God knows the intention of the Spirit is to intercede for us
in accordance with the divine will; probably: 'knows *that* the
Spirit intercedes', not (as *RSV*) 'because' . . .

28. God works for good with those who love him: *RSV*,
following *RV mg.*, adopts the reading of AB, now supported by
P[46] (cf. also Moffatt). That Paul could write: 'all things work
together for good' (*AV, RV*) is denied by some exegetes; Paul was
no facile or 'evolutionary' optimist. Barrett seeks to defend the
traditional rendering (*in loc.*). Stylistically, the repetition of 'God'
as subject so soon after the phrase 'for those who love God' is
difficult. (Note how the *RSV* avoids the repetition.) *NEB* takes
'the Spirit' as subject, unexpressed; it is the main subject in the
context: 'and in everything, as we know, he (the Spirit) co-oper-
ates for good with those who love God'. See further Dodd (Fontana
edn.), pp. 152ff., J. P. Wilson, *ET*, LX (1948–9), pp. 110ff., M.
Black, 'The Interpretation of Romans 8:28', in *Neotestamentica
et Patristica* (*Festschrift* for Oscar Cullmann, Leiden, 1962), pp.
166ff. Also H. G. Wood, in *ET*, LXIX (1957–8), pp. 292–5; J. B.
Bauer, in *ZNTW*, L (1959), pp. 106–12.

It is suggested (e.g. by Michel) that verse 28 is a *Lehrsatz* coming
out of a familiar *OT* and Jewish tradition; he compares Test.
Issachar iii.8, Gad iv.7, Benj. iv.5; also Ber. 60b. Gad iv.7 reads:
'For the spirit of hatred worketh together with Satan, through
hastiness of spirit, in all things to men's death; but the spirit of
love worketh together with the law of God in long-suffering, unto
the salvation of men.'

called according to his purpose: this is a necessary qualification for Paul, since, without these words, the impression might
have been given that divine 'co-operation' or 'furtherance' was
somehow a reward for loving God. (Similarly this co-operation is
'for or with a view to good', i.e. the good life, which again defines
the goal for which divine help is received.) Notice too the emphasis on the divine purpose (or plan, counsel), the divine calling,
the divine pre-knowledge (i.e., choice, selection, election; cf.
above, p. 34), divine 'pre-ordination'. Human freedom for Paul
is always exercised under the gracious sovereignty of God. (Cf.
Dodd, *in loc.*)

The Hebrew tradition out of which Paul's doctrine of the
sovereign grace of God in election was developed is well illustrated
in 1QS ii:22ff., iii:6, iv:15ff.: the God of knowledge created all

being according to his purpose and, at the end of time, by the
same purpose there is to be a divine election of mankind. See
D. Flusser, 'The Dead Sea Sect and Pre-Pauline Christianity',
Scripta Hierosolymitana (Jerusalem, 1965), p. 220. (Cf. 1QS
iii.15–16.) Cf. also K. Grayston, 'The Doctrine of Election in
Rom. 8:28–30', *Stud. Ev.*, II (1964), pp. 574–83.

29. For those whom he foreknew . . .: four stages in the
divine counsel or plan are set out: (a) the divine foreknowledge,
i.e. choice and election (the divine 'fore-ordination' is virtually
synonymous; cf. Ac. 4:28); (b) the divine call when the 'saints'
become aware of their election; (c) 'justification', the act of
salvation by faith; (d) the final 'glorification', defined as con-
forming to the image of the Son of God, the first-born of many
brethren—the Christian's hope of final 'adoption', the 'redemption of the body'.
image of his Son: cf. above, at Rom. 3:23; and A. R. C.
Leaney, 'Conformed to the Image of His Son', *NTS*, x (1963–4),
pp. 470–9); J. Kürzinger, *BZ*, II (1958), pp. 294–9.
first-born: a term which Paul no doubt found in his *paradosis*
(cf. Lk. 2:7; Col. 1:15, 18; Heb. 12:23). For a helpful note on it,
see T. W. Manson, *On Paul and John* (*Studies in Biblical Theology*,
38, London, 1963), pp. 130ff.

30. predestined . . . called . . . justified . . . glorified: a
climactic period (Michel, *Kettenschluss*). See also K. Grayston,
op. cit. (p. 120).

Security from Death **31–9**
These verses constitute something of the nature of a rhetorical
climax, in which the central argument about the Christian's
triumph over all the forces of evil—his groaning, travailing,
persecution, even death—is summarized by a Scriptural text from
Ps. 42:22 (cf. 2 C. 4:11). Salvation is certain, since everything is
undergirded by the love of God in Christ. It is a passage of
exalted feeling.

31. What then shall we say to this? The question implies a
break and summing up. Paul is still thinking out objections to his
argument, and finally disposes of them all in 31*b*. The writer is
possibly thinking in terms of a law-court; cf. verses 33 and 35,
where the same kind of rhetorical questions are asked, 33 with a
forensic allusion. Note again the climactic build-up of these

rhetorical questions and their answers. The dialogue is reminiscent of the *OT* 'law-suit pattern' (e.g. Isa. 50); cf. Leenhardt, p. 236, and C. Müller, *Gottes Gerechtigkeit und Gottes Volk, Forschungen zur Religion und Literatur des Alten und Neuen Testaments*, LXXXVI (Göttingen, 1964), pp. 57–72 (*Rechtsstreitgedanke*). See also C. Roetzel, 'The Judgement Form in Paul's Letters', *JBL*, LXXXVIII (1969), pp. 305–12.

32. did not spare his own Son but gave him up: Paul's answer is firmly based on a Christian *paradosis* about the death of Christ, formulated in traditional kerygmatic terms, e.g. 'gave him up' (*paredōken*); cf. Rom. 4:25 and Mt. 26:2, Mk 9:31, Lk. 24:7 of the 'surrendering up' of the Son of Man; Barth points out that it is the same verb which is used at Rom. 1:24, 26, 28 for God's 'surrendering up' of man to the divine judgement; so Christ was 'given over' to judgement. Gen. 22:16, the *akedāh*, or sacrifice, of Abraham's beloved son (so LXX) Isaac, probably contributed to the development of this theme (Michel, *in loc.*). Cf., further, N. A. Dahl, 'The Atonement—An Adequate Reward for the Akedah?', *Neotestamentica et Semitica* (M. Black *Festschrift*) (Edinburgh, 1969), pp. 15–29.

all things with him: the verb 'give' here (*charizesthai*) specially emphasizes the sheer goodness of this divine gift. 'All things' can hardly refer to absolute dominion over all things (*die Weltherrschaft*); more probably it embraces all the 'benefits' of salvation, eternal life, etc., which God freely bestows 'along with Christ'. The latter phrase is ambiguous: it may mean that Christ is also a freely-bestowed gift which goes with 'all things', or that God, along with Christ, is the free-bestower of all things.

33–4. may be variously punctuated (see U.B.S. Greek New Testament). *NEB* offers one of the main alternatives to *RSV*.

The style is modelled on Isa. 50:7–9, encouraging us to punctuate: 33, question: statement (exclamation) ('It is God who does the acquitting'); 34, question: statement (or exclamation), with the last relative clause resuming the subject and containing the main verb—'Jesus Christ, he it is—the one who died, nay rather rose from the dead—who is also at the right hand of God, who does the interceding for us'. The tenses, both of the participles as well as the main verbs are probably best understood as *futures*: it is to the Last Judgement Paul is referring.

Christ's death, and its sequel in resurrection, ascension and

intercessory ministry, is the demonstration of the love of God
(cf. verse 39).

33. God's elect: an old name for Israel (1 Chr. 16:13, Ps.
105:6, 43), but specially used in the later apocalypses and inter-
Testamental writings for the 'Elect Israel', or 'Remnant', and its
members (e.g., in I Enoch *passim* and at Qumran, e.g., 1QHab.
x.13, CD iv.3ff.). See Michel, *ad loc.*, and cf. Mk 13:20, 22, 27
et par.; Lk. 18:7; Rom. 16:13; Col. 3:12; 2 Tim. 2:10; Tit. 1:1;
1 Pet. 1:1; Rev. 17:14.

35. Cf. 2 C. 11:26f. Paul's experiences are typical. Seven forms
of tribulation are listed, but the number is probably without
significance (there are ten in verses 38–9). Cf. Ps. Sol. xv.7.

36. Ps. 44:22; cf. 2 C. 4:11.
For thy sake: God's or Christ's. In the context it could be either.

37. more than conquerors: a strong compound expression
here only in the *NT*: 'we are winning an overwhelming victory'.
The Christian's conquest of 'all these things' is not, however,
through his own efforts, but through 'the One who loved us'.

38. For I am sure: the 'hymnic' rhetorical style, present
throughout this passage, becomes specially noticeable in this
verse. We move *a minori ad maius*, i.e. to a climax. After the seven
afflictions comes a list which, beginning with 'death and life',
seems mostly to be grouped in pairs, and includes ten 'powers' of
evil: 'neither angels nor principalities', i.e. cosmic forces of evil
(cf. G. H. C. Macgregor, 'Principalities and Powers: the Cosmic
Background of Paul's Thought', *NTS*, 1 (1954–5), p. 17ff.) It is
unlikely that Paul is grouping 'death and life' among the cosmic
powers of evil, but they may here be personified; and 'life' no less
than death can come between us and the love of God. Cf. 1 C. 3:22.
things present . . . things to come: no doubt earthly calami-
ties, present or future (Michel). Cf. 1 C. 3:22.

39. height nor depth: explained by the Fathers as heavenly
and 'sub-terranean' powers. Modern exegetes explain as astro-
logical terminology: the 'height' refers to the sky above the
horizon, the 'depth' the sky beneath the horizon: here, however,
like 'principalities and powers', the words probably refer to
'celestial powers'. For the combination, cf. Isa. 7:11.
nor anything else in all creation is rather a free translation;
lit. 'nor any other created being'.

GOD'S PURPOSES FOR ISRAEL 9:1–11:36

In chapters 9–11 Paul deals with the problem of Israel's rejection
—her own rejection of the Gospel and, in consequence, her
rejection by God. See especially J. Munck, *Christ and Israel: an
Interpretation of Rom. 9–11* (Philadelphia, 1967); for more recent
discussion, see C. Müller, *Gottes Gerechtigkeit und Gottes Volk: eine
Untersuchung zu Röm. 9–11*, *FRLANT*, LXXXVI (Göttingen, 1964);
E. Dinkler, 'The Historical and the Eschatological Israel in
Rom. 9–11', *Journal of Religion*, XXXVI (1956), pp. 109–27; L. S.
Murillo, 'El "Israel de las Promesas": o Judaismo y Gentilismo
en la concepción Paulina del Evangelio', *Bib.*, II (1921), pp.
303ff.; D. W. Vischer, 'Das Geheimnis Israels', *Judaica*, VI (1950),
pp. 81–132.

Jeremias has argued (Gedankenführung, p. 148) that 9:1ff is a
reply to implied criticism of Paul. Cf. also H. J. Schoeps, *Theologie
und Geschichte des Judenchristentums* (Tübingen, 1949), pp. 135ff.

The argument has two main points: (a) the Gentiles owe their
salvation to the rejection of Israel; (b) in the long term, God's
purposes embrace His own people.

The section is a compact and continuous whole, possibly an
incorporated diatribe or missionary sermon (cf. Dodd, p. 148ff.),
distinctive in style as in content from 1–8. It is, however, a natural,
logical and necessary extension of the main argument. Chapter
8:38ff. gives the grounds for Israel's salvation, the unbreakable
bond of divine love in Christ. Such love could not fail to embrace
Israel, for whom the Gospel was first intended (1:16). The Gospel
was first and foremost for the Jew (1:16; 2:9ff; 3:9; 10:12), yet it
had been rejected by contemporary Judaism. In 3:1ff. Paul
included among the 'advantages' of the Jew God's loyalty, which
does not give up even an apostate people. This statement alone
implies that Israel, in spite of her defection and rejection, nevertheless remains the special object of God's 'steadfast love'.

These implications of 3:1ff. are not further pursued there, but
are taken up and developed in chapters 9–11.

Israel's Unbelief 9:1–5

1. I am speaking the truth in Christ: the vehemence of St
Paul's assertion that he speaks truly about his terrible grief and
unremitting agony about Israel (verse 2) suggests that he had been

accused of indifference to the fate of his compatriots (cf. Barrett, *ad loc.*). Paul speaks the truth *in Christ*, and his conscience supports him *in the Holy Spirit*. Has he the thought here of two witnesses corroborating his statement, Christ and the Spirit (cf. Dt. 17:6, 19:15, 2 C. 13:1)? The words can hardly be interpreted to mean: 'As one who lives in Christ (in the Holy Spirit)'.

3. **accursed and cut off from Christ:** an outcast under a ban or curse. The word was originally the same as that for an 'offering' to God (*anathema*). The Greek translation of the *OT*, however, required an expression to denote that which is offered to God *for destruction* (*ḥerem*). Cf. Lev. 27:28, 29; Gal. 1:8, 9; 1 C. 16:22, Cf. also, however, MM, *s.v.*: in Greek thought, 'the person on whom the curse was to fall was always devoted to the vengeance of the two Infernal Goddesses, Demeter and her daughter, "May he or she never find Persephone propitious."' Paul is thinking less of the vengeance to come on the 'accursed', as on the state of severance from his Lord; cf. 8:35ff. Paul may possibly have had the 'self-offering' of Moses in mind (Exod. 32:32) in declaring himself willing to be 'devoted' to utter destruction. That we have here also a familiar type of 'ban-formula' is probable (Michel); parallels from Sanh. ii.1, Sukka 20a, Josephus, *B.J.*, V.ix.4 (419). There can be no suggestion that this was a mere 'empty wish', incapable of fulfilment (so Zahn, who compares 8:38ff.): God was, for Paul, always free to accept his self-oblation; after all, He had accepted the propitiatory sacrifice of Christ; cf. further J. Munck, op. cit., pp. 29ff. Munck has drawn attention to the close parallels between this passage and Exod. 30:31-2.

4. **to them belong the sonship...:** on the concept of sonship (*huiothesia*), see above, on 8:15, and cf. L. Radermacher, *Neutestamentliche Grammatik*, 2nd edn (Tübingen, 1925), p. 36. For the idea of Israel or Israelites as particularly 'sons of God', cf. Hos. 11:1 (Mt. 2:15), Ps. Sol. 17:29, 30. 'Sons' means 'children', male or female (cf. above on 8:15).

the glory: i.e. the Shekhinah, or symbol of the divine presence, or the 'restored glory' of Adam (cf. note on 3:23).

the covenants: i.e. the divine 'charters' with Israel—the first given at Sinai, the new announced by Jeremiah and now granted in Christ. Cf. L. G. da Fonseca, '*Diathēkē*—Foedus an Testamentum', *Bib.*, IX (1923), p. 26; C. Roetzel, '*Diathēkai* in Romans 9:4', *Bib.*, LI (1970), pp. 377-90.

the giving of the law, the worship: *tôrāh* and *'abodāh*, originally the Temple cultus, then more widely 'worship'. According to *Pirqé Aboth*, i, 2, the world rests on three things: the *tôrāh*, worship, and the showing of kindnesses.

5. Christ. God who is over all be blessed for ever: *mg.* or, 'Christ who is God over all, blessed for ever'; this is widely supported. It is extremely doubtful, however, whether Paul would ever apply the name 'God' thus *simpliciter* to Christ. The reading of the *RSV* text, on the other hand, which suddenly introduces a doxology, is also decidedly unnatural. Dodd is inclined to favour the old Socinian conjecture (J. J. Wettstein, *Novum Testamentum Graece* (Amsterdam, 1751–2), *in loc.*) which gives a climactic line: 'to whom belongs the God over all, blessed for ever'. Cf. W. L. Lorimer, *NTS*, xiii (1966–7), p. 385f., who conjectures: 'of whom is God over all Who is blessed for ever' (cf. 2 C. 11:31). Cf. H. W. Bartsch, 'Röm. 9:5 und 1 Clem. 32:4: eine notwendige Konjektur im Römerbrief', *TZ*, xxi (1965), pp. 401–9. See especially Denney, p. 658, *ad loc.* SH (defending the tradition of *RSV mg.*), Michel, Barth, *ad loc.*, who adopts the conjecture without discussion: 'Whose is God that ruleth all things—blessed for ever, Amen'. See further, H. M. Faccio, *De Divinitate Christi iuxta S. Paulum: Rom. 9:5* (Jerusalem, 1945).

THE DIVINE PURPOSE IN ELECTION 6–13

The transition seems to be: Israel has rejected the Gospel, but this does not imply the failure of God's Word to his people (cf. 3:2ff.).

The argument is a favourite one of Paul's, first set out in Gal. 4:21–31, then again at Rom. 4. There has been no failure on God's part; his scriptural promises still hold—for the Israel of the Promise, not the national Israel, since mere physical descent does not count. The argument, conducted in characteristic rabbinical form, is supported by Gen. 21:12, 18:10, 14, and 25:23. The true Israel is the 'elected' Israel.

6. word of God: 'word', certainly in the sense of the divine 'oracles' of Scripture, containing the (messianic) promises; cf. the use of *logia* at 3:2. But 'word' here has a wider reference, meaning the whole plan and intention of God.

failed: cf. 1 C. 13:8 (*textus receptus*); Jas 1:11, Isa. 40:7, 'wither', 'fade'; Sir. 34:7 for the sense of 'fail', and equivalent to *naphal* = 'fall', and so 'collapse, fail'; see verse 11 below.

The construction of the first four words is a mixture of a phrase meaning: 'by no means' and 'it is not as if' (see Blass-Debrunner, §480(5)). 'It is impossible that . . .' (*NEB*).

not all who are descended from Israel belong to Israel: i.e. not all those who can trace their descent to the founding fore-father constitute the true Israel, the 'Israel of God' (cf. Gal. 6:16). We may also render: 'Nor is it as if all (Abraham's) children constitute (are) the Seed of Abraham.' This preserves the special meaning for 'seed'. For the phrase 'children of Abraham', Mt. 3:9. For 'seed of Abraham', cf. Jn 8:33.

7. descendants: lit. 'seed'. Cf. 4:13, 16, 18, and Gal. 3:16, 19, 29 (2 C. 11:22). Although 'seed' is a collective term for Paul, the Galatians passage uses it to refer to Christ as the 'Seed' of Abraham.

shall . . . be named: or 'divinely called' (*NEB mg.*). The argument is supported by Gen. 21:12. The passive may have been understood by Paul (as in verse 8: 'are reckoned') as an expression of *divine* action. It is God who will name their descendants from Israel: it is God who acclaims the 'children of the promise' as the true seed. The promise was made by one of Abraham's three angel visitants at Mamre, but it is a 'word of the Lord' he speaks (cf. Gen. 18:10, 14).

8. the children of the promise are reckoned as descendants: 'reckoned', 'counted', again *logizomai*. Cf. Barrett, p. 181: 'The word "counted" is of fundamental importance in this epistle . . . It points to the creative freedom of God, who creates "righteousness" by "counting" it, and annuls sin by not "counting" it (4:6, 8)'. See above, pp. 75ff; and C. Müller, *Gottes Gerechtig-keit und Gottes Volk: Eine Untersuchung zu Römer 9–11, FRLANT,* LXXXVI (1964), p. 184.

children of the flesh . . . children of God . . . children of the promise: These are familiar Pauline terms and ideas, belonging, no doubt, to the homiletical stock-in-trade of St Paul's Gentile preaching mission. 'Children of the flesh' recalls Ishmael. Isaac's descendants are 'children of the promise'—the promise made to Abraham after all hope had disappeared of further natural progeny—and these are likewise 'children of God'. Cf. Gal. 4:21–31.

9. The absolute priority of the promise is emphasized in this verse by a further quotation from Gen. 18:10, 14. Note the position, at the beginning of the sentence, of the emphasized

word, 'promise', in the Greek order; for 'this word of the promise'
is as follows: that God is miraculously at work in this election of
Isaac and his descendants is clear from the verb '*I* will come' (so,
rightly, *NEB*).

10-13 seem intended to meet the possible objection of Jewish
opponents that they are no Ishmaelites, but the true seed of
Abraham (cf. Dodd, *ad loc.*) At the same time, Paul is clearly also
reinforcing his argument of the sovereign act of God in election:
Jacob was elected, his elder brother Esau rejected, and this was all
revealed to Rebecca before their birth, and therefore also before
they could be judged on grounds of 'works' (see note on
verse 11).

11. that God's purpose of election might continue: i.e.
that the purpose of God which works by the principle of *election*
might stand; the Greek verb means 'remain', 'abide'; it is the
opposite of the word used at verse 6 ('fall', or 'fail'); God's word
does not collapse or fail; so likewise his plan of selecting cannot
do anything other than 'stand', i.e. 'prevail'.

The divine purpose has been the theme of 8:28. Cf. Eph. 1:11,
3:11, 2 Tim. 1:9, 3:10.

not because of works but because of his call: the Pauline
controversy, faith or works, is determinative of his thought here;
it was by a free act of gracious choice that Jacob—and so his
descendants, the spiritual Israel—was named: this choice was
made by God even before the birth of Isaac's progeny, before they
had any 'works' by which they could be judged.

12-13. The quotations are from Gen. 25:23, Mal. 1:2, 3. The
combination of a quotation from the Pentateuch with one from
the Prophets is common; together they seal the argument by
Scriptural authority. The formal introduction of the Malachi quotation, 'As it is written', shows that Paul probably thinks of this
as the climax and conclusion of his argument: 'love' here means
'prefer', 'hate' means 'reject' (or 'love less'). (See Leenhardt,
ad loc.).

For a valuable discussion of the *OT* background of 'election',
consult T. L. Vriezen, 'Die Erwählung Israels nach dem Alten
Testament', *Abhandlungen zur Theologie des Alten und Neuen Testaments*, XXIV (Zürich, 1953), pp. 41-50; and G. Schrenk in *TWNT*,
s.v. '*eklegomai*'.

GOD'S SOVEREIGN FREEDOM TO ELECT WHOMSOEVER HE CHOOSES
14-29

SOME OBJECTIONS REBUTTED AND A STATEMENT OF ISRAEL'S REJECTION
14-18

Paul meets the obvious Jewish objection that this highly arbitrary selection and rejection seems to imply injustice on God's side. Paul has an answer in Scripture, Exod. 33:19 and 9:16. In verses 19-29 the prophets are cited in support of the claim that God is absolutely sovereign in his dealings with man; cf. Isa. 29:16, 45:9; Wis. 12:12, Jer. 18:6, Wis. 15:7. Verses 30-33 conclude with a reflection on God's rejection of the national Israel and about such a rejection as a 'rock of offence'.

On the formal structure, it is noteworthy that vv. 14-18 are based on the *Tôrāh*, 19-21 on the *Prophets*, and 22-24 draw the theological consequences from this Scripture-based argumentation with references to both *Tôrāh* and Prophets (Michel, p. 212).

14. injustice on God's part: as almost always in Paul, words like *adikia* have a 'forensic' overtone: miscarriage of justice. The second phrase, 'on God's part', could have the further meaning: 'in God's assize', or 'court'.

15. Exod. 33:19. In citing Scriptural authority for his doctrine of God's sovereign will in election or rejection, Paul chooses a text which first shows that sovereign election as coming from a gracious, compassionate God; and this enables him further to introduce his doctrine of pure grace. See further v. 17 for its opposite, God's rejection.

I will have mercy on whom I have mercy: for this idiom, so common in Hebrew and especially in Arabic (*idem per idem*), cf. S. R. Driver, *Notes on the Hebrew Text of the Books of Samuel* (Oxford, 1913), on 1 Sam. 23:13, pp. 185f.

16. So it depends not upon man's will: lit. 'Consequently, (the divine mercy) does not come from one who has exercised his will or run hard morally . . .' The use of 'run' for moral effort is good Stoic language; see Bauer, s.v., *trechō*.

17. I have raised you up: i.e. to bring on to the stage of history. See H. H. Rowley, *Biblical Doctrine of Election* (London, 1964), chapter 5, esp. pp. 132ff.

showing my power: for the phrase (and the general idea of divine sovereignty), see Wis. 12:(16,) 17, etc.

18 sums up. Exod. 9:16 is chosen to illustrate God's sovereign will in rejection as well as in election. God's 'hardening' of Pharaoh's heart corresponds to or typifies His rejection of national Israel.

hardens the heart: i.e. makes obtuse and unresponsive, and so disobedient (and thus by implication 'rejects').

GOD'S WRATH AND MERCY **19-29**

If it is God himself who 'hardens' men's hearts, why then does he 'find fault'—i.e. impute blame—on the assumption that they are free creatures?

19. who can resist his will: who then is a 'free man'? (what becomes of man's free will?). This meaning seems to take the verb as a gnomic perfect. This is challenged (see SH *in loc.*). SH also renders: '*is* resisting God's will', explaining the tense as a perfect with a present meaning. Cf. Rom. 13:2 for a parallel. The question is then a rhetorical one, ironically put by Paul's imaginary opponent. The answer, on the argument just concluded, is: 'No one', since the man who rebels against God (Pharaoh) is only doing what God willed. The tense, however, may be simply a regular perfect tense: 'who has (ever) resisted His will?'. Cf. Wis. 12:12.

20. But who are you, a man: *NEB;* 'Who are you, sir, to answer God back?' This succeeds, as the *RSV* does not, in conveying something of the force of the vocative. 'You who are just a man', but also: 'You, fellow! Are you really (*menounge*) answering God back?'

21. The imagery of the potter and his clay is a familiar one in the prophets; cf. Isa. 29:16, Jer. 18:6; also Wis. 15:7, Sir. 36(33):12f.

one vessel for beauty ...: lit. 'for honour, for dishonour', i.e. one for what is esteemed, and another for what is not esteemed.

22. What if God, desiring ...: *NEB* renders in the same way, and it is difficult to find an alternative rendering for this involved and characteristically Pauline verse. There is no apodosis; and this suppressed apodosis requires to be understood after 'destruction': lit. 'Now if God, even though he wanted (the participle is concessive) to manifest his wrath and to make known his might, bore with much patience, the vessels of wrath, prepared for destruction, (what have you to object to this display of divine magnanimity and mercy?'—suppressed apodosis).

23. When Paul had completed the protasis, he loses the thread of the sentence he intended to complete and goes off on the tangential thought of the purpose clause. This was also a reason for God's 'forbearance' with the 'vessels of wrath': 'even (*kai*) in order to make known the riches of his glory . . .'

24. even us whom he has called: lit. '. . . for glory, whom he has called—*us*, not from the Jews only, . . .' The personal pronoun brings a climax to the argument. God's purpose culminated in *us*, Jews *and* Gentiles.

25. The argument is clinched by two quotations, the first from Hos. 2:23 (cf. 1:6, 8, 9), the second Hos. 2:1 (LXX 1:10). **As indeed he says:** cf. *NEB*: 'as it says'. The subject of 'says' is probably impersonal: 'as is said' (lit. 'as one says'). **her who was not beloved:** the figure of the nation as the bride of Yahweh.

26. This is a quotation from the LXX of Hos. 1:10. What is the place referred to, which was at one and the same time the place of Israel's rejection and her call again to sonship? Was it Jerusalem? Or has the apostle Palestine in mind? See H. A. W. Meyer, *Critical and Exegetical Handbook to the Epistle to the Romans* (Edinburgh, 1873-4) *in loc.* (especially n. 3). Is it possible that Paul did not intend the quotations to be understood *in a locative sense* at all? In the original Hebrew the word 'in the place of' means almost certainly in this passage 'instead of'; (cf. *RV mg.* to Hos. 1:10: 'Instead of that which was said unto them, "Ye are not my people", it shall be said . . .') Decisively against this is the adverb 'there', i.e. 'in that place'.

Paul may be thinking not only of the Gentiles here but, like Hosea, of the 'temporary lapse of Israel and their subsequent return'. (Barrett, *in loc.*)

27-9 consist of two further testimonia, Isa. 10:22ff. and Isa. 1:9, for the Remnant (assumed to be the Christian Church) as the true Israel.

27. cries out is the regular expression for inspired prophetic utterances. Cf. Jn. 1:15 and R. Bultmann, *Das Evangelium des Johannes* (Göttingen, 1941), *in loc.*

only a remnant: perhaps correctly: 'only the Remnant' cf. Lietzmann, *An die Römer* (*Handbuch zum NT*, 9th edn, 1933), *ad. loc.* The connection of 'remnant' with 'seed' is made at Isa. 10:22.

29. children: lit. 'seed' (*sperma*). Gal. 3 shows how Paul might have understood *sperma* in this sense.

ISRAEL'S FAILURE 9:30–10:13

THE STONE OF STUMBLING 30–3

30. What shall we say, then? The familiar formula is usually employed to state an objection raised by an imaginary opponent. Here it summarizes the foregoing argument in two paradoxical statements.

did not pursue: See SH, *in loc.* The words are correlatives ('pursue', 'overtake'), and the figure is taken from the race-course.

Does this mean that Gentiles who did not, as a matter of set purpose and policy, literally 'pursue' *dikaiosynē*—i.e. not only make it their chief aim and goal in life, but also 'chase' it—actually achieve (obtain) it? The figures of speech are of a pursuit and 'overtaking' of the elusive 'righteousness' by Gentiles.

The word *dikaiosynē* is used in the first occurrence in its widest sense of 'righteousness', including the sense of being accounted righteous by God, i.e. justification; in the second occurrence it is possibly used in the latter meaning only, 'justification' now fully defined as 'justification which is by faith', though some might say that this restricts the semantic range of the word.

31. did not succeed in fulfilling that law: lit. 'did not attain to the Law' (for the verb used in this sense, cf. 2 C. 10:14, Phil. 3:16). The latter phrase is a contraction for 'the fulfilment of the Law', or 'the justification which comes from the fulfilment of the Law'.

Between verses 31 and 32 an answer has to be supplied to the question raised about Israel's success in fulfilling the law; the answer is: 'They (Israel) did not succeed'. Then follows a further question.

32. as if it were based on works: 'as if' emphasizes the fact that it was 'by works' the Jews thought *dikaiosynē* could be attained; really it could only be done 'by faith'.

they have stumbled over the stumbling stone: it is assumed by St Paul as well known to his readers who the stumbling-stone is. Both the texts which follow (Isa. 8:14 and 28:16) are used elsewhere in the same connection (1 Pet. 2:6 uses the same non-LXX type of Greek text); they were probably familiar *testimonia*, employed by the early preachers and missionaries especially in their controversy with Jews (see C. H. Dodd, *According to the Scriptures*, p. 41ff.).

33. a stone that will make men stumble ...: at Isa. 8:14 it was Yahweh Himself who was originally the 'stone of stumbling'. At Isa. 28:16 God lays in Zion a precious foundation stone, and 'he who trusts therein shall not be put to shame'. Already the Targum interprets the precious foundation stone as 'a mighty King'. For Paul the stone of stumbling which is also the foundation-stone is Christ. Had this identification and interpretation already been made in the use of these *testimonia* before Paul?

With which verb are we to construe **in him:** 'believe' or 'be ashamed'? Should we read 'he that believeth shall not be ashamed in him'? The words 'in him' are not in the Hebrew, but they do appear in the LXX (cf. 1 Pet. 2:6). Have we here an early adaptation of the Greek *OT* text to Christian propaganda?

TRUE RIGHTEOUSNESS **10:1-13**

There is no break in the argument with the beginning of the new chapter. Paul pauses briefly to repeat his personal grief at his fellow-countrymen's failure to accept the Gospel (the parenthetic verses are 1-3). The rest of the chapter consists of a further exposition of the Pauline doctrine of 'righteousness' *sola fide*, now supported from Scripture by a fresh *catena* of texts from the Prophets and the Pentateuch.

1. my heart's desire: the *RSV* is right in taking the word *eudokia* here in its Biblical Greek sense (Hebrew *raṣōn*, 'desire'— the word never means 'desire' *except* in Biblical Greek); so *NEB* brings out even more fully the force of the word especially as here qualified, 'my deepest desire'. Cf., for other views, SH *ad loc*. It is difficult, however, to see how ideas of 'goodwill' fit this context; cf. G. Schrenk, *TWNT*, II, p. 736ff.

2. enlightened: lit. 'but not with discernment, percipience, recognition' as opposed to unawareness, ignorance (cf. v. 3), i.e., without discernment or recognition of the true source of *dikaiosynē* in faith. Cf. for the noun *epignōsis*, J. A. Robinson, *Ephesians* (London, 1903), p. 248. Cf. above, 3:20 ('recognition of sin', rather than a 'deepening awareness', knowledge of sin). The religious devotion or enthusiasm of the Jews ('zeal' used so absolutely Ps. Sol. iv. 3) was a blind devotion and unenlightened *Schwärmerei.*

3. establish: *NEB:* 'set up'. Paul is accusing the Jews of striving to set up their own (human) system of 'righteousness' by legal works.

did not submit: they did not commit themselves to the righteousness of God (revealed in the Gospel apart from the Law; cf. 1:17; 3:21). Since such commitment was to God, it was necessarily also a 'submitting' of oneself—hence the choice of verb.

4. end: for the hellenistic and *NT* use of the word, see Selwyn, *1 Peter,* on 1:9: Selwyn questions SH's very influential view that the word could only mean 'end', i.e. termination, here and never 'fulfilment', 'consummation' (cf. Mt. 5:17).

Vsere 4 gives a distinctive *NT* meaning of the term; the usage at 1 Pet. 1:9 conforms more closely to classical Greek (= 'the logical end of a process or action—its issue, consummation, perfection—and thus in philosophical writings its idea of chief good'); cf. 1 Tim. 1:5: 'the end of the commandment is love'. So the 'end', the climactic development (practically 'perfection', 'perfecting') of the Law is Christ. Cf. further, E. E. Schneider, '*Finis Legis Christus*', in *TZ*, xx (1964), pp. 410–22; R. Bultmann, 'Christus, des Gesetzes Ende', *Beitr. Ev. Theologie,* 1 (1940), pp. 3–27; F. Flückiger, '*Christus, des Gesetzes Telos*', *TZ*, xi (1955), pp. 153–7; R. Bring, in *Stud. Theol.,* xx (1966), pp. 1–36. Naturally such a meaning implies the cessation of the validity of the 'old Law'.

who has faith: i.e. to every believer Christ has superseded Law as a means of attaining 'righteousness'.

6–8. The original purpose of the *OT* passage was to meet the objection that the Mosaic code was impossible to keep; it is *not* something so far removed from reality that human nature cannot realize it. It is on the lips to utter it, and in the heart to carry it out (the 'commandment' or 'word of God', in the sense of the Mosaic code, the Law). Paul substitutes Christ for the Law: Christ is not so remote that he has to be brought down from Heaven or up from Hades; the Lord, Who has come down from heaven, has

also 'descended into hell' and risen from the dead—to be present
and available to Christian faith. The 'word of faith' (corresponding to the 'word of the Law') consists of the confession of Christ
'with the mouth' and genuine belief 'in the heart' that God
raised Him from the dead. This is the saving Faith-Righteousness.
See Selwyn, *1 Peter*, p. 320ff. Paul's 'drastic allegorising' is not all
his own invention (see M. Black, 'The Christological Use of the Old
Testament in the New Testament', *NTS*, xviii (1971), p. 9ff.[1])

6. the righteousness based on faith: or Faith-Righteousness. Is Paul personifying his *dikaiosynē sola fide*, making it (her)
utter the Scriptural text Dt. 30:11-14 in a Greek version adapted
to the writer's special exegetical purpose (for such personification,
cf. Prov. 1:20 (Wisdom), Lk. 11:49, etc.)?

10. For man believes: inward faith puts a man right with
God; confession of that faith brings him to salvation.

11. takes up again the closing verse of the testimony text from
Isa. 28:16.

12. repeats the thought of 3:22, the central plank in the
Pauline 'Gospel'.

bestows his riches: lit. 'abounding wealth'.

13. Jl 2:32. Note how St Paul can, without comment, equate
the Lord of the New Covenant with the Lord of the Old. For this
important aspect of the development of New Testament Christology, consult D. E. H. Whiteley, *The Theology of St. Paul* (Oxford,
1961), p. 106ff. The original Hebrew means, not simply 'make
appeal to Yahweh', 'invoke Yahweh', but implies that the
Israelite, in so doing, places himself on Yahweh's side, professes
allegiance to Yahweh, and so for Paul, the words mean 'to profess
oneself a Christian'. (Note also that this passage is concerned with
the 'Day of the Lord'.) The verse also contains a reference to the
Remnant.

---

[1] Cf. further F. F. Bruce, in *Soli Deo Gloria: New Testament Studies in Honor
of William Childs Robinson*, ed. J. McD. Richards (Virginia, 1968), p. 35ff.
See also S. Lyonnet, 'St. Paul et l'exégèse juive de son temps à propos Rom.
x. 6-8', in *Travaux de l'Institut Catholique de Paris*, iv, pp. 494-506. Cf. also
A. M. Goldberg, 'Torah aus der Unterwelt: eine Bemerkung zu Röm. 10:6-7',
BZ, xvi (1970), pp. 127-31. It has been suggested that Paul has in mind the
inaccessibility of Wisdom; see M. J. Suggs, ' "The Word is Near You": Rom.
x. 6-10 within the Purpose of the Letter', *Christian History and Interpretation:
Studies presented to John Knox*, ed. by W. R. Farmer, et al. (Cambridge, 1967),
pp. 305ff.

Israel's Sin Inexcusable 14–21

These verses meet an objector's argument that Israel can hardly be held responsible for rejecting the Gospel when she had never even heard it or known about its meaning (God's universal salvation). This is answered, first by a quotation from Ps. 19:4 ('their voice' must refer to the preaching of the earliest Christian (apostolic) missionaries), and then by two quotations from Dt. 32:21 and Isa. 65:1–2.

14. have not believed: an objector interposes: 'How could they [the Jews] confess Christ in whom they did not believe?' The tense is aorist, and probably refers to the Jews' historic rejection of Christ. The second part of the objection is more serious: How could there be real belief in one about whom the Jews had not heard?

The argument is carried forward and upward in a series of steps leading to a climax. How could they hear, if there was no herald, i.e. no one to proclaim the *kērygma*? But they had heard, and had known what the Gospel implied for the Gentile world; Moses prophesied their jealousy, Isaiah the election of a new People and the rejection of Israel.

15. unless they are sent: how could there be any to proclaim if they were not commissioned to go forth and preach? The 'sending' refers to the official commissioning and despatching of the missionaries, Christians or, before them, Jews (cf. Ac. 13:3).

16. they have not all heeded the gospel: the 'not all' stands in contrast to the statement at verse 11 about 'everyone who believes'. The following quotation from Isa. 53:1 stresses the universality of unbelief. Such unbelief is in accordance with *OT* prophecy. A negative response to the Gospel is common to both prophetic and apostolic witness.

17. so faith comes from what is heard: This verse is a brief concluding summary, and not just a repetition of verse 14. Cf. J. Munck, *Paul and the Salvation of Mankind* (London, 1959), p. 93, and p. 93, n. 131, for a survey of interpretations of this verse.

18. This verse meets the objection that some may not have heard the Gospel ('their words', i.e. 'about Christ', verse 17). This is ruled out by a quotation of Ps. 19:4 (LXX), stressing the universal proclamation of the Gospel; it has gone out, through the apostolic mission, to the ends of the earth. All Jews are acquainted with it. Cf. Munck, op. cit., pp. 96ff. (the mission to the Jews has been completed).

19–21. Again, I ask, did Israel not understand? In the light of the answer to this question given in the two quotations which follow (from Dt. 32:21, Isa. 65:1), the question must mean 'Did Israel fail to understand the universal nature of the Gospel (cf. verse 12, and Dodd, *ad loc.*)? They ought to have understood in view of the words of Moses, first of all declaring that God would stir up their jealousy against a 'non-nation', and enrage them against a people with no understanding. Isaiah even went further, in his declaration that God would be found by those who did not seek him, and reveal Himself to those who did not, like the Jews, enquire after Him.

THE REMNANT 11:1–10

God has not rejected Israel. Paul himself is living proof of this, and there are others. Those who have not been brought into the Church are those who, for the present, at any rate, are 'hardened'. Now, however, as in the past history of Israel, although the masses are 'hardened' there is a remnant which will be saved.

1–2. rejected: a direct allusion to the language of 1 Kg. 12:22 and Ps. 93:14 (LXX). The proof that Israel has not been 'thrust away' is Paul himself, an Israelite of Israelites (cf. his boast at Phil. 3:3f.). This personal form of appeal and apologetic—it is also a form of witnessing—continues similar personal references, e.g., at 9:3, 10:1. The Benjamites were the Israelite 'aristocracy'; cf. Finkelstein, *The Pharisees* (1963), I, p. 39. The variant reading 'inheritance' (*klēronomia*) for 'people', supported by P46, G and some Old Latin MSS., is clearly a text influenced by the parallel at Ps. 93:14 (LXX).

2. whom he foreknew: practically His chosen people. Cf. 8:29 for this familiar Biblical expression, probably selected here to suggest that the divine 'election' still held good—for the new 'Israel'.

of Elijah: lit., 'in (the case of) Elijah'; a rabbinic usage. Cf. Cant. R. i.6.

how he pleads with God against Israel: (so also *NEB*) This could be a wrong translation; the verb here (*entynchanei*) means 'brings a complaint' to God against Israel (1 Mac. 8:32, 11:25; cf. 1 Enoch ix:3).

3. A quotation, practically verbatim, from the LXX of 1 Kg. 19:10, 14. Does Paul mean to compare himself with Elijah, as also being the Remnant in person? If so, he soon corrects himself.

4. What is God's reply: lit. 'What does the "oracle" (1 Kg. 19:18) say to him?' The word for 'reply', 'oracle' (*chrēmatismos*) occurs only here in the *NT*; but also at 1 Clem. xvii. 5 (2 Mac. 2:4, 11:17). This rare and solemn word clearly is consciously selected to give prominence to the authoritative word of God that follows. Cf. further, A. T. Hanson in *NTS*, xix (1972–3), pp. 300–2.

6. grace would no longer be grace: A number of MS. authorities, supported by Syr and some early Fathers (e.g., Chrysostom, Theophylact) expand in various ways; e.g. Chrysostom (= א𝕔 BΨ): 'but if it were of works, it is no longer grace, since works are no longer works (*sic*).'

7–8. hardened: cf. above, p. 134. It is incorrect to stress the passive, as if Paul was avoiding any suggestion that God did the 'hardening'; indeed, the opposite is true, and the passive here could be an idiomatic Hebraic locution to avoid the use of the divine name; but it is God who is the real subject. See above, p. 41; and cf. Mk 6:52; Jn 12:40; 2 C. 3:14. 'Paul does not shrink from the conclusion that it was God's will (determined ultimately by his mercy) that this should be so, and confirms the conclusion by Old Testament quotations' (Barrett, *in loc.*). See, further, A. Škrinjar, in *Bib.*, xi (1930), p. 295, n. 2.

8–10. Paul clinches his argument and conclusion by his customary *OT* authorities—a quotation from the Pentateuch (Dt. 29:4), supported by the Prophets (Isa. 29:10) and the Writings (Ps. 69:22f., 35:8). The quotations are woven together, *charaz*-fashion (see above, p. 64) from *Tôrāh*, Prophets and Writings, thus providing a solemnly authoritative climax and Scriptural coping-stone to the argument. The first word from Dt. 29:4 is a condemnation of Israel, the second ('And David says') is virtually an invocation of David, pronouncing a curse on Israel. The imagery in the quotation should not be pressed.

9. their feast: better, perhaps, 'their feasting', rather than simply 'their table-fellowship'. Israel's great festivals themselves will be her ruination. Rabbinical exegesis equates 'table' with altar, so that if Paul is thinking in these terms 'table' would here signify the ceremonial religion of Judaism.

10. for ever: or, 'continually' (?); see C. E. B. Cranfield, *Stud. Ev.* II (1964), pp. 546–50.

THE REJECTION OF ISRAEL IS NOT FINAL 11–24

11. stumbled so as to fall: the first figure was possibly suggested by *skandalon* (verse 9; 'pitfall', lit. 'stumbling block'); the Biblical 'fall' implies final destruction. One may recover from a 'stumble', and Israel's 'stumble' or 'stumbling' was not to have the result of final destruction. Both verbs are often used in a moral sense (SH, *in loc.*).

By no means: stronger, 'Heaven forbid!' (cf. above, p. 63).

trespass: 'by their false step' (SH).

to make Israel jealous: recalling 10:19 and Dt. 32:21. Cf. Ac. 13:45f.

12ff. For the style of these verses (parallelism, balance of clauses, etc.), cf. note on 5:12ff.

12. riches for the world: i.e. an enrichment of (for) the world; cf. 10:12.

their failure: lit. 'their defeat'. *Hēttēma* is rare in Biblical Greek (Isa. 31:8 and 1 C. 6:7). In view of its contrast, however, with lit. 'fullness', 'full inclusion', the meaning 'deficiency' (lit. 'the lesser quantity') is also possible.

how much more: for this argument *a minori ad maius*, cf. 5:9.

full inclusion: cf. Rom. 11:25 where the same word (*plērōma*), applied to the Gentiles, supports the interpretation: 'until the full number of the Gentiles comes in'. The meaning, then, presumably is that, if the deficiencies (failures) of Israel enriched the Gentile world, their full inclusion—i.e. full enrolment in the Church, the Kingdom of God—will bring an even vaster increase of wealth to the world.

However, the word has also eschatological overtones (cf. the parallels at verse 15): some take it as synonymous with *teleiōsis* ('consummation'). There may also be hellenistic philosophical parallels; see J. B. Lightfoot, *St Paul's Epistles to the Colossians and to Philemon* (London, ⁸1886), pp. 255ff. For the eschatological-apocalyptic use of the word, perhaps in a sense like 'their Final Inclusion' (in the People of God), see J. Jeremias, *Parables of Jesus*, trans. S. H. Hooke (London, 1962), p. 152, n. 92; D. W. Vischer, 'Das Geheimnis Israels' (1950), p. 120, assumes that Paul is using the terminology of the money market. Israel's debt or loss was the enrichment of the world. When the whole debt is paid up, and Israel makes its full contribution to mankind's spiritual resources, then what an enrichment that will be! Such an interpretation, however, seems forced and artificial. On the whole, 'full' (or 'final') inclusion, or even 'final total' or 'total number' (see, further, note on 11:25 below), is preferable.

13. to you Gentiles: i.e. to the Gentile component of the Roman Church, and, no doubt, through them to the whole Gentile world.

magnify . . .: I bring my office (as Gentile apostle) to honour (see Bauer). 'I make much of my office (to see if I may provoke to envy my own flesh and blood . . .)' (Moffatt).

14. my fellow Jews: (see *NEB:* 'men of my own race'); better, and more literally, with Moffatt, 'my own flesh and blood'.

15. rejection . . . acceptance: i.e. by God. Cf. the corresponding contrast at v. 12: 'failure', 'full inclusion', which helps us to define the parallel terms. God 'accepts' (Rom. 14:3), Christ 'accepts' (Rom. 15:7) by an act of 'grace' what is 'unacceptable', in this case the apostate Israel (and likewise Christians each other (Rom. 15:7)). Cf. the gloss on Sir. 10:21: 'The fear of the Lord is the beginning of acceptance (*proslēpsis*); obduracy and pride are the beginning of rejection (*ekbolē*).'

reconciliation of the world: i.e. the reconciliation of the Gentiles ('world' = Gentiles) to God. This was the result of Paul's ministry ending in the salvation of the Gentiles (cf. 2 C. 5:18, 19).

life from the dead: i.e. the climax of the eschatological drama of salvation, the 'general resurrection', conceived, not as any special renewal of Israel such as that envisaged by Ezekiel (37:1-10) or Hosea 6:2-4, but the kind of resurrection from the dead which the Targumist envisages in interpreting Hos. 6:2-4— one which, on Paul's understanding of it, was a resurrection of the faithful and elect, both Jew and Gentile.

16. dough offered as first fruits: the reference is to the custom of the harvest offering. By the offering of the 'first fruits' of the dough, i.e. probably the first loaf baked, the whole mass of dough is consecrated (Num. 15:17ff.) Israel, as a whole, is consecrated through the Patriarchs (the 'holy root'; and cf. verse 28). The Fathers explain the 'first-fruits' (*aparchē*) as 'Christ' on the basis of 1 C. 15:20: the figure is a not uncommon one in the *NT*,

and is variously applied (e.g. Rom. 8:23, 16:5; 1 C. 16:15;
2 Th. 2:13; Jas 1:18; Rev. 14:4).

THE ALLEGORY OF THE ENGRAFTED WILD OLIVE 17-24

The process here described is said to be entirely unnatural (cf.
Dodd, *in loc.*), and that this is admitted by Paul himself (verse 24).
The opposite process is said to be usual: the wild olive (*agrielaios*)
becomes the cultivated olive (*kallielaios*) by the engrafting on it
of a cutting from a cultivated olive.

On the other hand, the engrafting of a fresh cutting from a wild
olive into an old olive-tree does not seem to have been unknown,
or possibly even uncommon, in the ancient world (cf. Michel, p.
275ff., who also cites parallels from Philo for a similar figure of
speech applied to Israelites and proselytes (*de Exsecr.* 6)). See also
SB, III, p. 291.) Paul is building on earlier traditional figures of
speech about Israel and its Gentile converts. According to Yeb.
36a (SB, *loc. cit.*) Israel had twice had a fresh cutting engrafted
into it, viz. Ruth and Naomi. The analogy, however artificial, is
a vivid and telling one. Moreover, if the Jewish-Christian congregation which formed the nucleus of the Roman Church had its
beginnings as an 'off-shoot' of the synagogue of the Olive Tree in
Rome (Intro., p. 22, n. 2: *synagōgē elaias*), the allegory would
be even more appropriate; cf. further, M. M. Bourke, *A Study
of the Metaphor of the Olive Tree in Romans* 11 (Washington,
1947).

17. to share the richness of the olive tree: *mg.* 'rich root'.
The word 'root' has, according to the *RSV* (possibly correctly)
been scribally inserted or interpolated into the text. Textual support for *RSV* is good, and includes P^{46}, D*, G, it.d, f, g, though the
alternative, with 'root' in the text, has slightly better support. If we
read 'root' in the text, the genitive must be qualitative: 'a root of
fatness' = a fat root; but we may also construe: 'the fat proceeding from the root'.

18. do not boast over the branches: *NEB:* 'make yourself
superior to the branches'; the verb is stronger than 'give yourself
airs', and more like 'bragging about your superiority'—so 'be
contemptuous of'. ('Become proud' (verse 21) is practically a
synonymous and equally strong expression.) 'If you do find
yourself "glorying" in your position' (the verb 'boast' is not
necessarily used in a pejorative sense) 'then [remember—this

verb has to be supplied] it is not you that supports the root, but the root that supports you.'

Were these Gentile Christians 'spiritual enthusiasts' (*pneuma-tikoi*), as the Corinthians at 1 C. 2:6ff.? Cf. Michel. It is very doubtful if the evidence exists to support this attractive possibility, any more than the assumption that the Gentile Christians at Rome were anti-Semitic.

19. In this question and answer style of the diatribe, the Gentile Christian 'comes back' with: 'You will then say (*ereis*), *So* the branches were broken off for the sake of *my* engrafting.'

20. That is true: true, indeed (*kalōs*)—Paul's reply is ironical. But Israel was cut off on account of her unbelief, while your present security ('you stand fast') is entirely due to your faith. (In that case, it is implied, you have no reason for self-glorifying.) **stand fast:** the word here used (lit. 'to stand') is employed in this connection especially in a sense the opposite of that of the verb 'to fall' (i.e. 'to fail'). 'To stand (fast)' is to enjoy a state of inward stability (or security) as a Christian; passages with such a meaning are Rom. 5:2; 1 C. 7:37; 10:12; 2 C. 1:24; Jn 8:44. The Hebrew *'āmad* is also used in a similar figurative sense, but the Pauline term has taken on a meaning of its own in relation to the 'firmness' of the Christian in his faith and calling.
become proud: cf. 12:3, 16; cf. 1 Tim. 6:17. These words are quoted frequently as a *sententia* by the Fathers; they read like a sentence from the Wisdom literature.

21. neither will he spare you: the variant reading of Western witnesses (supported now by *P46*) is stronger: 'Will he *really* (*mē pōs*) spare you?'

22. severity: the word in Greek (*apotomia*, lit. 'severing off') carries on the figures of speech of the branches being 'lopped off': but the word, of course, is regular in the meaning 'severity', 'hardness' (the opposite of 'mildness, gentleness, kindness' as a trait of character).

22-4 prepare the way for the Pauline *mystērion*, his eschatological 'secret', now disclosed at verses 25-6. It is God's ultimate purpose, when the 'fullness of the Gentiles' is reached, that He will reverse His judgement—the rejection of Israel has been, in any case, only a partial rejection (verse 25)—and all Israel will be saved. Paul introduces this final 'mystery' by the argument that, if the wild olive could be engrafted against nature, then the cultivated plant

can, by the power of God, be engrafted back into the new Israel,
its own natural 'olive plant'. In customary fashion, Paul concludes
and clinches his argument from Scripture (verses 26, 27, a contraction of Isa. 59:20-21 (cf. Ps. 14:7), Isa. 27:9, and Jer. 31:33-4).

COMPLETION OF GOD'S PLAN 25-32

25. wise in your own conceits: a matchless translation
capturing exactly the nuance of Pauline thought and emotion.
The expression in Greek (lit. 'clever in oneself') may have been an
idiomatic one for 'too clever by far in his own esteem' or 'wise in
his own conceits'.

a hardening has come upon part of Israel: lit. 'has partially
come to Israel'. Virtually 'a partial hardening' (*NEB*: 'this
partial blindness has come upon Israel . . .'). Israel's unbelief is
not a total 'obduration', but partial, only affecting some—no
doubt many—'Israelites'; Paul has to allow for the many
'Israelites' who had become Christians. Cf., further, O. Glombitza,
'Apostolische Sorge. Welche Sorge treibt den Apostel Paulus zu
den Sätzen Röm. 11:25ff.?', *Nov. Test.*, VII (1965), pp. 312-18.

until the full number of the Gentiles: According to the
rabbis, after the Fall the precise number of mankind was decreed
until the Last Judgement, and the latter could not take place till
this number was complete. At 2 Esd. 4:36, Rev. 6:11, 7:4; 14:1
it is the number of the saints that has to be 'fulfilled', or 'filled up'.
Here the number of the Gentiles (cf. 2 Bar. xxiii. 4, 5,). The term
begins to be used as a semi-technical apocalyptic term in Paul
(see above, p. 143).

come in: some understand 'into the Kingdom of God', and it is
argued that the term 'enter' is beginning to be used thus absolutely
at Mt. 7:13, 23:13, Lk. 11:52. It may be, however, that the word
here is used (as so frequently in the LXX for *bō'*) in the simple
sense 'has come', i.e. 'has arrived', and so 'been realized'.

26-7. The Deliverer will come from Zion: In his usual
style Paul sums up with a concluding Scriptural quotation (or combined quotation, Isa. 59:20-1 (Ps. 14:7), 27:9 (Jer. 31:33-4))
which recalls the prophecy of the coming out of Zion of *the*
Deliverer, to remove—turn away back—his impieties from Jacob;
it recalls also the ancient covenant promise of forgiveness.

The first part of the prophecy ('out of Zion will come the
Deliverer') seems to refer to the saving of Israel at the Parousia,

Zion being understood to mean the 'heavenly Jerusalem' (cf. Gal. 4:26). The prophecy may be understood, however, from the point of view of the prophet, to refer to the coming 'out of Israel' of the Christ and to the redemptive 'work' of Christ on behalf of Israel—achieving her forgiveness and inclusion in the 'New Covenant'.

The LXX reads: 'on account of Zion', the Hebrew: 'and a Redeemer shall come *to* Zion'. The Pauline 'variant' may come from Ps. 13:7, 52:7 (LXX): 'O that deliverance (salvation) for Israel would come out of Zion'. Paul may have changed the preposition in the interests of his soteriology; Isaiah had promised that the Messiah would come *out of* Zion and bring salvation to Israel. 'Zion' would then most probably signify the 'City of David'. See also, L. G. da Fonseca, in *Bib.*, IX (1928), p. 28.

28. As regards the gospel . . . as regards election: i.e. from the point of view of the Gospel, from the point of view of *their* election, 'beloved for the sake of their forefathers'.

The sentence has a characteristic rhetorical structure of clauses: *a b c, a b c;* the balanced structure is continued to verse 32. To the rhetorical style of the Greek schools Paul has added the parallelisms of Hebrew tradition. Cf. Barrett, *ad loc.*

enemies of God: simply 'with reference to the Gospel, enemies'. The interpretation of the versions 'enemies of God' (cf. *NEB*) is justified, but the Pauline shorter form does not exclude the further sense of 'enemies of the Church'. So also, 'beloved' can refer to Jews who are 'beloved' even to Christians as the elect of God.

for the sake of their forefathers: cf. B. Reicke, 'Um der Väter willen (Röm. 11:28)', *Judaica*, XIV (1958), pp. 106–14.

29. the gifts and the call of God are irrevocable: God cannot 'repent' of his decisions (cf. 2 C. 7:10; Ps. 109:4 (LXX)). It is about Israel's special 'divine' vocation ('the call of God') that St Paul is primarily thinking when he declares it to be 'irrevocable', 'irreversible'—something on which God cannot change his mind, because he is God (cf. Rom. 3:3ff.); but he thinks of Israel's vocation as among the special gifts God has bestowed on Israel—indeed the sum and purpose of them all. Is there a hendiadys: God's gracious endowments by virtue of which she was 'called'? Cf. C. Spicq, '*Ametamelētos* dans Rom. 11:29', *RB*, /LXVII (1960), pp. 210–19.

30. See M. Dibelius, *op. cit.* (above, p. 86).

31. they also may receive mercy: *mg.*: add 'now'. At verse
25 Paul seems to speak of the final salvation of Israel as still lying
in the future; and this makes the reading of 'now' here difficult;
this was felt by a number of scribes who omitted the adverb, P⁴⁶
(*vid*); A, D, G, etc. We would expect the adverb *pote*, 'once', 'some
future day', to correspond to this adverb in the parallel clauses
in verse 30.

The 'now' is, however, the more difficult reading. Paul could
be contrasting the former disobedience of the Gentiles, who have,
through Jewish apostasy, come to enjoy a present mercy, with the
present apostate Jewry, to whom, however, the door of mercy is
always open, even now: '. . . in order that God might show
mercy, to them too—now!'

32. consigned: the figure is a military one; cf. Ps. 77:62
(LXX): 'He gave his people over unto the sword'. 'Used (in this
verse in Romans) with the pregnant sense of giving over so that
there can be no escape' (SH). For a similar figurative use, cf. Gal.
3:22. The literal meaning of the verb is 'to imprison' (1 Mac.
5:5), then in general of the 'delivering up', synonymous with
paradidōmi. The figurative sense, of 'being delivered up captive to',
is clearly intended by St Paul in both passages where he uses the
term. The sense here is: 'All men without exception were, as it
were, "locked up in unbelief" that God might show his mercy
to all.'

all men: should we interpret in terms of 'universalism', i.e.
every single individual without exception, or as 'all', looked at
collectively, like the phrase 'fullness of the Gentiles', or 'all
Israel'? SH is quite definite: 'The reference is not here any more
than elsewhere to the final salvation of every individual' (p. 339).

Doxology 33-6

Verses 33-6 are described as a *Hymnus* ('hymn') by Michel. They
are, in fact, more of the nature of a concluding doxology (famil-
iarly Pauline, cf. Rom. 16:25) cast in *OT* language (verses 34-5
combine elements from Isa. 40:13; Job 15:8; Jer. 23:18; Job
41:11), and continue the 'poetic' style of the section. The out-
burst is prompted by St Paul's having just fully revealed the
'mystery' of verse 25, the divine purpose for Israel, salvation
through an apostasy serving God's purpose for the Gentiles.
'God works in a mysterious way His wonders to perform.'

33. the depth of . . .: cf. H. M. Dion, 'La Notion paulinienne de "Richesse de Dieu" ', *Sciences Ecclésiastiques*, XVIII (1966), pp. 139-48.

riches and wisdom . . .: some prefer to make 'wisdom' and knowledge depend on 'wealth': '. . . the depth of God's wealth both of wisdom and knowledge'. Most modern interpreters tend to take 'wealth' independently, meaning all the infinite resources of God, in goodness (cf. for this figure of speech, Rom. 2:4; 9:23).

35. that he might be repaid: *NEB* is better: 'Who has ever made a gift to him, to receive a gift in return?'—another way of saying that the goodness of God is not a repayment for services rendered; it is a free, outgoing, undeserved gift.

36. The formula 'from-through-to' is said to be a Pauline adaptation of a hellenistic prayer (cf. Michel, *ad loc.*). Michel claims that Paul avoids the mystical 'in him'. God is the Creator, Redeemer, and the eschatological God of Creation and Redemption; cf. 1 C. 8:6. The threefold form ('from-through-to') is reflected in the 'riches-wisdom-knowledge', and in the threefold question in verses 34-5—an illuminating example of St Paul's rhetorical composition in a 'hymnic' passage.

PRACTICAL EXHORTATIONS 12:1-15:13

There follows Paul's concluding *paraenesis*—practical exhortations based, for the most part, on the doctrine of the Epistle; they are applications of the fundamental tenets of the doctrine of justification *sola fide* and the 'life in Christ'. The central idea is that of the peace and concord of the Church in the world. The same type of *paraenesis*, characteristically Pauline, is found in 1 Th. 4, 2 Th. 3:6ff., Gal. 5, Col. 3, and Eph. 4.

CHURCH MEMBERSHIP 12:1-8

1. I appeal . . . by the mercies of God: This kind of formula (with *dia*) may mean little more than: 'I urge you, for the love of God, to present yourselves' . . .; but cf. Barrett, p. 230ff. The 'exhortation' to obedience is consequential on the Christian experience of the 'mercies of God'. Alternatively, we may explain that here and at verse 3 ('. . . by the grace given to me I say') it is Paul, the Apostle to the Gentiles, who is speaking, but in both cases he declares that it is by the mercy and grace of God alone, which so exceptionally has been shown to him, that he can so charge his hearers.

your bodies: cf. 6:13. Paul means their *whole selves*, but his choice of term perhaps reminds his readers that they are still 'in the body'.

living sacrifice: this may imply a contrast with the 'dead' sacrifices of 'irrational' worship, i.e. the dead bodies of sacrificial animals (cf. SH). Cf. Rom. 6:13 (cf. Michel, *ad loc.*); and further, P. Seidensticker, *Lebendiges Opfer (Röm. 12:1). Ein Beitrag zur Theologie des Apostels Paulus (Neutest. Abhand.*, xx, Münster, 1954).

spiritual worship: cf. *NEB* text: 'the worship offered by mind and heart'; and *mg.*: '. . . for such is the worship which you, as rational creatures, should offer.' 'Spiritual worship' (*logikē latreia*) is said to refer in hellenistic literature to the act of spiritual thanksgiving which replaced the offering or sacrifice in early forms of worship (so Michel). 'Spiritual' seems the best rendering, provided we include the worship of all that is highest in man—mind, spirit, will. It is possible too that the word had associations, among Roman 'spiritual' enthusiasts (the *pneumatikoi*), with a 'higher life' above the physical; and this could account for Paul's choice of the term 'bodies' to emphasize that it is the whole man, in his bodily life, that is the holy and acceptable offering.

2. conformed . . . transformed: note the Greek distinction between *schēma* (outer (passing) fashion) and *morphē* (inner transformation, and in Platonic thought the 'real'). Cf. SH and J. B. Lightfoot, *Epistle to the Philippians* (London, [10]1891), pp. 130f.

renewal of your mind, that you may prove: the second clause may be consequential or purposive, more probably the latter. The object of such spiritual dedication and transformation is to enable the Christian to discover, by a process of trial and error ('testing'), the good, well-pleasing, perfect will of God.

It is *the mind* in which this inner 'transformation' takes place; and this is in keeping with the rational or 'spiritual' nature of our service. Cf. Heb. 5:14 ('. . . *perceptions* trained by long use to discriminate between good and evil') and Phil. 1:9–10: 'love' which grows richer 'in *knowledge* and *insight* of every kind' bringing 'the gift of true discrimination' (*NEB*).

True dedication of spirit is to engage powers of mind, in the quest for perfection, or rather for the perfect will of God for us. Cf. Mk 12:30.

See also H. E. Stoessel, 'Notes on Rom. 12:1-2: The Renewal of the Mind and Internalising the Truth', *Interpretation*, XVII (1963), pp. 161-75.

world: *mg.*, '*age*', i.e. this present evil age under the dominion of Satan and the powers of evil.

3. For by the grace given to me: cf. the opening of verse 1. The two phrases are parallel.

every one among you: there are no exceptions.

to think of himself . . . judgement: no English translation can bring out the word-play in the original *phronein* ('to think'), *hyperphronein* ('to think overmuch of oneself'), *sōphronein* ('to be sober-minded', not only in one's self-esteem, but in the sense also of leading a righteous, godly and sober life). Cf. Phil. 2:2-3.

each according to the measure of faith: Michel draws attention to the Hebrew idea of the Spirit being apportioned by God 'according to measure (weight)', i.e., capacity (cf. SB, II, p. 431: 'one prophet prophesied *one* book, another (like Jeremiah) *two*'). Is this what the apostle means by the 'measure of faith'? Eph. 4:7, 'the measure of the gift of Christ (to each Christian)', may explain the phrase; cf. verse 6; lit. 'according to the proportion of faith'. Cf. SH, p. 355: 'Faith "being the sign and measure of the Christian life" is used here for all those gifts which are given to man with or as a result of his faith.' Pallis, *ad loc.*, takes the phrase in a passive sense: 'the measure of that which has been entrusted to us by God', i.e. to the limit of the capacities we have been entrusted with (by God) (Lat. *fideicommissum*). Cf. Polybius v. xli. 2: 'This Hermeias was a Carian who had been set over the affairs of Seleucus, Antiochus's brother, who had committed this trust (responsibility) (*pistis*) into his hands'. This sense of *pistis*, i.e. 'responsibility', fits the Pauline context; the reference is to every man's 'measure of responsibility' within the Church, the Body of Christ. So, likewise, at verse 6: 'the proportion of our responsibility'. For other examples of *pistis* in this and related senses, cf. Josephus, *Antiq.* II. v. 1 (61); Test. Ash. vii. 7; Sir. 45:4; Mt. 23:23.

Is Paul perhaps using this familiar idea of 'measure' (with its associations with 'fitting measure') to curb the excesses of 'spirituality'? See, further, J. N. Birdsall, '*Emetrēsen* in Rom. 12:3', *JTS*, XIV (1963), p. 103f.; C. E. B. Cranfield, '*Metron pisteōs* in Rom. 12:3', *NTS*, VIII (1961-2), pp. 345-51.

4–5. The comparison of a community with a living body is a commonplace of ancient literature (e.g. Livy, ii.32: Senate and people are said to belong together as much as stomach and limbs; cf. the use Paul makes of the figure at 1 C. 12:12; Eph. 4:15; Col. 1:18).

5. so we, though many: Semitic use of 'many' inclusively when we prefer 'all', i.e. 'so we all . . .' See above, p. 90.

7. in our serving: the *diakonia* here is usually interpreted of general service in the Christian community or including the 'service of tables' (Ac. 6:2), the care of the sick or the poor (cf. 2 C. 8:4); the order—after 'prophesying' and before 'teaching' (the latter follows 'prophecy' at 1 C. 12:27)—may be without any significance. See, however, note on verse 8.

teaching . . . exhortation: both go together, and no doubt include 'counselling' (*nouthesia*, 1 Th. 5:12ff.). Notice the use of the participles, tending to emphasize function rather than status.

he who gives aid: *NEB*: 'if you are a leader'. The verb is ambiguous. In the second sense it is used by Justin Martyr of the *proestōs*, or president, who officiates at the celebration of the Eucharist (1 Apol. lxv. 5). Cf. also for such Church 'leaders', 1 Th. 5:12.

8. liberality: *NEB*: '. . . give with all your heart'. It is doubtful if either is correct, though the sense of 'liberality' is also claimed for 2 C. 9:11, 13. The Testament of Issachar (cited by SH) gives the clearest meaning: *haplotēs* means 'purity, or simplicity of heart', i.e. a self-forgetful attitude, entirely innocent of any ulterior motive. Cf. R. H. Charles, *Testaments of the Twelve Patriarchs* (London, 1908), Issachar III, p. 102f.

Paraenetical Maxims 9–21

These verses represent a more or less self-contained unit of Christian *sententiae*, very much in the style of the Hebrew Wisdom literature; cf. Barrett, *ad loc.* The main theme is *agapē*. Barrett thinks that there may even have been a Hebrew source at St Paul's disposal. The use of participles with the force of imperatives is a feature of Hebrew style, especially when these are used to express, not direct commands, but rules and codes; cf. Selwyn, *1 Peter*, and appended note on 'Participle and Imperative in 1 Peter' by D. Daube. They are by no means all logically connected; occasionally the only connection appears to be that of a *Stichwort* (a key-word), where word-association, not logic or meaning, is the link (e.g. between verses 13 and 14, the use of the term *diōkein* (in two different senses: in verse 13 'practising (hospitality)', in verse 14 'persecuting'). There is no formal *schēma* in the verses (so Lagrange: 9–16 love to Christians, 17–21 love to all men; but verse 14 belongs to 'love to all men'); the *agapē* theme is renewed at 13:8–10. The form of the *sententia* is sometimes a negative formulation followed by a positive exhortation (e.g. verse 17). On 12: 9–13:10, see A. Viard, 'La Charité accomplit la Loi', *Vie Spirituelle*, LXXIV (1946), pp. 27–34.

9. The transition from verse 8 reminds us of the transition to 1 C. 13:1ff. at 1 C. 12:31; here too reflections on *agapē* follow a similar passage on the exercise of 'spiritual gifts'. *Agapē* is the precondition in the Christian community for the exercise of all *charismata*.

genuine: lit. 'without hypocrisy'. It is perhaps better to render by a negative equivalent; hypocrisy is just what Christian *agapē* can become. This description of *agapē* (or *philadelphia*) appears to have been in the paraenetical tradition; cf. 2 C. 6:6, 1 Pet. 1:22. The idea is also related to 1 C. 13:4.

hate . . . hold fast: *NEB*: 'loathing . . . clinging to'; *AV*: 'abhor . . . cleave to', perhaps bring out better the force of the original. These are both strong expressions, conveying a passionate hatred of evil and zeal for good, the latter here to be defined as at verse 1, i.e. the pursuit of the will of God.

10–13 yield five pairs of parallel *sententiae*, beginning with 'brotherly love' (verse 10), and concluding with 'hospitality' (verse 13); the rhetorical structure is in the style of such writing.

10. with brotherly affection: lit. 'be warmly affectionate' (*philostorgoi*). The Christian shows the same love to his fellow-Christian as he does within his own family; it is a caring concern. The word here used—verb, adjective, and noun—has special associations with the intimate, tender love of family; see H. G. Liddell and R. Scott, *Greek-English Lexicon*, rev. edn (Oxford, 1940), s.v. If 10*a* is *philadelphia*, 10*b* is *agapē*.

11. zeal: Mentioned here only and at 2 C. 7:7 as a Christian characteristic and a genuine sign of the spirit's working.

aglow with the Spirit: *NEB*: 'in ardour of Spirit'; the same expression is employed to describe the ardent spiritual zeal of apostles at Ac. 18:25 ('fire' is a familiar Biblical figure for the

Spirit's consuming power: Isa. 4:4; Mt. 3:11 and par.; Ac. 2:3),
and, for similar figures of speech, 1 Th. 5:19; Rev. 3:15.

serve the Lord: a variant 'serve the opportunity' is attested (a
contraction *KR* (*Kyriō*, 'Lord') may have been misread as *kairō*
(opportunity), or vice versa), *NEB mg.*: 'meeting the demands of
the hour'. 'To serve the time' in Greek means 'to be an oppor-
tunist'.

'Lord' is better attested textually, and gives a less difficult
meaning; some, however, prefer the harder reading on the
grounds that it is more in keeping with the context; besides, St
Paul was not opposed to opportunism.

12. hope: i.e. of the final revelation at the Parousia, when
the Christian would exult in the (restored) glory of Adam.
Cf. note on 5:2.

patient in tribulation: patience (endurance, long-suffering) is
inspired by 'hope'; cf. Rom. 5:2f, where we find the same order:
hope—patience (endurance). The 'tribulation' was not necessarily
identical with persecution; but, as verse 14 implies, it must have
included it.

constant in prayer: the phrase is an old one—no doubt well-
established in Christian paraenesis; see Ac. 1:14, 2:42, 1 Th.
5:17, Eph. 6:18; cf. Col. 4:2. Paul practised what he preached;
cf. Rom. 1:9–10. In the practice of prayer, the synagogue was the
school of the Church; Judaism in Paul's day not only produced
in Pharisaism a system of legalism covering all possible behaviour;
it also produced prayers covering every moment of the entire day.
Such prayer was naturally especially evident in time of persecution.

13. Contribute to the needs of the saints: *koinōneō*, to share
out one's property. For the verb and its cognates, cf. Phil. 4:15;
Rom. 15:26; 2 C. 9:13; Heb. 13:16. A variant, obviously late
and secondary, reads: 'sharing in the commemoration(s) of the
saints' (*mneiais* for *chreiais*, with D*, G it vg, etc.).

14. This *logion* (cf. Mt. 5:44 par. Lk. 6:28) stands alone in its
context, but is further developed in verses 17ff. Michel describes
the sayings as a Pauline Targum-like version of the original
dominical *logion*, which no doubt by Paul's time had become
firmly embedded in catechetical tradition; cf. 1 C. 4:12, 1 Pet.
2:23. 'Blessing' and 'cursing' (the latter of 'enemies') was a
regular feature of synagogue worship; 'cursing' recalls the
synagogue custom of formally 'cursing' its opponents; Jesus'

Word abolishes it (cf. Jas 3:9ff.). The unity of theme between
this verse and verses 17 to 21 give the impression of a dislocation
in the text; verse 16 certainly follows more logically on verses
9-10. The variant 'you' after 'persecute' is strongly attested, but
appears to come from a reminiscence of Mt. 5:44.

15. The Christian *sententia* here compressed is a commonplace
of Jewish and hellenistic moralists. Parallels are cited from Sir.
7:34: 'Do not fail those who weep, but mourn with those who
mourn.' The Christian injunction is a positive one; cf. 1 C.
12:26, Phil. 2:17-18.

16. live in harmony with one another: recalls verse 3.
The injunction is frequent in Paul; cf. Rom. 15:5, 2 C. 13:11,
Phil. 2:2, 4:2. Was it a necessary exhortation in these early
congregations?

do not be haughty, but associate with the lowly: lit. 'do not
be carried away by the high and mighty, but go along with the
humble.' Alternatively we may interpret, with special reference
to the ideas and claims of the Christian enthusiasts, whose minds
were to such an extent on higher things—the *charismata* of prophecy and tongues—that they despised the humbler aspects of
Christian service. Cf., further, A. Fridrichsen, 'Humilibus con-
sentientes', *Horae Soederblomianae* I. i (1942), p. 32.
associate with: the verb here is a strong one for those who are
'carried away' by their enthusiasm. The Christian is to be 'carried
away', not by 'high-minded' but empty speculations, but by the
humble tasks in the community (2 Pet. 3:17, Gal. 2:13).
never be conceited: a Pauline adaptation of Prov. 3:7 (LXX:
'Be not wise in thine own eyes!'). This is not the only echo in
tradition of this verse. See SB, III, p. 299.

17. Repay no one evil for evil: cf. 1 Th. 5:15, 1 Pet. 3:9.
Again, evidently a well-known Christian injunction firmly
embedded in the paraenetical tradition. The *OT* deprecates the
returning of evil for evil (Gen. 44:4; Jer. 18:20; Prov. 17:13).
There is frequent discussion in late Judaism of the question of
retribution (cf. Prov. 20:22); but this never appears to have
gone further than negative injunctions such as: 'Do not rejoice
over the misfortune of thine enemy', or 'Return not evil for
evil' (SB, I, p. 368; III, p. 299. Michel, *ad loc.*). In this Christian
injunction, the negative injunction is always followed by a positive
—here represented by verses 17b and 18.

take thought for: *NEB*, better: 'Let your aims be such as all men count honourable.' Paul is supporting his paraenesis (as he does his arguments) by an adaptation of Prov. 3:4 (LXX) (cf. 2 C. 8:21). The original of Prov. 3:4 has: 'So shalt thou find favour and good understanding in the sight of God and man'; Paul adapts it to the sense above. The words can also be construed as 'harbouring the best of intentions towards all men', and this is more nearly parallel to the thought of verse 18.

18. so far as it depends upon you: Others may not be prepared to live at peace with you; then your attitude must be that defined in verses 19ff. The *AV*, 'so far as lieth in you', suggests that we may not always be ourselves capable of peaceable relations with others, a thought which is not in the text. This thought of peace-making no doubt ultimately stems from the teaching of Jesus (Mt. 5:9, Mk 9:50). Paul repeats the exhortation at 1 Th. 5:13, 2 C. 13:11, etc.; but he is thinking here of the Christian virtue as exercised beyond the Christian congregation (as at Heb. 12:14); cf. Epict. IV. v. 24. The Hebrew foundations of the thought of these two verses 17 and 18 are found at Prov. 3:4 and Ps. 33:15 (LXX); cf. Dodd's comment (p. 199).

19. For the literary form, see above, p. 154; on the theme, cf. K. Stendahl, 'Hate, Non-Retaliation and Love: 1QS x. 17-20 and Rom. 12:19-21', *HThR*, LX (1962), pp. 343-55.
Beloved, never avenge yourselves: The form of address ('Beloved') is an indirect reminder of the Christian's obligation to *agapē* (including love of enemies).
leave it to the wrath of God: (*mg.* Greek: 'give place'); *NEB mg.*, literally, 'leave a place for divine retribution'; *RSV* is an idiomatic and exact rendering of the meaning of the (originally Hebrew) idiom: 'give place to' (cf. Eph. 4:27, Lk. 14:9, Sir. 13:22, for this Biblical locution).
it is written: as usual the Christian *didachē* is authoritatively summed up by a Scriptural text or interwoven texts (see note on p. 64). The first, Dt. 32:35, is the Pentateuchal prohibition of vengeance, on the grounds that it is a divine prerogative.

20. The second text, Prov. 25:21f, comes short of the Christian attitude of love to one's enemies, since the motivation is still revenge. For the figure 'coals of fire' in recent discussion, see W. Klassen, 'Coals of Fire: Sign of Repentance or Revenge?', *NTS*, IX (1962-3), pp. 337ff. The repetition of Dt. 32:35 at

Heb. 10:30 suggests that this verse had a firm place in Christian catechesis. Cf. also M. J. Dahood, *CBQ*, XVII (1955), pp. 19–24; S. Morenz, 'Feurige Kohlen auf dem Haupt', *Theol. Ltzg.*, LXXVIII (1953), pp. 187–92.

21. sums up (both verse 20 and verses 17–21) negatively and in a succinct and pregnant *sententia*, the basis of all Christian behaviour towards others.

OBEDIENCE TO RULERS 13: 1–7

The group of maxims ending at 12:21 resumes and is completed at 13:9–10; 13:1–7 consists of Christian teaching on the attitude of Christians to the civil powers. For recent literature and views, consult O. Cullmann, 'Zur neuesten Diskussion über die *Exousia* in Röm. 13:1', *TZ*, x (1954), pp. 321ff.; cf. also O. Cullmann, *The State in the New Testament* (New York, 1956), and C. D. Morrison, *The Powers that Be* (*Studies in Biblical Theology, 29*, London, 1960). E. Wolf, 'Politischer Gottesdienst', *Festschrift K. O. Schmidt* (Göttingen, 1961), pp. 51–63; V. Zsifkovits, *Der Staatsgedanke nach Paulus in Röm. 13* (Vienna, 1964); H. v. Campenhausen, 'Zur Auslegung von Röm. 13. Die dämonistische Deutung des Exousia-Begriffs', *Aus der Frühzeit des Christentums* (Memorial volume for A. Bertholet, Tübingen, 1950); E. Käsemann, 'Grundsätzliches zur Interpretation von Röm. 13', *Beitr. Ev. Theol.*, XXXII (1961), pp. 37–55; C. E. B. Cranfield, 'Some Observations on Rom. 13:1–7', *NTS*, VI (1959–60), pp. 241–9; A. Strobel, 'Zum Verständnis von Röm. 13', *ZNTW*, XLVII (1956), pp. 67–93; O. Michel, 'Das Problem des Staates in neutest. Sicht', *Theol. Ltzg.*, LXXXIII (1958), pp. 161–6; E. Bammel, 'Ein Beitrag zur paulinischen Staatsanschauung', *Theol. Ltzg.*, LXXXV (1960), pp. 837–40; G. Delling, *Röm. 13: 1–7 innerhalb der Briefe des Neuen Testaments* (Berlin, 1962).

Verse 1a lays down the general thesis of Christian submission to the supreme authorities, i.e. clearly the governing or civil authorities, wherever the Christian congregation or Christian believer is located; the repetition of this injunction at verse 5 shows that it is the central thought of the whole passage, which is argued out in the style of the Wisdom literature as a rational appeal to the individual conscience. Verse 1b gives the theological grounds for such 'submission', that such authorities are in exist-

ence as ordained by God. Verses 2 to 4 draw the consequences of
verse 1b, and form an independent literary unit.

The passage leaves the clear impression that St Paul is ad-
dressing his remarks to a definite situation or situations which had
arisen in relations between some early Christian communities
and the state or local authorities. Christians may even have been
refusing to pay taxes.

The connection of 13:1–7 with its context—12:19–21 and
13:8ff.—is not immediately obvious; it is sometimes explained
as an 'interpolated' section of teaching. The logical link, however,
is with 12:19–21, where the fundamental Christian ethic, to leave
all retribution to God, is unambiguously stated: '. . . do not avenge
yourselves, beloved, but leave a place for divine retribution.
"Retribution belongs to me," says the Lord, "I will repay." '

The Christian ethic is clear: good is to be returned for evil.
But this does not mean that there is no redress of wrongs or
retributive justice in this life. God deals out this retribution, and
he does so *in this world* through his divinely constituted authorities,
the civil magistrates. Paul, at this point, fills in a gap in the
Sermon on the Mount which leaves open the question: 'If we
suffer wrong and do not seek revenge, but return good for evil,
does the offender get off scot-free? Is the injustice to be righted
only at the Last Judgement?' 'No', Paul replies. 'It is for this end
civil law exists, to mete out divine justice on this earth. And this
kind of law no man can take into his own hands.' St Paul's
argument is reinforced if the 'authorities' (*exousiai*) are for him,
like the 'principalities and powers', divine agencies. Cf. SH,
p. 366: 'The idea of the civil power may have been suggested by
verse 19 of the preceding chapter, as being one of the ministers of
the divine wrath and retribution (verse 4); at any rate the juxta-
position of the two passages would serve to remind St Paul's
readers that the condemnation of individual vengeance and
retaliation does not apply to the action of the state in enforcing
law; for the state is God's minister, and it is the just wrath of God
which is acting through it.'

1. **governing authorities:** i.e. of the state, the state 'authorities', abstract for concrete, and equivalent to 'rulers' at verse 3.
Some interpret in terms of the 'principalities and powers' of
1 C. 15:24, Col. 1:16, 2:10, 15, thus including the 'State' in
these higher 'spiritual' entities. These 'higher powers' are then

conceived as demonic agencies, and no doubt also envisaged as personal beings. Rulers (emperors) can be conceived as evil deities incarnate (2 Th. 2:8); Cf. Cullmann, *The State in the NT*, p. 95ff. (A variant text—supported by P^{46}, D*, G^{it}—has: 'To *all* the higher powers subject yourselves'.)

be subject to: a strong word expressly used in this connection; cf. Tit. 3:1.

there is no authority except from God: a doctrine both Jewish and hellenistic (Dan. 2:21, 37f.). The idea persists in rabbinical Judaism; even though Rome destroys the Temple, and slays the pious Israelite, she is nevertheless the heaven-appointed ruler (SB, III, pp. 303f.).

have been instituted by God: lit. 'are ordered (*tetagmenai*) by (under) God. Verse 2 speaks of resistance to the divine order (*diatagē*).

2. he who resists the authorities resists what God has appointed: Moffatt: 'anyone who resists authority is opposing the divine order'. The second verb is even stronger than the first: it is used especially of the 'resistance' of rebellion or revolt. Cf. Josephus, *Antiq.*, XIV. xv, 5 (424).

will incur judgement: a Hebrew or Semitic locution—a closer rendering bringing out the force of the original would be 'will receive (bring) judgement for (on) themselves'.

3. good conduct: abstract for concrete, i.e. those who behave themselves.

4. he is God's servant: a consequence of the principle of verse 1 that temporal authority is instituted by God. The words here are in a prominent position opening the sentence (with the emphasis on the genitive: '*God's* servant he is') and are repeated, stressing this fundamental thought, later in the verse. Cf. also note on verse 6.

to execute his wrath: lit. 'bringing retribution to the evil-doer', a retribution which effectively constitutes the out-workings of the wrath of God.

5. conscience: as in Stoic thought, 'conscience' is the individual's sense of right and wrong, his moral judgement, his recognition of the inherent claims of the good, and the grounds for rejecting what is wrong. It also includes the recognition of the divinely given authority of the state in executing justice which may include the *ius gladii*. See above, p. 58.

6. ministers of God: the word used for 'ministers' has liturgical associations. Is Paul seeking to convey that the state authorities have a sacred task to perform?

taxes . . . revenue: i.e. direct and indirect taxation, the first probably the poll-tax, the second duties and taxes on goods (see Michel, *ad loc.*).

attending to this very thing: the verb 'to attend to' (*proskartereō*) has also special associations with liturgy, cf. of constant occupation with prayer, e.g. above, Rom. 12:12; Ac. 1:14; cf. also Ac. 2:46.

7. Pay (*apodidonai*) . . . **their dues:** The words recall the Word of Jesus at Mk 12:17. These closing paraenetic chapters of Romans contain several versions of Words of Jesus interpreted and adapted by Paul for his own special purposes, e.g., Rom. 12:14, 17, 21;13:9.

respect . . . honour: to this outward conformity in payment of taxes, etc., Paul adds the inward attitude of 'fear and respect'. In this we can detect the influence of tradition (cf. SB, III, p. 305), as well as of a Christian attitude to the State recommended by the early Church (1 Pet. 2:17). Cf. further, A. Strobel, 'Furcht, wem Furcht gebührt: zum profangriechischen Hintergrund von Röm. 13:7', *ZNTW*, LV (1964), pp. 58–62.

BROTHERLY LOVE AS CONSUMMATION OF THE LAW 8–10

There is no division in thought between verses 7 and 8; indeed, on the contrary, verse 7 leads logically into verse 8 and prepares the way for this striking Pauline aphorism. (*NEB* begins a new paragraph at verse 7. Bengel, however, notes at verse 8 *nova pars adhortationis*.) The train of thought of 12:14 is resumed after the intervening section on the Christian's attitude to the State.

8. owe no one anything: The Greek word 'to owe' (*opheilein*) evidently here shares the ambiguity of its Aramaic equivalent *ḥobh*, Michel, *ad loc.* (cf. A. Friedrichsen, *Theol. Studien u. Kritiken* (1930), p. 294ff.): it means, literally, 'to be in debt to', but also 'to be under an obligation to', and so 'to have a duty towards' (cf. 15:27 and the note on 1:14 above, p. 42). Furthermore, it seems hardly coincidental that the same consonants give the word in Aramaic 'to love', *'aḥebh* or *ḥabbebh*. (See M. Black, *Aramaic Approach*[3], p. 182.) The paronomasia is reproduced in the Peshitta Syriac: *walᵉʾenash medem la teḥubun 'ella ḥad leḥad* *lemaḥabbu.* As Meyer points out (*Jesu Muttersprache* (Leipzig, 1896), pp. 125ff.; see also E. Nestlé, *Philologica Sacra* (Berlin, 1896), p. 49ff.), this proverbial-like saying was just the kind to lend itself to a 'punning' word-play. Paul is probably reproducing in Greek an Aramaic *sententia*, possibly a Christian one, conceivably even a dominical pun.[1] Lietzmann would confine 'one another' to fellow Christians, but this seems an illogical narrowing of the scope of this universal Christian obligation, especially following verse 7: 'Pay all . . .'. We should be in debt to no one (including the tax authorities): our obligation to everyone, however, is *agapē*. On 8*b*, see D. G. Hughes, in *Estudios Biblicos*, II (1943), pp. 307ff.

for he who loves his neighbour has fulfilled the law: the perfect is that of a general truth; 'fulfilling the Law' is the same as 'doing the Law' (2:13): *agapē* produces the results aimed at by the Law. See W. Marxsen, 'Der *heteros nomos* Röm. 13:8', *TZ*, XI (1955), pp. 230–7.

9. Here we have a brief summary of the 'second' Decalogue (i.e. Dt. 5:16ff.), the addition 'and any other commandment' serving the purpose of 'etc.'. These summaries were well-known. The order of the commandments here follows the same tradition as at (LXX B) Dt. 5:16; Mt. 19:18; Mk 10:19, Lk. 18:20; Jas 2:11; Clem. Alex., *Strom.* vi. 16. Such summaries were no doubt useful for catechetical purposes as well as for reference. Whether any significance attaches to the use of a summary placing of the seventh Commandment first in a paraenesis on *agapē* is not certain.

Philo divides the Decalogue into two sets of five commandments, the first set being concerned with 'the divine', the second with 'the human' (*de Decal.* xxiv). It is the second set Paul is summarizing. Was this division already known to him?

in this sentence: i.e. Lev. 19:18. What is meant is that every injunction, exhortation, and whatever in the Law concerns human relationships, are all comprised in this comprehensive 'portmanteau' rule. In every human situation *vis-à-vis* others the obligation to *agapē* is paramount.

10. fulfilling of the law: the sentence in the original is ar-

---

[1] In an original Aramaic the *ei mē* would probably correspond to the adversative *'ella* (=*alla*; cf. Michel, p. 324, n. 4) and the infinitive alone, independently of the previous infinitive, implies obligation. Cf. l*e* *mahabba* (Dt. 33:3, Frag. Targ.): Owe no man anything/But love one another.

ranged in a chiastic order: subject/predicate/predicate/subject, the sentence beginning and ending with 'love'. So *NEB:* 'Love cannot wrong a neighbour; therefore the whole law is summed up in love' (*mg.:* 'or the whole law is fulfilled in love'.) 'Fulfilled' (*RSV, NEB mg.*) is better, since the word refers to the active carrying out of this commandment *usque ad finem*, while the love which is the fruit of such obedience is the whole, rich fullness of the Law.

The noun 'fulfilling' (*plērōma*) has a wide variety of associations; see above, pp. 143, 147; a close parallel to its meaning here is its use of a 'complete', 'finished' performance. Cf. Theophrastus (*Char.* xxvii. 7) of the full performance of a dramatic entertainment.

A Reminder of the Imminent Parousia 11–14

These verses echo 1 Th. 5:1–11, but there is a change of tone. In 1 Th. the tone is one of intense, almost excited, urgency; here the tone is more that of an earnest preacher, but not that of the herald of an imminent catastrophe; cf. C. H. Dodd, in *Bulletin of the John Rylands Library*, xviii (1934); 'The Mind of Paul: Change and Development', p. 69ff.; 'Gospel and Law', p. 28f.; also Selwyn, 1 *Peter*, pp. 396f.

11. Besides this you know what hour it is: cf. *NEB;* lit. 'And (do) this, knowing . . .', i.e. 'and get on with this all the more for knowing . . .'

wake from sleep: 'sleeping', 'waking', 'day', 'night', 'light', 'darkness' are familiar images in the apocalyptic eschatology, Jewish and Christian, of the period, for the passing of the 'period of wickedness' and the 'dawn' of the messianic era (Kingdom of God). Cf., e.g., Eph. 5:14, (8), 1 Th. 5:4, etc., and in Qumran (sectarian) Judaism (e.g., 1QS i. 9, ii. 16, iii. 13, 1QM i. 1, Test. Lev. xix. 1, Joseph. xx. 2, etc.).

salvation here clearly means the final 'deliverance' from evil, sin, and death, to be realized at the Parousia. Cf. 8:23–4.

12. the day is at hand: cf. Mk 1:15. Very early morning, as dawn breaks, and at sunset, are the periods of maximum activity in the East, because of the heat of the day. Thus we learn that King Agrippa I was already, along with the populace, in the theatre at dawn (Josephus, *Ant.* xix. viii. 2 (344)). It was the busiest period of the day in the Temple, as preparations were made for the daily offering; it was then the *Shema'* was recited; it was then the Essenes made their devotions, turned towards the rising sun (Josephus, *BJ*, II. viii. 5 (128)). Then was also the time for Christians to be awake and about their Lord's business. The suggestion that the words 'in the day' are intended also to convey the idea that Christians are now to behave as if the Last Day had come is somewhat far-fetched.

cast off: the metaphor is that of putting off garments. The expression in the connection and context belongs to a set of formulae evidently connected with baptism and possibly deriving from a primitive baptismal liturgy; cf. Selwyn, p. 396ff. The figure is used less frequently of the putting on of the 'armour of light', cf. 6:13, 'arms of righteousness', than of the 'donning of Christ' (or the 'new man'), e.g., Gal. 3:27; Eph. 4:24; Col. 3:9, 12.

It is possible that the imagery was first suggested by the undressing of the catechumen at baptism, and by the donning, after the ceremony, of a (white?) baptismal garment, symbolic of new life.

13. as in the day: cf. 1 Th. 5:5: Christians are 'children of the light' and 'children of the day', not 'of the night' or 'of darkness'. Lagrange detects a suggestion of the Roman idea that 'in the night everything is permissible'.

revelling and drunkenness . . . : cf. 1 Th. 5:7.

debauchery: *koitai* is morally neutral, meaning simply 'sleeping together'. It is negatively qualified by *'licentiouness'* (*aselgeiai*), evidently a frequent type of excess in the hellenistic world; it is listed and condemned at 2 C. 12:21, Gal. 5:19, 1 Th. 4:3; Eph. 4:19, 1 Pet. 4:3, 2 Pet. 2:18.

ATTITUDE TO CHRISTIANS, WEAKER IN THE FAITH **14:1–15:13**

The fellow-Christian here is the Jewish Christian still harbouring legalistic scruples about feast-days or food, and still, no doubt, finding it difficult to accept Gentile participation in the Gospel (cf. A. George, *Les Écritures, Source de l'Esperance* (*Romains* 15:1–6), *Bible et Vie Chrétienne*, XXII (1958), pp. 54ff.). These are the 'weaker brethren'; Paul identifies himself with the 'strong', those able to exercise their Christian freedom, but he pleads for a charitable exercise of it. The argument is that it is the same Lord with whom we all have to do, and it is to Him each must give account. We are not, then, to sit in judgement on our brother, but rather to make up our minds not to place a stumbling-block in his path; and

this we do if we give offence to a 'weaker' brother for whom
'clean' and 'unclean' are still questions of conscience.

1. weak in faith: for this kind of debility or impotence, cf.
4:20, where it is also contrasted with strength and vigour (cf.
below 15:1). Cf. also 2 C. 12:10, 13:9.

welcome: *NEB*: 'accept'. The word is used in the papyri of
'receiving' into a household (once of 'accepting' for the army).
See MM, s.v. Here it is not only receiving fellow-Christians with
a 'weak' faith into the household of faith, but taking them as
full partners. Cf. verse 3 of God's acceptance of all such; 15:7,
Christ's acceptance. Cf. also Phm. 17.

for disputes over opinions: *NEB*: 'attempts to settle doubtful
points' (*diakriseis*, 'resolvings (by judgement)'; *dialogismoi*, 'con-
troversies'). Paul is here recommending unconditional acceptance
of the 'weaker' brethren into the 'fellowship' (including 'table
fellowship'); even arguments about Christian freedom are not to
be allowed to jeopardise the brotherly relationship of *agapē*.

2. vegetables: cf. verse 21. The controversy evidently had to
do with eating meat. Were these people the ancestors of the later
Encratite heretics? Cf. also 1 Tim. 4:3ff., where these *abstinentes*,
like their Marcionite descendants, abstained from marriage as
well; see, further, note at verse 21.

3. despise: *NEB:* 'hold in contempt'.

welcomed: cf. above, verse 1. 'God has taken him into his
household (*familia dei*)' (Michel). The same argument is repeated
with reference to Christ at 15:7. The figure of speech is con-
firmed by the use of 'household servant' at verse 4.

4. the servant of another: i.e. of Christ.

stands or falls: the household servant (note that he is *oiketēs*, not
doulos) is responsible only to the *pater familias*, his master; so is
the Christian to his Lord. There is also the meaning that whether
a Christian 'weak in faith' is adjudged worthy or unworthy is a
matter between himself and his Master only; he may well have
compensating qualities which the 'strong in faith' in this connection lack.

is able: better, *NEB*: 'has power to enable', used also of God at
2 C. 9:8 and of Christ at 2 C. 13:3.

5. esteems one day as better than another: clearly in
addition to food laws—and evidently connected with these—
there were differences about festival days. These could be about

Jewish festivals, or differences relating to the transition from the observance of the Sabbath to the Lord's Day. The controversy could also have been connected with fasting on feast-days. Belief in 'lucky' (good) and 'unlucky' (bad) days was also prevalent.

6. in honour of the Lord: the dative (*tō Kuriō*) may have the force given by the *NEB:* 'has the Lord in mind'; both senses are possible. Such 'days' were days of special thanksgiving; even he who fails to keep such a day, if he does it with a good conscience, in the name of Christian liberty, is giving thanks to God.

gives thanks to God: Is there an implied allusion to grace before meat?

EQUALITY BEFORE GOD 7–12

Like other similar passages in Paul, this gem of Christian teaching, where an argument is built up to a doctrinal climax by literary features such as balance of clauses (negative, then positive) and by polar opposites—life, death, embracing all attitudes in life— the whole clinched from Scripture, arises in the course of the discussion of a long-forgotten controversy in the Roman Church on clean and unclean foods, the observance of Sabbaths, feast-days, etc. For the 'hymnic' style, cf. 2 Tim. 2:11–13.

7–8. None of us lives to himself . . .: Cf. D. M. Baillie, *God Was in Christ* (London, ²1956), pp. 204ff.: '. . . the very essence of sin is self-centredness.' Behind St Paul's proverbial and Hebraic *sententia* lies the hellenistic as well as, no doubt, Jewish reflection. Terence sees the dangers of self-sufficiency (*Adelphoe*, v. iv. 9) and Plutarch (*Vita Cleom.*, 31) declares that it is 'a disgraceful thing to live and to die for ourselves alone'. The problem is to find an alternative to self-centred living.

8. to the Lord . . . so then . . . we are the Lord's: we only live and die, Paul declares, 'for the Lord' (dat. of advantage), or 'before the Lord', and therefore responsible alone 'to the Lord, the reason being that we belong to the Lord; we are his servants' (verse 4; cf. 1 C. 6:19f.).

9. lived again: *NEB:* 'came to life again' (the oldest reading). Christ's death and resurrection alone establish his right to be Lord of the living and the dead.

10. Judgement belongs to the Lord. Christians have enough to do minding their proper business.

judgment seat of God: the variant 'Christ' is explained as due

to the influence of 2 C. 5:10. Origen noted that Paul wrote 'God'
to the Romans, but 'Christ' to the Corinthians. Sanday argues that
God is here mentioned as Judge because He judges the world
through Christ.

11. As I live, says the Lord: there are two salient features
in the Pauline 'quotation' of Isa. 45:23 which owe nothing to the
LXX or MT: (a) the asseverative formula prefacing the
quotation, 'As I live', probably derived from Isa. 49:18, which
is introduced by St Paul, not just as a formula of asseveration (an
'honest to God!'), but with the clear intention of identifying 'the
Lord' in the quotation with the Lord Christ who 'lived again'
(verse 9; lit. 'came alive', i.e. rose from the dead), and is the
Lord both of the dead and the living (verse 9). It is to the Risen
and Living Lord that every knee shall bow; (b) the second part
of the quotation should be rendered: 'and every tongue shall praise
God'—universal worship of the Risen Lord is to be accompanied
by universal thanksgiving to God. (On the basis of the Pauline
exegesis of Isa. 45:23, see the present writer's article 'The
Christological Use of the Old Testament in the New Testament',
in *NTS*, xviii (1971–2), p. 8.)
give praise to God: *mg.* 'confess', i.e. to acknowledge God (so
NEB); it is also suggested that the *testimonium* Isa. 45:23 was
understood as 'will confess (me) as God'. Cf. Phil. 2:10–11. Perhaps SH are right in rejecting this line of interpretation (taking
'God' of Christ in his divine nature), on the grounds that it is
contrary to Pauline usage (cf. however, Heb. 1:8). It is, however,
very important to see how easily St Paul passes from Christ to
God; cf. SH, p. 389. It is also possible to understand 'sins', and
interpret: 'confess (their sins) before God'; cf. Mk 1:5. The
rendering 'give praise to' is, however, clearly preferable.

12. to God: The omission of these words by mss. like 1739, G,
B, and the early Fathers might possibly be explained as neces-
sitated by reading 'Christ' at verse 10; it could also, however, be
an addition dictated by the change from 'Christ' to 'God' there;
cf. J. Hugh Michael, in *JTS*, xxxix (1938), p. 154.

THE RULE OF LOVE 13–23

13. decide: the same Greek word as for 'pass judgement'
(*krinein*). Cf. Mt. 7:1.
stumbling block or hindrance: both words are typical, and

when combined give a characteristically Biblical locution. The messianic use of the expression is quite independent of the usage here or in parallel passages, e.g. at 1 C. 8:9. Cf. Hermas, *Mand.* ii. 4, where 'religiosity' (*semnotēs*) of a kind different from that discussed here is the stumbling-block.

14. I know and am persuaded in the Lord Jesus: Paul gives the fullest possible apostolic emphasis to his conviction. Is he thinking of the dominical teaching at Mt. 15:11, Mk 7:15? First, the general principle of Christian 'freedom' is thus categorically laid down; then follows the qualification: it is better to tolerate another's prejudices than to advocate the truth at the expense of a breach of *agapē*. Cf. 1 C. 8:7-13.[1]

15. is being injured: *NEB*: 'is outraged'; the literal rendering, 'is pained', is as adequate as any. It is the grief and pain caused by outraged feelings Paul is stressing as a breach of charity. **walking in love:** better, *NEB*: 'guided by love' (lit. '(is no longer) walking *according* to love'). Cf. Eph. 5:2; lit. 'walking in love'. *Agapē* provides the standard of Christian conduct; it is also the inner disposition of the Christian believer.

for whom Christ died: that Christ died for mankind is the core of Paul's Gospel (cf. 5:6, 8). The repetition of this 'advice' here in the same terms as at 1 C. 8:11 may indicate that Paul used this stereotyped expression regularly in this connection. The solemn form the injunction takes shows how seriously the apostle regarded any breach of charity of this kind. By giving such offence, or in leading a 'weaker' brother astray, when his conscience was still troubled by such things (cf. 1 C. 8:10), the 'strong' Christian believer was undoing the work of Christ—destroying one whom Christ had saved.

16. spoken of as evil: a strong verb in Greek; lit. 'be something men curse'.

17. For the kingdom of God: Paul has several 'Kingdom of God' sayings, mostly bearing the character of general truths, e.g. 1 C. 4:20; 15:50; Gal. 5:21 (in the later two cases it is conceived as a kind of inheritance). 'Kingdom of God' is virtually here *regula dei* (like *regula fidei*), as in the rabbinical idea of taking on oneself the 'yoke' of the *malkuth* of God. In other words, it is here a spiritual absolute, though naturally also eschatologically

[1] For a useful discussion of the problems of this verse (and section), cf. O. E. Evans, 'What God requires of man', *ET*, LXIX (1957-8), pp. 199-202.

conceived; the righteousness, peace, and joy are the righteousness, peace, and joy of faith.

joy in the Holy Spirit: it is best to take the last phrase as defining 'joy'. Joy is the outward manifestation of the Spirit; cf. 1 Th. 1:6, Gal. 5:22, Ac. 13:52.

18. he who thus serves Christ: or, 'he who in this (Holy Spirit) serves Christ'. Probably to be understood, as *RSV*, more generally: he who serves Christ also by 'righteousness, peace and joy in the Holy Spirit', rather than by insisting that God's rule refers to kosher distinctions, or by uncharitably claiming that it does not—he is well-pleasing to God, and approved by men. 'This principle cuts both ways, for it hits Jewish-Christian kosher-complexes as hard as the freedom of the enlightened' (T. W. Manson).

19. peace: the phrase and ideal is a characteristically Hebrew one (see SB, 1, pp. 215ff.) which passed into Christianity (in a similar sense, Heb. 12:14, 1 Pet. 3:11, Rom. 12:18).

mutual upbuilding: peace is the foundation of any community's strength. The ideal of community, 'compactly built together' by the Gospel and its exponents (through word and life), is a central Pauline thought, especially in the Corinthian correspondence (1 C. 14:3, 5, 12, 26; 2 C. 12:19, 13:10). That *oikodomē* ('upbuilding') here means, correctly, the *ecclesia Christi* is argued by E. Peterson, in *Bib.*, xxii (1941), p. 441.

20. work of God: 20*a* corresponds to 15*b*; Cf. 1 C. 8:11: 'Do not let what you eat cause the ruin of one for whom Christ died.' The 'work of God' could conceivably refer to the individual man as 'the noblest work of God', or refer to the 'community' which has been built up. Other commentators, e.g. Michel, *ad loc.*, tend to interpret it, in line with verse 15*b*, of the 'work of Christ', in his death, resurrection, etc.

it is wrong: the general sense is that 'all things are pure'; cf. Mt. 15:11. Nevertheless, it is no good thing—indeed the very opposite, a wicked thing (*kakon*)—for anyone to give offence by his 'freedom' in eating anything set before him.

21. it is right not to eat meat or drink wine: abstention from meat and/or wine was a not unfamiliar feature of ancient ascetic practices; cf. the Rechabites in the *OT*, e.g. Dan. 10:3. The latter reminds us of the practices of the Egyptian *Therapeutai* (Philo, *Vita Contempl.* 37) and possibly also the Essenes. Judaism was probably not uninfluenced in this connection by Pythagorean (Orphic) practices (cf. Philostratus, *Vita Apollonii* 18, where wine is not in the category of things ceremonially impure, but condemned because it impairs the mind and disturbs the mystical union with the gods).

Was there an ascetic Jewish-Christian group in Rome, or was wine objected to as having been 'dedicated' by a libation to a pagan deity (Michel), like the 'meat offered to idols' (1 C. 8)? The probability is that there was a stricter group of *abstinentes* in the Roman church, abstaining from meat and wine, if only as a protest against pagan excesses.

your brother stumble states the principle of Paul's own conduct, enunciated at 1 C. 8:13.

Mg., 'be upset' or 'be weakened'. The longer text is not badly attested (B, D, G), but finds only a few supporters. For the conjecture: 'not even one thing by which your brother stumbles' (*mēde hen hō* (Hoffmann), *hen, en* (Mangey), see Michel.

22–3 state certain conclusions; cf. 14:2. An alternative text would read: 'Do you have (this) faith? Then keep it to yourself and God.' The 'faith' in question is the liberal doctrine that 'all things are pure'.

happy is he . . .: The translation is very obscure. Paul is stating, sententiously, as *NEB mg.* rightly renders: 'Happy is the man who does not bring judgement upon himself by what he approves.' The liberal-minded Christian approves of non-discrimination in food and drink; but if this attitude leads a brother into trouble, then such a Christian does bring judgement on himself. T. W. Manson: 'Happy he who does not condemn himself by what he approves (or when he puts himself to the test)'. cf. John Oman: 'Man is known not by what he has but by what he reverences.'

23. But he who has doubts: T. W. Manson: 'He who wavers in his opinion is self-condemned, if he eats (regardless of tabu).' 'Faith' here is (Christian) conviction. The doing of anything, such as eating non-kosher food, is sinful if it does not proceed from the conviction that 'all things are clean' since such a man is doing what he is still inwardly convinced is wrong. See, further, R. Aroud, 'Quidquid non est ex fide peccatum est (Rom. 14, 23)', *Mélanges H. de Lubac* (Editions Montaigne, 1964, 2 vols).

On the position after verse 23 of the Doxology at 16:25–7, see Introduction, p. 26ff.

THE ACTION OF LOVE 15:1-13

There is no sense division between 14:23 and 15:1; the chapter division has been determined by a rule of thumb without taking account of the contents.[1]

Verses 1-13 represent the third section of St Paul's exhortation on Christian 'freedom', or the relation of the 'strong' to the 'weak' about ritual matters. Verses 1-6 and 7-13 are to a certain extent parallel in thought, both concluding with a prayer (verses 5-7, 13): common to both is the reference to the lowly service of Christ in the interest of the 'upbuilding' (*oikodomē*) of the Christian community. The liturgical character of the second section is more marked; teaching, exhortation, and doxology are all present.

1. bear with the failings of the weak: the reference is probably more general now, namely to Jewish Christians whose 'weaknesses' the emancipated Christian must 'bear'. Earlier the 'strong' have been exhorted not to lead the 'weak' astray; now, more positively, Paul enjoins them to adopt the attitude of the Isaianic servant which was also Christ's, to 'bear' (i.e. tolerate in charity) these immature Christians. There seems to be an unmistakable allusion in these words, 'bear', 'weaknesses', to the Christian's duty as a 'servant of the Lord' outlined at Isa. 53:4 (cited at Mt. 8:17).

2. please his neighbour: contrasted with self-pleasing; cf. verse 3. Christ did not 'please himself'; the phrase is virtually synonymous with 'living for oneself' (cf. 14:7). Its opposite is stated at 1 Th. 2:4: 'pleasing God'. Cf. 1 C. 10:33 for St Paul's own attitude: 'I try to please all men in everything I do'—the context is a similar one. There is an indirect allusion to the obligation of Lev. 19:18. Cf. earlier at 14:19; all is for the good of the congregation.

3-6. Verse 3 recalls, not only the attitude of the Servant-Christ, but his long-suffering, forbearance and fortitude; the same qualities are enjoined on the Christian (verse 4)—and they are also the attributes of God Himself (verse 5). Paul frequently uses the same or similar expressions of God and Christ.

---

[1] On the last two chapters, consult especially R. Schumacher, 'Die beiden letzten Kapitel des Römerbriefes', *Neutest. Abhandlungen*, XIV. iv; C. H. Turner, in *JTS*, x (1909), pp. 365ff. Cf. also J. B. Lightfoot, *Biblical Essays* (London, 1893), pp. 285-374.

3. reproaches: Ps. 69 was evidently widely used as a Christo-logical *testimonium* in the early Church (cf. Rom. 11:9-10, Ac. 1:20, Jn 2:17, 15:25, Lk. 12:50, Mk 15:36). The insults directed at God, the Psalmist believed had fallen upon himself; likewise Jesus bore men's reproaching of God.

4. for our instruction: cf. Rom. 4:24, 1 C. 9:10, and especially 1 C. 10:11. This is the purpose of Scripture. The formulae here used belong to an *OT* and rabbinical type; cf. Bruce Metzger, 'The Formulas Introducing Quotations of Scripture in the New Testament and the Mishnah', *JBL*, LXX (1951), p. 297ff.

steadfastness: *NEB:* 'fortitude', i.e. following the example of the patience and long-suffering of Christ Himself. The sense is that Scripture is there in order to enable us to maintain our Christian hope with Christ-like patience, encouraged by its words.

encouragement: the encouragement comes from the Scriptures, but it is only because they speak of Christ. The Scripture which is prophecy of Christ is also precept for us. Cf. 1 C. 10:11 and Wrede, *Paul*, p. 80; also J. Hugh Michael, in *JTS*, XXXIX (1938), p. 154. Michael suggests that the first 'through patience and comfort of the scriptures' should be omitted; it erroneously repeats (by vertical dittography) the same phrase at verse 4. Cf. 1:17 above, p. 46.

5. to live in such harmony . . .: *NEB:* 'that you agree with one another'. The Greek phrase is the same as at Phil. 2:5: 'Let that *mind* be in you that was also in Christ'; for the expression, cf. Rom. 12:16, 2 C. 13:11, Phil. 2:2, 4:2. The petitionary prayer is that God should create in them the same outlook as Christ had—the same spirit. At 2 C. 13:11, the expression is followed by: 'be at peace (with one another)' (*eirēneuete*).

with one another: i.e. with both groups—liberals and conserva-tives, 'Jews' and 'Gentiles', 'formalists', 'ritualists' and the advocates of 'freedom'. Only such unity of spirit can lead to common thanksgiving.

7. welcomed you: *NEB:* 'accepted'. Cf. 14:1, 3, but here of both sides 'accepting' one another, including, no doubt, wel-coming one another to common meals. If these had been inter-rupted or ceased, then the reference could be to the 'acceptance' of each other once more, in a new beginning at the Lord's Table. Christ had 'accepted' them, the unacceptable; He had even died for sinners (5:6; 14:15); also He had 'received' them into His Body, the Church (Eph. 2:13).

8. servant to the circumcised: cf. Gal. 4:4; Wrede, *Paul*, p. 160. The Servant of the Lord as regards his own people, but also to show the 'reliability', 'trustworthiness', of God.

confirm: i.e. to 'realize' the promises made to the Fathers, yet also to enable the Gentiles to glorify God for His mercy, as is written, etc.

9-13. There follows a *catena* of *OT* verses (cf. *supra*, p. 64, and SH, p. 77). They are Ps. 18:49 (2 Sam. 22:50), Dt. 32:43, Ps. 117:1, Isa. 11:10. It is Paul's usual way of clinching his argument by invoking the authority of Scripture, here using a conventional form of Scripture quotation.

The verses not only sum up the conclusion of the argument between Jewish and Gentile Christian, but also the main theme and purpose of Romans—the furthering of the *Gentile* mission of the Apostle to the Gentiles.

13. Schumacher (p. 67) remarks that the main subject matter of the epistle in its teaching and exhortation is concluded in this closing petition invoking the divine blessing. We have here to think of Paul pausing momentarily in his dictation to utter this heartfelt petition.

Paul ends his Christian 'instruction' to the Romans by stressing Christian hope, though not in isolation from faith and the other 'fruits of the spirit': 'peace and joy', 'joy and peace' are closely associated (cf. above, 14:17, and Gal. 5:22)—they are specially emphasized in a situation where the Christian fellowship had evidently been disrupted by the tensions between the 'strong' and the 'weak' parties.

in believing: so far from these words being a gloss (cf. Michel, *in loc.*) they recall the central theme of the Epistle. Faith is the way into the kingdom of joy and peace.

so that by the power of the Holy Spirit you may abound in hope: an alternative is to translate: 'so that you may abound in hope—all in the power of the Holy Spirit', the latter referring, not only to hope, but to joy and peace in which we also abound 'by the power of the Holy Spirit'.

THE CONCLUSION OF THE EPISTLE 15:14-16:27

PERSONAL: THE APOSTLE'S PLANS 14-33

The Roman letter is concluded by a personal section which
corresponds to the personal introduction at 1:8-17, to a degree
suggesting to some point by point correspondence (Michel, *in loc.*).
(These two 'personal' portions bracket the main epistle.) Paul
returns to his plans to visit Rome: that he had a firm intention to
do so *deo volente* (cf. 15:32f.) is clear from 1:10 and 15:22-4. He
repeats in this closing personal part his duty and obligations as
Apostle to the Gentiles (1:5, 14ff., cf. 15:15-16), stressing again
his apostolic office and authority. Verses 22-3 outline his travel
plans after his forthcoming visit to Jerusalem: 30-3 remind the
reader of the extreme dangers of this visit (cf. Introduction, p. 20).
Cf. J. Knox, 'Rom. 15:14-33 and Paul's Conception of his
Apostolic Mission', *JBL*, LXXXIII (1964), pp. 1-11.

14. I myself: or, 'I too (as well as others)'. The emphasis,
'even I, myself', suggests that Paul did not expect to be believed
that he could have such a high regard for the virtues of the Roman
Church. 'I am convinced; yes, indeed, I am.' No doubt his
hearers believed he had been influenced against them.

goodness ... knowledge: no doubt terms inclusive of all the
Christian virtues and qualities of the Roman Church. The choice
of words suggests that Paul sets out to compliment the Roman
Church on its Christian virtues, but also on its Christian 'knowledge', i.e. its mature Christian wisdom requiring no help from
any outside source. 'Goodness' can only be understood of moral
qualities (but cf. Michel); for the noun, cf. Gal. 5:22, Eph. 5:9,
2 Th. 1:11. The choice of 'goodness' suggests that Paul deliberately selects a vague, general term. The object of these compli-
mentary references is now, as at chapter 1, to prevent the hearers
from taking offence.

15. on some points: *NEB:* 'at times', i.e. in some of his
arguments or modes of expression he had been more than bold.
very boldly: lit. 'rather boldly', i.e. much too boldly. Though
not the founder of the Roman Church, Paul can write to them
'much too boldly', only by virtue of his apostleship 'of grace' to
the Gentiles.
by way of reminder: Paul again strikes an apologetic note;

he had nothing to teach the Roman Church they did not already know.

grace given me by God: cf. Gal. 1:16.

16. offering of the Gentiles: the Gentile Christians are the 'offering', and Paul is the priest who offers them to God; cf. Phil. 2:17, where Paul adds the thought of pouring out his blood (life) as the libation accompanying the offering. Cf. Isa. 66:20, where the Diaspora Jews are the 'offering' (*minḥā*) which the Gentiles will bring to Jerusalem (SB, III, p. 153).

The 'offering' of the Gentiles is necessarily unclean; but it is cleansed and sanctified by the Holy Spirit, and so 'well-pleasing' to God. Is Paul thinking of the Christian's baptism?

in the priestly service: *hierourgein* means 'to exercise priestly functions'; cf. 1:9 and 12:1f. Cf. C. Wiéner, '*Hierourgein* (Rom. 15:16)', in *Stud. Paulin. Congressus*, 1961, II (Rome, 1963), pp. 399–404.

17. In Christ Jesus, then, I have reason to be proud: Paul boasts of the success of his apostolic mission from vv. 17–21, but his 'boasting' is 'in Christ Jesus'. He boasts of what Christ and the Holy Spirit have accomplished in word and deed, through his ministry.

18. to win obedience from the Gentiles: the main purpose of the Epistle to the Romans. Cf. 1:5.

19. by the power of signs and wonders . . . : a further explication of 'word and deed' (verse 18). These 'signs and wonders' and 'power of the Spirit' were the marks of an apostle (cf. 2 C. 12:12, Heb. 2:4). Note the chiastic arrangement: word, deed; signs, etc.; spiritual power. The 'signs' are wrought by the apostles; it is the Spirit who inspires the Word.

Paul was only interested in reaching the unevangelized portions of the Levant, and repeats his earlier principle of not entering the 'territory' of another (cf. 1 C. 3:10).

Illyricum: the 'inclusive' geography (from Jerusalem to the edge of the Roman world) is not mentioned simply to supply grounds for St Paul's 'boasting'. It may have been less ambition than eschatology which determined this representative area, just as it was the apostle's desire to preach the Gospel 'to the ends of the earth' which motivated his planned visit to Spain (cf., especially, J. Munck, *Paul and the Salvation of Mankind*, trans. F. Clarke (London, 1959), esp. p. 51ff.).

Illyricum was an extensive Roman Province stretching along
the Adriatic from Italy and Pannonia in the North to Macedonia
in the South.

fully preached the gospel of Christ: cf. Col. 1:25 (*AV:* 'to
fulfil the word of God'). We are possibly dealing with a familiar
expression (so Michel), but one not necessarily meaning the same
in every context. Could it mean here that Paul's boast was that he
had 'filled the whole of the Mediterranean East with the Gospel
of the Messiah' (obj. gen.)? *NEB* is probably correct: 'I have
completed the preaching of the Gospel of Christ from Jerusalem
as far as Illyricum.' Cf., further, A. S. Geyser, 'Un Essai d'Explication de Rom. 15:19', *NTS*, VI (1959–60), pp. 156–9.

20–21. In customary fashion, Paul concludes this argument by
a Scriptural quotation (Isa. 52:15), singling out for special
emphasis the thought of the previous verse—Paul's policy of not
entering the 'territory' of others.

21. who have never been told of him: The quotation
originally referred to the Servant of the Lord; now it is applied to
Christ as the Lord's Servant-Messiah; cf. 10:16 (Isa. 53:1). Paul
is a missionary of the Servant-Messiah to the world, which, till his
kērygma, had neither sight nor hearing of such a one.

PAUL'S PLANS TO VISIT ROME **22–3:**

These verses read very much like an ordinary, non-literary, personal
letter of the period: the style is simple, paratactic, and parent-
hetical.

22. hindered: a familiar word in Paul (e.g. 1 Th. 2:18,
Gal. 5:7) for any let or hindrance from human or other agency.
Is there any suggestion that obstacles had been placed in the
apostle's way to any visit to Rome, on the grounds that it was the
province of other 'apostles'? (Perhaps Paul considered Rome big
enough for all?) The whole passage assumes a sensitive awareness
to the possibility that he might be considered an intruder. He is
careful to emphasise that it is only a visit in passing on the way to
Spain, and is not 'trespassing' on the preserves of others.

24. Spain: the Pillars of Hercules marked the limits of the
oikoumenē. Paul's plan is eschatologically conceived: the Gospel
must first be preached 'to the ends of the earth' before the End
comes (see note above, p. 175).

At the same time, that there is nothing to suggest, however,

that Paul's plans were not real ones: Spain was frequently visited
from Rome (Pausanias, *Hell. Peri.*, x.iv.6, *CIL* II, no. 1982 (p. 268):
cf. Cicero, *Tusc.*, i.45; the tourist centre was Gades, site of the
famous Temple of Melkart, the Phoenician Hercules). Ac. 19:21ff.
confirms the plans of the Apostle outlined here; Rome was a
populous centre of the Roman Empire, and there were probably
several active synagogues there (Schürer, II. ii, p. 242).

to be sped on my journey: i.e. not only to be given an encouraging farewell, but no doubt also direction, and means, and
letters of introduction; cf. Ac. 20:38, 21:5. The phrase was
probably a polite formality in current speech (1 C. 16:6; 2 C.
1:16). Dodd, *ad loc.*; SH, p. 411.

enjoyed your company for a little: i.e. 'had some satisfaction
out of my visit to you', implying that more of their company
would have been even better—again, probably a familiar polite
locution in current use.

25. with aid for the saints: or, 'in order to be of service to'.
Cf. J. J. O'Rourke, 'The Participle in Rom. 15:25', in *CBQ*, xxix,
Vol. 29 (1967), pp. 116–18.

26. have been pleased to make: i.e. have freely decided for
themselves that it was, after all, no more than their duty. Note the
emphatic repetition of this at verse 27: Paul clearly wishes to
emphasise that this is no Jewish-Christian 'tax', like those payable
by Diaspora synagogues to the Temple, but a freely offered
contribution.

the poor among the saints: *NEB:* 'the poor among God's
people'. The genitive is partitive, so that the 'poor' here are the
physically poor; i.e. the term can hardly be understood here as a
terminus technicus for the Jerusalem congregation (cf. Michel, *ad
loc.*). Cf., however, Gal. 2:10 and, for 'poor' in this specialized
sense (applied also to the Qumran sectarians), see Kittel, *TWNT*,
s.v. Is Paul here recalling this familiar appelation while reminding
his readers that it was also literally true? For 'saints' as a *terminus
technicus*, see note on 1:7.

30. to strive together ... prayers: lit. 'to agonize together
with me'. For prayer as an 'agonizing', 'wrestling' with God, cf.
Col. 4:12; the image no doubt could go back to Gen. 32:24ff.
(Jacob). Others think of the struggle being against evil or opposing powers (SH); cf. Mt. 26:42 par. Cf. Col. 4:12 for the thought
of a 'shared striving' in prayer.

31. delivered from: especially of physical danger. Used by Paul again at 2 Th. 3:2; cf. Mt. 6:13 of spiritual deliverance.
unbelievers: the chief danger, the hostile Jews who rejected the faith of Christ. The participle 'those who are unbelieving' suggest an active disbelief.
my service: *diakonia*. A variant, *dōrophoria* ('gift-bringing') occurs in the Western text; it has the overtones of 'oblation', but is clearly secondary.

If Paul could be certain of the attitude of the 'unbelieving Jews', one would have expected that he would not be uncertain about the friendly reception of the Jerusalem Christians. But they were probably as suspicious of a Gentile mission as were the Jews, so that Paul cannot even be certain that his 'collection' from the Gentile churches would be acceptable. Cf. Ac. 21:21.

32. be refreshed in your company: i.e. enjoy a kind of spiritual holiday after Jerusalem.

A PERSONAL NOTE 16:1–27

For the problem of the connection of chapter 16 with the rest of the Epistle, see Introduction, p. 26ff. The lists of studies by Lightfoot (*Philippians*, p. 172ff.) and SH are still the most comprehensive.

PERSONAL GREETING 16:1–16

1. Phoebe is usually considered to have been the bearer of the letter. If this is a separate letter, it could almost be classed as a letter of recommendation (as common then as now, cf. 2 C. 3:1); even as it is, as part of Romans, it serves this purpose. The Christian lady in question appears to have been a Greek Gentile Christian (a Jew would scarcely have such a name), probably of some social standing or influence, for she is described as a *prostatis*, or *patrona* (cf. Schürer). This would seem originally to have designated an officially recognized person who had to deal with the rights of 'aliens' and freed slaves. Here the sense may be a general one; the Roman Christians are asked to 'stand by' her ('help her'), as she has 'stood by and for' many, including the apostle himself—possibly in some legal matter; see note on verse 2. As a 'deaconess' (cf. 1 Tim. 3:11), she had also an official function in the congregation at Cenchreae, the port of Corinth. This seems the only *NT* reference to a deaconess. It has been conjectured that

Phoebe's duties were concerned especially with women, the sick
or 'aliens', or with assisting women at baptism, but there is very
little foundation for these speculations. Cf. further, C. H. Turner,
in *The Ministry of Women* (London, 1919), p. 93ff., M. D. Gibson,
'Phoebe', *ET*, xxiii (1911–12), p. 281, C. C. Ryrie, *The Place of
Women in the Church* (New York, 1958), pp. 86ff.

2. receive her in the Lord as befits the saints: i.e. 'give
her a Christian welcome', 'welcome her *christiano more*' (Bengel);
'in the Lord', the phrase occurs again at 11b, 12, 13. All that
Christians are or do is *en kyriō* ('in the Lord'), especially their
heavy labours for others (e.g. 12: 'those that labour in the Lord'—
the verb is a strong one).

help . . . in whatever she may require from you: lit. 'in any
affair where she may need you'. The word for 'help' seems to
imply the kind of help a *prostatis*, or patron, could give, possibly
legal aid ('affair' may have this meaning), i.e. assistance, especially
that rendered to aliens entering a country, and particularly
Jewish aliens. This may well have been the kind of 'assistance' Paul
himself had received from Phoebe at Cenchreae when he arrived.

greet: the verb (*aspazesthai*) is repeated fifteen times in this
'greetings' section.

3. Prisca and Aquila: the Jewish Christian couple Paul met
in Corinth (cf. Ac. 18:2, 26). The order of the names—wife first—
is striking: it occurs again at 2 Tim. 4:19; cf., however, 1 C. 16:19
and Ac. 18:2 (Aquila-Priscilla), 18:26 (Priscilla-Aquila). (The
diminutive form 'Priscilla' occurs only in Acts.) They had
been refugees in Corinth after the publication of the Edict of
Claudius in A.D. 52. They accompanied Paul from Corinth to
Ephesus, where evidently they had a residence, like the residence
which they had left in Rome, where the local Christian community met (1 C. 16:19; cf. Rom. 16:5). At 2 Tim. 4:19 they
appear again in Ephesus. (But cf. Introd., p. 27.) The position of
Priscilla *vis-à-vis* Aquila may be explained on the grounds that she
was a wealthy Jewish-Christian matron in her own right, able
to act as hostess to the Church in these two centres.

If Hort is right in suggestion that Prisca (Priscilla) was a member
of a high-born Roman family, this might account for the order;
SH thinks they were both 'freed-men'. Aquila came from Pontus
in Asia Minor (Ac. 18:1, 2). Their connection with the Roman
Church seems probable (SH). The site of their 'house church' in

Rome is pointed out at the Church of Ss Aquila and Prisca on the
Aventine, but the identification does not bear closer examination.
There is also a legendary tenth-century *Acts of Prisca* (perhaps
significantly named as the leading partner); see, further, SH,
pp. 418–420.

4. risked their necks: a current Greek idiom (probably
colloquial). See A. Deissmann, *Light from the Ancient East*, pp.
119ff. Is this a reference to a definite incident such as might have
happened during the 'riots at Ephesus' (Ac. 18)?
all the churches: the service of this devoted couple to the ex-
panding Church must, indeed, have been great.

5. church in their house: 5*a* goes with verse 3: the greeting
to Priscilla and Aquila includes their house-church. In the first
two centuries the Church had no buildings of its own, but met in
private houses, usually of a well-to-do family (or widow)—cf.
Ac. 12:12; 1 C. 16:19; Col. 4:15; Phm. 2. Cf. also Clement,
Recogn. x.71.

It has been suggested that the persons greeted in verses 3–16
were members of the 'house-congregation' of Priscilla and Aquila.
This would certainly account for Paul's knowing so many Roman
Christians since this 'house-church' may have moved from Rome
to Ephesus in A.D. 52.

**my beloved Epaenetus, who was the first convert in Asia
for Christ:** a literal and correct translation, but concealing the
cultic metaphor of 'first-fruits', the first offering of the harvest,
perhaps conferring on Epaenetus a position of special honour
in the community. Cf. Clement, *Ad Cor. Ep. I* xlii. 4, where
these 'first-fruits' become the earliest church leaders, bishop,
deacons.

Clearly a Greek (the name is common), he may have belonged
to the household of Priscilla, and have been their first convert in
Ephesus. The adjective 'beloved' does not necessarily imply that
Paul had a specially warm personal affection for him (cf. verses 8,
9, 12): the term appears as a general epithet for Christians who
were well-liked.

6. Mary, who has worked hard among you: from the name,
possibly, but not certainly, a Jewish-Christian, unless we read
(with P^{46}, ℵ, etc.) Miriam. Four women in this chapter are said
to have 'laboured' for the Roman congregation; it was a 'Christian
work' ('in the Lord'); cf. v.12. Were they official deaconesses?

7. Andronicus and Junias ...: possibly, from their names, freed-men, but clearly Jews by birth. Did some or all of the persons greeted on this list belong to 'Caesar's household'? Cf. SH, *ad loc.* Cf. also Phil. 4:22.

my fellow prisoners: in either a literal or a metaphorical sense. Cf. Col. 4:10, Phm. 23. It seems more likely that Paul meant this literally, though when and where Andronicus and Junias were in prison with him it is impossible to say (cf. 2 C. 11:23). Schlatter (*Gerechtigkeit*, p. 399) thinks the time referred to was when, along with Paul, they belonged to the Antioch congregation; their conversion (older than Paul's) and description as 'distinguished among missionaries' require us to make such an assumption. What evidence, however, is there of imprisonment in this period?

they are men of note among the apostles: i.e. 'themselves distinguished missionaries'.

they were in Christ before me: the perfect tense (*gegonasin*) implies that they still are.

8–9. Ampliatus and **Urbanus** are common names in themselves, but are also found in lists of the imperial household (Lightfoot, *loc. cit.*).

Stachys is a comparatively rare name but attested, and at least one person with this name held important office in the imperial court in St Paul's time (Lightfoot, *loc. cit.*).

10. Apelles: also a name associated with the Roman court (SH). It was also the name of a well-known tragic actor, a native of Ascalon, favoured by the Emperor Gaius.

those who belong to the family of Aristobulus: probably slaves and/or freedmen. Aristobulus was possibly the person of this name who was a grandson of Herod the Great and brother of Agrippa I, who ended his life, as a private individual, in Rome (see Lightfoot, *op. cit.*, and Josephus, *BJ*, II.xi.6 (221–2); *Antiq.* xx.i.2(13). On his death, which probably preceded the writing of Romans, it is likely that, in accordance with established practice, Aristobulus's household was taken over by the Emperor Claudius, of whom Aristobulus appears to have been a friend and adherent. Paul's phrase corresponds to *Aristobuliani;* no doubt such a household would be mainly composed of Jews; **Herodion,** next to be mentioned as a fellow-kinsman (i.e. a Jew), bore a name which one would expect among slaves or freedmen of the Herodian class. (The conjecture that it was this high-born Aristobulos who is here referred to is described by S. Sandmel (*Interpreter's Dictionary of the Bible* (1962), s.v. Herod, p. 593) as far-fetched.)

It was obviously through such 'households', where Jews, and later Jewish Christians, were numerous and influential, that the Gospel penetrated into the higher echelons of Roman imperial society.

11. my kinsman Herodion: obviously a member, probably a freedman, of the Herod family, clearly unconnected with the preceding *Aristobuliani* and the following *Narcissiani*.

the family of Narcissus: i.e., again, the Narcissians. Lightfoot thinks the reference is to the slaves of the powerful freedman whose wealth was proverbial (Juvenal, *Sat.*, xiv. 329), and who wielded great influence with Claudius. He was put to death by Agrippina just after the accession of Nero. His 'household' would also have been incorporated in the imperial economy.

12. Tryphaena and Tryphosa: two sisters (possibly twins)— or, at any rate, near relatives—for it appears to have been customary to designate such with names from the same root. The second name is commoner than the first.

Persis, singled out by Paul for special praise, is a typical slave's name.

13. Rufus . . . also his mother and mine. Was this the Rufus of Mk 15:21, the son of Simon of Cyrene? Cf. SH, p. 427. He was probably a freed slave. His mother, whom Paul may have known in Palestine or Asia Minor, is specially honoured by the apostle's skilful compliment; in fact, at some time, she may have protected Paul, rendering him some service.

eminent in the Lord: lit. 'elect in the Lord', but meaning probably more here than an 'elect one', i.e. a Christian; Rufus was evidently a notable Christian. Could there possibly be an allusion to the service his father had rendered?

14. and the brethren who are with them: for the names, see SH, Michel. This last greeting suggests that those here mentioned formed a small group or community by themselves.

16. Greet one another with a holy kiss: the 'holy kiss' was part of the liturgy; cf. 1 Th. 5:26; 1 C. 16:20; 2 C. 13:12; 1 Pet. 5:14; Justin, *Apol. I*, 65: 'We greet one another with a kiss when we have ceased from prayer.' In 1 Pet. 5:14, the 'kiss of *agapē*' may recall that the 'holy kiss' was part of the Eucharist. Cf. Selwyn, 1 *Peter*, p. 244, R. Seeberg, in *Dictionary of the Apostolic Church*, ed. J. Hastings (1915–18), II, p. 443.

It has been thought that Paul's letter was probably read to the congregation assembled to celebrate the Eucharist, and that the brotherly kiss would terminate the reading (Michel, p. 382). By conveying the greetings of 'all the churches of Christ', Paul makes this a specially authoritative greeting. It is the Apostle to the Gentiles speaking.

A STERN WARNING AGAINST FACTIOUSNESS AND FALSE DOCTRINE
17-20

Cf. Gal. 6:11-16 (also Phil. 3:19ff.). The apostle may have had in mind the divisive influence of judaizing or gnosticizing tendencies, e.g., behind the 'weak' brethren of 14:1ff., may have been a judaizing movement. Cf. W. Schmithals, 'Die Irrlehrer von Röm. 16:17-20', *Studia Theol.*, XIII (1959), pp. 51-69.

Paul's language is strong, bordering on anathema (Michel thinks this particular paraenesis (cf. verse 17) belongs in a cultic setting); cf. especially verse 18: 'their own appetites'; *RSV mg.*: 'their own belly' (Phil. 3:19). If this is understood as the sin of gluttony, it is difficult to see how it fits into the context. Older commentators may not be so far wrong in taking the reference to be to the Jewish obsession with 'meats'; but it is also possible that the word includes a reference to 'libertarians'.

A number of commentators have held that these verses (17-20), falling between the lists of greetings, could only have been written to a Church which Paul himself had founded.

18. appetites: Greek *koilia*. The interpretation of Michel who takes *koilia* (lit. 'belly') as synonymous with *sarx* ('flesh') seems doubtful.

by fair and flattering words: lit. 'fine speech and praise (blessing)'. The Romans defined the man who made fine speeches as one to speak well, yet act ill; Cf. SH, *ad loc.* The use of the second word in the sense of 'flattery' is rare: its associations in Biblical Greek are cultic ('blessing'). Is Paul punning and playing on words? The first word, *chrēstologia*, would sound like *Christologia*. (The pun *Christos, chrēstos* ('good, kind') was well established in the early Church; cf. 1 Pet. 2:3, Justin, *Ap. I*, 4, F. W. Beare, 1 *Peter* (Oxford, 1958), p. 90). Were they people who had 'Christ' often on their lips, and went in for a specious kind of *eulogia* ('blessing'), but whose doctrine was false and conduct libertarian?

19. obedience is Christian obedience, i.e. the obedience of faith (defined at 1:5).

wise as to what is good . . . : experts at goodness, simpletons at evil. The thought is clearly dominically inspired; cf. Mt. 10:16, Phil. 2:15.

20. the God of peace: cf. 15:33. It is the 'God of peace' also who will thus remove the discord in the Church. The verse is both prediction and prayer for the Roman Church.

soon has implicit eschatological overtones, referring to the Parousia.

PERSONAL GREETINGS 21–3

These verses list the greetings of Paul's companions, headed by **Timothy,** singled out as Paul's colleague ('fellow worker'); the inseparable aide-de-camp of the apostle is usually mentioned at the beginning of letters (2 C. 1:1, Phil. 1:1, Col. 1:1, 1 Th. 1:1, 2 Th. 1:1, Phm. 1). The three following names, **Lucius, Jason, Sosipater,** were clearly Jewish Christians ('my kinsmen'). Lucius, a Roman name, recalls Lucius of Cyrene (Ac. 13:1), but it could also be 'Luke, the beloved physician'. The other two are also Greek names; there is no evidence really to connect them with the Jason of Acts 17:5–7, or the Macedonians charged with 'the collection for the saints' (Ac. 20:4). **Tertius** and **Quartus** are both familiar Roman forms of name.

Gaius (1 C. 1:14) must have been a wealthy Christian, since he appears as the host to the Christians no doubt frequently travelling via Corinth (older commentators explain that the whole Church met in his house). **Erastus** is 'city-treasurer': whether the city is Corinth or Ephesus, the high position of this convert is noteworthy. In Corinth (or Ephesus), as well as at Rome, Christianity was penetrating all strata of society; cf. H. J. Cadbury, 'Erastus of Corinth', *JBL,* L(1931), pp. 42–58.

THE DOXOLOGY 25–7

For the position of the doxology in the epistle, see Introduction, p. 27f.

That the closing doxology is of later literary vintage than the original letter to the Romans is widely recognized. It conforms to a liturgical-literary scheme familiar at Eph. 3:20, Jude 24, and Polycarp, *Ep. Philipp.,* xx. 2 (all beginning with the words: 'To

Him who is able'; for the hymnic style, see E. Norden, *Agnostos Theos* (Leipzig/Berlin, 1923), p. 255, n. 3; and G. Harder, *Paulus und das Gebet* (Gütersloh, 1936), pp. 45, 79. Cf. also E. Kamlah, in *Theol. Litzg.*, LXXXI (1956), p. 492.) Its central thought, the final revelation of the 'mystery' kept secret for long ages, may derive from the later Paulines (or deutero-Paulines), Col. 1:26, Eph. 3:9; certainly all three passages have the same theme. The final editor of the Romans doxology however, has, worked in a number of expressions from Romans itself (e.g., 1:2, 5, 2:16). Harnack held that the phrases 'and the proclamation of Jesus Christ', 'through the prophetic writings', 'made known', were editorial additions by which the original doxology had been 'laboriously and inadequately "catholicised"' (*Marcion* (²1924), p. 165).

The central theme, shared with the deutero-Pauline Colossians and Ephesians, and touched on at Rom. 11:25, is of the divine *mystērion*, or 'secret', hidden through countless ages, now revealed through prophetic writings in the eschatological present.

25. strengthen you according to my gospel . . .: the idea of an inner 'confirmation' of 'corroboration' (cf. 1:11, 1 Th. 3:2, 13, 2 Th. 3:3, etc.), no doubt in sound doctrine and sure convictions, is to be 'according to my gospel and the preaching of Jesus Christ'. Alternatively, one may interpret the two expressions 'my gospel' and 'the preaching of Jesus Christ' as a kind of hendiadys, and take the preposition with the verb as instrumental: '. . . who is able to strengthen you through my proclamation of the gospel of Jesus Christ'.

26. according to the command of . . . God: God has authorized by divine command the revelation of the secret plan of salvation—and its purpose is to bring to faith and obedience *all* the Gentile nations. Cf. 1:5 for the phrase 'the obedience of faith', another accommodation to the Roman epistle.

prophetic writings: i.e. of the old Biblical literature (*OT* and apocalyptic writings of the inter-Testamental period). The meaning 'inspired' for 'prophetic' (and so embracing inspired Christians writings) is probably to be rejected.

27. to the only wise God be glory for evermore through Jesus Christ! Amen: a traditional type of formula. Cf. 1 Tim. 1:17; Jude 25; 2 Mac. 1:25. An alternative text to *RSV* reads: 'to the only wise God through Jesus Christ, to whom be glory

for evermore' (cf. *NEB mg.*). This is the more difficult and the
better supported text, and is to be preferred (it is supported by
P^{46}, ℵ, A, C, D, etc.); but the true antecedent of the relative is
'God', not 'Jesus Christ'; the ambiguity in the position of the
relative no doubt led to its removal or to the substitution of the
personal pronoun (*autō*, 'to him'); cf. J. Dupont, in *Ephemerides
Theologicae Lovanienses*, XXII (1946), pp. 362–75.

INDEX OF AUTHORS

The names of authors of standard or well-known commentaries, such as those of Sanday and Headlam, C. H. Dodd, C. K. Barrett, etc., some of which are quoted *passim*, are not included.

GENERAL INDEX

Achaea, 19
Adoption and 'sonship', 129
Ambrosiaster, 22
anathema, 128
Andronicus, 21
Anthropology, Pauline, 100ff.
Antinomianism, 62, 92
aparchē, 'first-fruits of the Spirit', 122
Apostle, use of term, 34
Aquila, 21, 27
Aristobulus, 23
Aristotle, 50, 57
arrabōn, 'first instalment' of the Spirit, 122
Arrian, 61
Augustine, St, 86, 87

Babylonian captivity, 43
Baptism, Pauline doctrine of, 92ff.
'Body', Pauline doctrine of the, 108ff.

Cenchreae, 19
charaz, catena of quotations, 64, 173
Chrysostom, 36, 142
Cicero, 176
Claudius, edict of, 21
Clement of Alexandria, 162
Clement of Rome, 180
Coals of fire, 157
Corporate personality, 93
Cranmer, 69

Day of Atonement, 69f.
Decalogue, the 'second', 162
Derbe, 21
Diatribe, Stoic, 29, 61
Dittography, vertical, 46
doxa, the, 66
Doxologies, 149
Doxology, closing, 27, 184f.

Epaenetus, 26
Ephesian ministry, 20
Ephesus, 19
Epictetus, 61, 105, 157
epistolary catechesis, 18
epistolē, 18
Erasmus, 69
Exile, 43, 67

'Flesh', Pauline concept of, 108ff.
'Freedom', Christian, 168

Gades, 176
Gaius, 19

Gallio, 20
gezera shawa, 76
'Glory' (*shekhinah*), the, 129

Hercules, Phoenician, 176
Hercules, Pillars of, 176
ḥerem, the, 128f.
Hermas, 167
Herod, 82
Herod family, 23
hilastērion, 69f.
Hippolytus, 38

Isocrates, 57

Josephus, 60, 67, 69, 93, 129, 152, 160, 163, 164, 181
Junias, 21
Justin Martyr, 153, 182, 183
Juvenal, 182

Kingdom of God, in Paul, 168
Kiss, holy, 182

Last will and testament, Paul's, 20
Lehrbrief, 18
Lehrstil, 90
Livy, 152
Luther, 30
Lycaonia, 21
Lystra, 21

Macedonia, 19
Many, inclusive use of, 90
Marcion, 28, 185
Measure of faith or 'measure of responsi-
bility', 152
Melancthon, 69
Melkart, Temple of (in Gades), 176
'Mystical union', 93
Mysticism, Pauline, 115ff.

Natural Law (*lex naturalis*), 57
Natural Theology, 50
Nero, 27

Origen, 28, 68, 86, 101, 114, 166
Ovid, 105

Paraenetical maxims, 153
Parousia, the imminent, 163
Pausanias, 176
Personality, corporate, 93
Pesher, Pauline, 138f., 166